Palgrave Studies in Communication for Social Change

Series Editors
Pradip Thomas
University of Queensland
Australia

Elske van de Fliert
University of Queensland
Australia

Communication for Social Change (CSC) is a defined field of academic enquiry that is explicitly transdisciplinary and that has been shaped by a variety of theoretical inputs from a variety of traditions, from sociology and development to social movement studies. The leveraging of communication, information and the media in social change is the basis for a global industry that is supported by governments, development aid agencies, foundations, and international and local NGOs. It is also the basis for multiple interventions at grassroots levels, with participatory communication processes and community media making a difference through raising awareness, mobilising communities, strengthening empowerment and contributing to local change. This series on Communication for Social Change intentionally provides the space for critical writings in CSC theory, practice, policy, strategy and methods. It fills a gap in the field by exploring new thinking, institutional critiques and innovative methods. It offers the opportunity for scholars and practitioners to engage with CSC as both an industry and as a local practice, shaped by political economy as much as by local cultural needs. The series explicitly intends to highlight, critique and explore the gaps between ideological promise, institutional performance and realities of practice.

More information about this series at
http://www.palgrave.com/gp/series/14642

James Pamment · Karin Gwinn Wilkins
Editors

Communicating National Image through Development and Diplomacy

The Politics of Foreign Aid

Editors
James Pamment
Lund University
Lund, Sweden

Karin Gwinn Wilkins
University of Texas at Austin
Austin, TX, USA

Palgrave Studies in Communication for Social Change
ISBN 978-3-319-76758-1   ISBN 978-3-319-76759-8   (eBook)
https://doi.org/10.1007/978-3-319-76759-8

Library of Congress Control Number: 2018934653

Cover credit: Shui Ta Shan

Printed on acid-free paper

This Palgrave Macmillan imprint is published by the registered company Springer International Publishing AG part of Springer Nature
The registered company address is: Gewerbestrasse 11, 6330 Cham, Switzerland

CONTENTS

Notes on Contributors

Andreas Åkerlund is Senior Lecturer in History at Södertörn University, Sweden. He has investigated various aspects of Swedish public diplomacy from a historical perspective. His dissertation ("Mellan akademi och kulturpolitik," Uppsala, 2010) dealt with Swedish language lecturers in Germany from 1906 to 1945. His recent book (*Public Diplomacy and Academic Mobility in Sweden*, Lund, 2016) is a long term study of the scholarships of the Swedish Institute, focusing policy, granting practice as well as the grantees themselves. He is currently finishing a report on the Swedish Institute's Visby program on behalf of the Swedish Governmental Migration Studies Delegation (Delmi).

Banu Baybars-Hawks is a professor and Chair of the Public Relations Department in the Faculty of Communications at Kadir Has University in Istanbul, Turkey. She received her Ph.D. from the University of Tennessee, Knoxville, in 2002. Her research has appeared in numerous journals such as the *International Journal of the Humanities*, the *International Journal of Civic, Political, and Community Studies*, and the *Journal on Systemics, Cybernetics and Informatics*, among others.

Senem B. Çevik is Lecturer at the University of California, Irvine in the International Studies Program. Her research focus is public diplomacy and strategic communication. Her current research is on the role of development assistance on nation brands and the domestic component in public diplomacy practice.

Nadia Kaneva is Associate Professor at the Department of Media, Film, and Journalism Studies at the University of Denver, USA. Her research explores the intersections of culture, identity, and power in the age of globalization and commercial media. One specific focus of her work is nation branding in post-socialist and post-conflict contexts. Nadia is the editor of three books: *Mediating Post-Socialist Femininities* (Routledge, 2015), *Branding Post-Communist Nations: Marketizing National Identities in the "New" Europe* (Routledge, 2011), and *Fundamentalisms and the Media* (Bloomsbury, 2009), co-edited with Stewart M. Hoover. Her research appears in numerous academic journals and edited collections.

Kyung Sun (Karen) Lee is a doctoral candidate at the University of Texas at Austin. Her research analyzes articulations of national identity, internationalism, and globalism and their relations in the discourses and material practices of development, nation branding, and public diplomacy. Her articles have appeared in the *International Journal of Communication*, *Journalism Studies*, and her recent work is forthcoming in the *Journal of Contemporary Eastern Asia*.

Toby Miller is Research Professor of the Graduate Division, University of California, Riverside; Sir Walter Murdoch Professor of Cultural Policy Studies, Murdoch University; Profesor Invitado, Escuela de Comunicación Social, Universidad del Norte; Professor of Journalism, Media and Cultural Studies, Cardiff University/Prifysgol Caerdydd; and Professor in the Institute for Media and Creative Industries, Loughborough University London. The author and editor of over 40 books, his work has been translated into Spanish, Chinese, Portuguese, Japanese, Turkish, German, Italian, Farsi, and Swedish. His most recent volumes are *Greenwashing Culture* (2018), *Greenwashing Sport* (2018), *The Routledge Companion to Global Cultural Policy* (co-edited, 2018), and *Global Media Studies* (co-authored, 2016).

James Pamment is Associate Professor and Head of the Department of Strategic Communication at Lund University, Sweden. He is an external faculty member at the USC Center on Public Diplomacy and Vice Chair of the Public Diplomacy Interest Group at the International Communication Association. Pamment researches on the role of strategic communication in state influence across borders, including diplomacy, public diplomacy, information operations, and development communication. He is author of *British Public Diplomacy & Soft Power: Diplomatic Influence & Digital Disruption* and *New Public Diplomacy in the 21st Century*, and editor of the forthcoming *Countering Online Propaganda and Violent Extremism* (w/C. Bjola).

Efe Sevin is Assistant Professor of Strategic Communication at Reinhardt University (Georgia, USA). His current research focuses on the role of place branding and public diplomacy campaigns on achieving development goals and foreign policy objectives. His most recent book, *Public Diplomacy and the Implementation of Foreign Policy in the US, Sweden and Turkey*, was published by Palgrave Macmillan in 2017.

Larisa Smirnova is a Russian academic who has worked in China since 2009. She is Senior Research Fellow at the Central Economics and Mathematics Institute of the Russian Academy of Sciences. In 2013–15, she was awarded a Confucius China Study Plan stipend for research on fighting corruption. She is a former employee of the World Bank and of the United Nations, and a graduate of Moscow Lomonosov State University (Ph.D. in Politics, 2015), the National School of Administration of France, and the Moscow State Institute of International Relations (MGIMO).

Olga Lucía Sorzano is a visiting lecturer in Sociology at the City University of London, where she recently completed her Ph.D. in Culture and Creative Industries. She also has a B.A. in Economics and an M.Sc. in Economic and Social Policy Analysis. Olga Lucia has extensive experience of policy-making in Colombia in social policy, cultural diplomacy, and international relations through her work at the National Planning Department and the Ministry of Foreign Affairs. Her current work is focused on the analysis of invisible figures and unrecognized art forms such as the circus.

Rebecka Villanueva Ulfgard is Associate Professor of International Studies, Instituto Mora, Mexico City. She holds a Ph.D. in Political Science from Linnaeus University, Sweden. Her research areas focus on Mexico and international development cooperation, Mexico's civil society and New Multilateralism, and theories of international relations and development. She has published on these topics in English and Spanish for international journals and editorials. Currently she is the lead coordinator of the book series *Governance, Development, and Social Inclusion in Latin America* for Palgrave Macmillan/Springer.

Karin Gwinn Wilkins (Ph.D., University of Pennsylvania) serves as Associate Dean for Faculty Advancement and Strategic Initiatives with the Moody College of Communication at the University of Texas at Austin, where she also holds the John P. McGovern Regents Professorship in Health and Medical Science Communication. Wilkins is also the Editor-in-Chief of *Communication Theory*. Wilkins has won numerous awards for her research, service, and teaching, and chaired the Intercultural/Development Division of the International Communication Association. Her work addresses scholarship in the fields of development communication, global communication, and political engagement.

Di Wu is a Ph.D. candidate at the American University. Her research is positioned at the intersection of foreign policy and strategic communication, with a focus on the relational and network approach to public diplomacy. Her geographic interest lies in China, East Asia, and USA–China relations. Wu has published on soft power, public diplomacy, nation branding, and USA–China relations. Her publications include one book chapter on "Chinese Political Leadership Transition" and two papers in *Public Relations Review*: "China's Public Diplomatic Networks on the Ebola Issue in West Africa" and "Assessing Resource Transactions in Partnership Networks."

LIST OF FIGURES

CHAPTER 1

Introduction: New Dimensions in the Politics of Image and Aid

James Pamment and Karin Gwinn Wilkins

This edited collection draws upon interdisciplinary research to explore new dimensions in the politics of image and aid. While development communication and public diplomacy are established research fields, there is little scholarship that seeks to understand how the two areas relate to one another (Pamment 2015, 2016a, b). However, international development doctrine in the USA, the UK and elsewhere increasingly suggests that they are integrated—and should become *more* integrated—at the level of national strategy. Similarly, ambiguous concepts such as soft power and nation brands are suggestive of changes in how nations represent their identities and interests to one another. But what are the modalities of these changes when viewed through the lens of international development? How do these strategies interact

J. Pamment (✉)
Lund University, Lund, Sweden
e-mail: james.pamment@isk.lu.se

K. G. Wilkins
University of Texas at Austin, Austin, TX, USA
e-mail: karin.wilkins@austin.utexas.edu

© The Author(s) 2018   1
J. Pamment and K. G. Wilkins (eds.), *Communicating National Image through Development and Diplomacy*, Palgrave Studies in Communication for Social Change, https://doi.org/10.1007/978-3-319-76759-8_1

in practice? And what can this teach us about the changing nature of twenty-first-century development communication?

The approach taken in this volume is to consider a variety of cases drawing upon a combination of theoretical and conceptual lenses that each in its own way combines a focus on *aid* with attention to *image*. The cases in this volume consist of empirical contributions in regions as diverse as Kosovo, Korea, Mexico, Turkey, Afghanistan, Somalia, Sweden, Colombia, Russia, and China. They seek to explore foreign policy trends originating with some of the most powerful Northern donors in order to see how they are influencing patterns of national development. Together, these cases establish a new body of knowledge on how contemporary debates into public diplomacy, soft power, and nation branding are fundamentally changing not just the communication of aid, but also its broader strategies, modalities, and practices.

Research in this direction builds on recognition of intersections between public diplomacy and development communication, each of which engages in strategic intervention meant to benefit the public good. While development communication as a field does not always articulate the importance of politics and political interests, we see this as an integral component of communication for social change, in its implementation as well as articulation. Equally, discussions of diplomacy and the pursuit of national interests often foreground (geo-)politics, while underplaying how these activities directly or indirectly empower and disempower societies and individuals to shape their own development. In order to analyze the layers of overlap between these different approaches, the central conceptual framework is grounded in our understanding of the interactions across strategies promoting soft power, public diplomacy, development communication, and nation branding.

Soft Power

Soft power is key in articulating critical intersections across public diplomacy and nation branding, emphasizing the geopolitics that guide strategies such as nation branding. In the late 1970s, Keohane and Nye (1977, p. 19) sketched an image of a world connected by "networks of rules, norms, and procedures that regularize behavior." This context of "complex interdependence" paved the way for new theories of "how holders of power could wield that power to shape or distort patterns of interdependence that cut across national boundaries" (Keohane and Nye 1998,

p. 82). One of those theories was Joseph Nye's (1990) soft power thesis, an approach that has inspired a range of studies on international influence and attraction (e.g. Nye 2004, 2008; van Ham 2010; Hayden 2012; Thussu 2013).

Theorizing interdependence between different areas of international affairs was integral to Nye's earliest uses of the term soft power. In his seminal article from 1990, Nye outlines soft power as a means of *transposing* power between areas of international relations. He claims that "the fragmentation of world politics into many different spheres has made power resources less fungible, that is, less transferable from sphere to sphere." Consequently, "other instruments such as communications, organizational and institutional skills, and manipulation of interdependence have become important ... interdependence is often balanced differently in different spheres such as security, trade, and finance" (Nye 1990, pp. 156–158).

Nye's (1990) soft power thesis acted as an influential meditation on how the USA could maintain global leadership in a post-Cold War international system through its superior range of "power resources—military, economic, scientific, cultural, and ideological" (p. 155). An international environment of "unevenly balanced mutual dependence" means that actors should seek "to set the agenda and structure the situations in world politics" through "co-optive power" (ibid., pp. 158, 166–167). Explicit to Nye's theory is the notion of steering flows of knowledge in order to shape experiences of international engagement, all the while utilizing structural advantages to reproduce preferred ideologies:

> Co-optive power is the ability of a country to structure a situation so that other countries develop preferences or define their interests in ways consistent with its own. This power tends to arise from such resources as cultural and ideological attraction as well as rules and institutions of international regimes. (Nye 1990, p. 168)

Scholars of development communication will recognize aspects of this approach from the perspective of cultural imperialism. Cultural imperialism forms a robust body of research into the interaction between states, boundary-spanning actors, and international power relations (Schiller 1992 [1969], 1976; Boyd-Barrett 1977; Tunstall 1977; Nordenstreng 1984). It raises questions of how political, economic, and technological advantages seated in the West affect international flows of communication, and how influence over international regulation and distribution is leveraged to reinforce the attractiveness and competitiveness of Western values, goods, services, and structures. Herbert Schiller's much-cited definition of cultural imperialism may therefore be neatly juxtaposed with Nye's description of soft power to demonstrate some of the similarities between concepts:

> [Cultural imperialism] describes the sum of the processes by which a society is brought into the modern world system and how its dominating stratum is attracted, pressured, forced, and sometimes bribed into shaping social institutions to correspond to, or even to promote, the values and structures of the dominant centre of the system. (Schiller 1976, p. 9)

Cultural imperialism research declined during the late 1980s to be superseded by a focus on globalization; however, useful reflection has taken place over the flaws in its methodologies by many of the authors previously working in the field (cf. Boyd-Barrett 1977, 2007; Tomlinson 1991, 1997; or Mattelart 1979, 2002). For example, Thompson argued that a contemporary study of how nations and other transnational actors exert power through communication should acknowledge that there are many players impacting upon these practices, and not just one uncontested national or regional policy. Furthermore, transnational communication patterns engage with long-term patterns of cultural interaction, which means that any effects are likely to be unpredictable and formed out of a variety of longer-term influences. Cultural imperialism furthermore undervalues the creative ways in which audiences are able to appropriate knowledge and culture, often relying on reductionist methodologies of how influence takes place (Thompson 1995; van Elteren 2003). He concludes that "this thesis is unsatisfactory not only because it is outdated and empirically doubtful, but also because it is based on a conception of cultural phenomena that is fundamentally flawed." Herbert Schiller and his contemporaries would need to demonstrate the "multiple, shifting ways in which symbolic power overlap[s] with economic, political and coercive power in the process of globalisation" (Thompson 1995, pp. 172–173).

These critiques provide a helpful point of contact with debates about soft power. For example, a number of scholars have identified themes surrounding diplomacy and communication under the pressures of globalization, such as the greater participation in diplomatic affairs by corporate, nongovernmental and civil society actors, facilitated by the increased efficacy of transnational advocacy networks (Sharp 1999; Kelley 2010; Hocking et al. 2012). Others have observed the intensified role of mass media in such an environment and, in particular, their agenda setting and information transfer functions (Manheim 1994; van Ham 2010; Hocking 2006; Entman 2004; Hayden 2012; Pamment 2014). Some have questioned the role and purpose of the state in light of corporate influence, international trade patterns, and competitive nationalism (Hocking 2005; Kaneva 2012; Jansen 2008; Anholt 2007). Perhaps most importantly, the theoretical grounds underpinning the "problem of influence"—that is to say, the practices through which influence can be considered demonstrable and attributable to deliberate acts of persuasion—have been brought into question through an acknowledgment of changing communication symmetries and asymmetries (Melissen 2005; Pamment 2013; Hayden 2012, 2013). While the two fields of inquiry do not share the same political motivations (with the field of cultural imperialism strongly asserting the rights of citizens of developing countries and the study of soft power assuming a governance perspective), there remains a shared interest in the communicative practices associated with attraction, influence, cooperation, and competition in a globalized international context.

Despite these conceptual overlaps, foreign aid has not assumed a pivotal role in explications of soft power (e.g. Nye 1990, 2004; Hayden 2012, 2015; van Ham 2010; see Pamment (2015) for a detailed discussion). However, an implicit theme in soft power theories is the extent to which different forms of aid test the defining line between "hard" and "soft" forms of power. The voluntary transfer of resources from a donor to a recipient country may have the primary objective of supporting economic or humanitarian development, but it can also offer secondary benefits to the donor country derived from patterns of interaction: a preference for a particular language, culture, values, institutional structures, and so on. This would appear to meet Nye's general concept of transposing relative advantages between sectors. This suggests that foreign societies and multilateral institutions are the subject of efforts to influence rules, standards, norms, knowledge, frameworks, and ultimately the behavior that takes place in and through those sites (Neumann 2013). Aid is one set of resources among others to achieve these soft power goals. Thus, soft power fits within a pattern of supporting national and diplomatic objectives through different layers of influence without the reputational damage that formal command power entails.

PUBLIC DIPLOMACY

Public diplomacy (PD) refers to the efforts of an international actor to understand, inform, and influence foreign audiences in support of desired policy goals. It is predicated on the principle that government-to-government relations in a given foreign policy area may be influenced by engagement with foreign citizens and groups outside of government whose opinions, values, activities, and interests may help to sway a government's position. PD coexists awkwardly with Articles 12 and 13 of the Havana Convention (1928), which discourage diplomats from participation in the domestic or foreign politics of the state in which they exercise their functions. By consequence, one influential diplomatic studies scholar has claimed that PD is "foreign propaganda conducted or orchestrated by diplomats," and therefore that it is an activity which is manifestly "not diplomacy" (Berridge 2002, pp. 17, 125). The consensus among most contemporary scholars working in the field, however, is that diplomacy is an integrated field drawing upon a range of techniques and strategies including PD. Scholars have for example observed the impact of new communication technologies in enabling multiple stakeholders from across and outside of government to share in the co-creation and co-delivery of policy, as well as a movement away from one-way information flows and towards dialogue, relationship-building, and engagement (Melissen 2005).

The term was coined by former US diplomat Edmund Gullion in 1965, though its use in newspaper sources has been observed from as early as 1856 (Cull 2009). The term replaced the bland "information" and pejorative "propaganda" to include promotion, political advocacy, culture, exchange, and broadcasting activities under one convenient budgetary heading. In his comprehensive history of the United States Information Agency (USIA) between its creation in 1953 and dissolution in 1999, Cull (2008) details the many ways in which PD was used to influence the conduct of foreign affairs. The USIA's work is generally held in high regard as one of the strongest and most effective templates for conducting PD. Indeed, some claim that it was "essential" to winning the Cold War (Nye 2008). The USIA's mission was:

- To explain and advocate US policies in terms that are credible and meaningful in foreign cultures;
- To provide information about the official policies of the USA, and about the people, values, and institutions which influence those policies;

- To bring the benefits of international engagement to American citizens and institutions by helping them build strong long-term relationships with their counterparts overseas;
- To advise the president and US government policy-makers on the ways in which foreign attitudes will have a direct bearing on the effectiveness of US policies.

Due to the multifaceted nature of these activities, PD has been relatively difficult to conceptualize as a whole, and it is often described in relation to, or more specifically as a tool of, soft power (Melissen 2005; Gilboa 2008). There have been many attempts to provide an overarching framework for all PD activities, but they have not led to disciplinary consensus. Arguably the most successful is that of Cull (2008), who identifies five core components: listening, advocacy, culture, exchanges, and international broadcasting. This definition is particularly useful in the context of the USIA's activities during the Cold War, and for enabling comparison of how other examples relate to the USIA's approach. The components may be understood as representing the following:

- Listening: information gathering, media monitoring, and public opinion polling in order to inform decision-making;
- Advocacy: explaining and arguing for policies, ideas, or interests in ways intended to influence public and elite opinion;
- Exchange diplomacy: scholarships and sponsored visits, usually between individuals with leadership, educational, military, or cultural importance, to support mutual understanding and contribute to long-term relationship building;
- Cultural diplomacy: using cultural resources, achievements, and collaborations to support mutual understanding and contribute to long-term relationship building;
- International broadcasting: making use of media technologies such as radio, television, and digital platforms to provide news and information for foreign publics.

The close association of these techniques to diplomacy underscores that PD is part of a toolset to achieve foreign policy goals. However, this view of culture as an instrumental resource is deeply contested. Many cultural diplomacy actors, such as the Goethe Institute and British Council, have an arm's length relationship to their governments in order to protect their independence from explicit policy interests. The British Council in particular has stridently argued that cultural relations represent a special form of long-term engagement with foreign societies that reflects mutual respect and a genuine will to collaborate with and learn from others. This is not considered purposive communication on the grounds that genuine mutuality cannot exist when participants are framed as working within defined strategic objectives. On the contrary, mutual understanding should be an end in itself (Pamment 2016d). Similarly, international broadcasters such as the Voice of America, Radio Free Europe, and the BBC World Service have traditionally enjoyed complete editorial independence in their programming. Foreign policy considerations have rather been at the level of infrastructure, for example in the decision to broadcast in certain languages and in certain countries. Many proponents of soft power argue that it is a form of goodwill that emanates from society at large, and hence that governments should avoid intervention in these areas. From this perspective, PD reflects the *actualization* of soft power resources, whether or not this is used to achieve an organizational goal.

This links PD to cultural imperialism debates, and to broader research agendas relating to North–South power relations and social justice in development. As with development communication (see below), PD has undergone a "participatory turn" in which the needs of citizens are ideally foregrounded ahead of governance concerns. For some scholars, PD is a form of social empowerment that represents the "diplomacy of the people" in action via interconnected transnational activist networks (Castells 2008). For others, it is the means by which powerful actors package international policy areas to set the agenda in public debates, in order to extend their influence in shaping desired policy outcomes (Comor and Bean 2012). It is clear then that PD overlaps and intercedes in development issues by activating soft power resources in ways that are complex and unpredictable, but that nonetheless situate communication and power relations at the center of struggles over *influence*.

DEVELOPMENT COMMUNICATION

Development programs are intended to promote positive social change through strategic intervention. Communication comes into play as a tool toward achieving designated change, as well as a way of understanding the discourse engaged in this process. The field of development communication has shifted from an emphasis on effects of communication campaigns to attention to process, with many scholars advocating participatory and dialogic approaches, as well as recognition of context. It is the context that allows us to explore the politics of campaigns, evidenced through the economics of resource allocation as well as the consequences of development collaboration, particularly across nations.

Historically, the notion of development has been seen as the interventions of wealthier countries in the territories of those countries with relatively fewer resources. Following World War II, development communication emerged as a foreign aid strategy, designed by Northern and Western institutions to promote modernization among less wealthy countries. Early approaches articulated by Daniel Lerner, Wilbur Schramm, and others advocated the promotion of media toward modernization. According to these scholars, through individual attention to mediated news as well as fiction, consumers would become more modern, meaning capitalist and democratically inclined, constituents.

These theories equating development with modernization were advanced mostly from US-based academic and development institutions. During the 1970s, scholars in Latin America and Asia initiated critiques of these models of development for being ethnocentric, linear, acontextual, and hierarchical. These critiques were grounded in broader concerns with cultural imperialism and dependency, drawing attention toward global conditions rather than the internal national contexts highlighted in earlier models. The processes of development, along with media production and distribution, were then recognized as privileging those with political and economic capital to the detriment of those without these resources.

Advocates toward participatory development emerged at this time, highlighting the importance of community involvement in critical decisions about social and economic strategies. Development institutions interested in creating efficient and effective projects understand participation as a necessary tool toward achieving a defined end. Other development institutions concerned with the ethical aspects of participation are more likely to conceive of participation as an end in itself, regardless of project outcomes.

Participatory goals may be constrained, however, by resistant power structures. The conceptualization of participatory development can be seen as overly idealistic, lacking attention to economic and political resources necessary for citizens to engage in their strategic initiatives.

Connecting development more directly to political agendas is part of the current critical scholarship in the field, necessary for our conceptualization as well as our understanding of development communication. Although the focus of development communication has changed over time from concerns with modernity to dependency, cultural imperialism, globalization, participation, and resistance, these shifts have not evolved in a linear fashion. Many underlying concerns with power, whether conceived within political-economic structures or within community contexts, or whether posited as hegemonic or pluralist processes, remain.

Development communication typically addresses programs designed to communicate for the purposes of social change, or what can be called "communicating *for* development." Social marketing is one of the central strategies used in health communication campaigns within development work, for example. In addition to communication approach, communication technologies may be seen in and of themselves as part of development. Historically radio has played a central role in this narrative, whereas current attention to digital media and phones are celebrated as integral to modernization.

More recent critical approaches of development concern "communicating *about* development," questioning the way that social change projects articulate assumptions about problems, solutions, and communities. The ideological assumptions of development, as an industry and as a particular institutional practice, are deconstructed and critiqued in this approach. The underlying question becomes how development practice communicates particular ideological assumptions, and, moreover, what the implications may be in terms of power dynamics (Pamment and Wilkins 2016). Power can be understood as a negotiated and fluid process through which some agencies have the economic, cultural, and other resources to dominate and advance their agendas, whereas other groups have the potential to subvert and resist. The power to situate a problem at an individual or structural level, for example, has serious long-term implications.

In conjunction with closer analysis of PD and stakeholder communication in relation to development, the notion of "communication *of* development" is also an important consideration. From this perspective, the branding, marketing, and promotion of aid activities to foreign citizens and domestic stakeholders is conducted to support an actor's reputation and image. This places aid within the remit of PD and nation branding, first as part of the storytelling of national interests in relation to aid activities in foreign countries, and second in the formal accountability work explaining aid expenditure to domestic audiences. The power to frame aid donor activities is one that is claimed by the donor in order to shape patterns of interaction and to boost domestic support for these activities.

Key to our analyses in this book is an emphasis on understanding development and diplomacy as practice. These strategies are conceived, funded, and implemented by organizations following political agendas. Development organizations themselves are part of this process, particularly as bilateral agencies directly connect to national interests. In this book, we focus on the communication strategies of nations, thus emphasizing bilateral donors as coordinators and facilitators within this cacophony of agencies. Even with this emphasis, we recognize emerging trends in privatization of the development industry, contributing to the assertion of social marketing models in campaigns directed toward host countries as well as toward global elites. We furthermore acknowledge the importance of foreign policy objectives in the shaping of international development practices, on the understanding that many activities have multiple, often ambiguous, contradictory and complex outcomes.

Public appearance matters to bilateral development agencies wishing to elevate their status. These donors wish to project the appearance of doing good in the world, justifying their work and their funding, and so through investing in public relations. Development donors want to project an image of their beneficence in the world and dedicate resources toward strategic communication campaigns to look good in the process. They justify this investment as a way to convince others of their legitimacy and their value, to attract resources, particularly when public opinion indicates declining support for foreign aid.

The public image of development intervention can be construed through analysis of discourse, situating communication as a way of looking at constructions of development rather than as a tool for development (Wilkins and Mody 2001; Pamment 2015; Wilkins 2016). Following up on earlier discussions of approaches to this field, studies of communication about development have tended to explore the implicit narratives engaged in the selection and articulation of problems, characterizations of targeted communities, and assertion of institutional solutions as interventions. Population programs, for example, might be suggesting that women are responsible for fertility decisions, thus justifying programs directed toward women alone, rather than understanding the complex gendered dynamics within which people connect sexually and decide on contraception, or the social norms that guide decisions about relationships and families (Wilkins 2016). This approach to development as a discourse situates these narratives within implicit political ideologies.

The central argument here is that development communication involves both a level of implicit politics embedded in its discourse, as well as a level of explicit politics, articulated through strategic communication campaigns highlighting the value of bilateral donors. These campaigns aim to make nations appear virtuous, and their interventions necessary and effective.

It has therefore been argued by Pamment (2015) that the dominant paradigms in both fields relied on a common conception of *process*: namely, that information propagated through media channels can alter how foreign citizens know and experience the world around them, and that this transformation could lead to positive social change. Information and news were seen in terms of persuasive messages based around "facts"; the media channels were positioned as neutral tools of propagation; foreign citizens were considered passive targets who could be moved to action by information; influence hinged on an ontological transformation that simply reproduced given attitudes, values, ideas, and behavior; and social change was in essence a tool of foreign policy.

Both fields have developed upon their theories of *process* in recent decades. In contemporary development communication theory, media channels and platforms are ambiguous in helping or hindering change, but never neutral; the notion of information is rejected in favor of situated knowledge emerging "bottom-up," ideally through the transformative experience of co-intentional learning; foreign citizens are considered to be actors determining their own transformation within their own communities; and social change is about justice and self-determination.

This may be contrasted with theories of the "new" public diplomacy, which mirrors to some degree this theoretical shift. According to such approaches, media channels and platforms are enablers and meeting places, but their role in shaping relationships is still perceived from a functionalist perspective; information is considered in the form of messages supporting dialogue, and all dialogue is good; foreign citizens are both targets and participants located in complex networks; transformation is still about attitudes, values, ideas, and behavior but assumes the form of a negotiation over their co-option; and social change remains a tool of policy, but one spread out across a number of multilateral, non-governmental, and private actors with different but overlapping agendas.

Taken together, development communication, public diplomacy, and soft power represent a series of significant overlaps that will be explored further in Chapter 2. A key component of this intersection is, however, the relationship between power and image. In this respect, an additional term to consider is "nation brands."

NATION BRANDS

Simon Anholt (1998) is usually credited with coining the term "nation brand," although his insights developed on major trends in the study of economic prosperity throughout the 1990s. For example, Michael Porter cogently theorized the notion that national cultures can be utilized instrumentally to support economic competitiveness in 1990. Anneke Elwes's (1994) pamphlet *Nations for Sale*, written for an advertising agency, argued that Britain's image had become a "dated concept" reliant on the fictionalized imagery of its heritage rather than reflective of its contemporary creative industries and cultural diversity; both Porter and Elwes were key influences on Mark Leonard's manifesto for New Labour's rebranding of Britain, *Britain™*, which can be credited with inspiring Cool Britannia (Porter 1990; Elwes 1994; Leonard 1997). Indeed, drawing upon a body of research into culture and economic development throughout the 1970s and 1980s, Aronczyk (2013, pp. 34–61) observes a distinct trajectory toward calculating the competitive value of culture and developing the means to measure, evaluate, and manage a nation's attractiveness to foreign investors. It should be clear that such an approach is valuable both for developed countries seeking to differentiate themselves in the global marketplace and for developing countries seeking additional investments.

Anholt (2007, p. 4) defines a brand as "a product, service or organization, considered in combination with its name, its identity and its reputation," and brand*ing* as "the process of designing, planning and communicating the name and the identity, in order to build or manage the reputation." Nation branding, by extension, "propose[s] that national reputations can be managed through branding techniques imported and adapted from commercial practice" (Kaneva 2015, p. 179). A critical research agenda on nation brands emerged first in the context of US attempts to market its interventionist military agenda post-9/11, and later in response to the accession of parts of post-Soviet Central and Eastern Europe to the European Union (van Ham 2002; Kennedy and Lucas 2005; Aronczyk 2008, 2013; Jansen 2008; Ståhlberg and Bolin 2010; Volcic and Andrejevic 2011; Kaneva 2011a, b). In the case of Eastern Europe, nation branding was seen as a development project to help these countries assimilate into the EU, and consultants were sent under an aid remit (Kaneva 2011a). Studies connecting nation branding to PD are also common, since often the initiatives are coupled to foreign policy, and particularly foreign trade goals (Szondi 2008).

Critical approaches to nation brands "are not concerned with advancing a theory of nation branding that could inform its applied practice," but rather focus on questions of power, identity, nationhood, and neoliberalism (Kaneva 2011a, p. 127; Aronczyk 2013). Generally, these studies utilize empirical cases to interpret techniques of using cultural assets instrumentally, with a focus upon the perceived effects for the branded nation in areas such as national identity and the influence of economic elites. However, beyond public opinion surveys and the general positioning of foreigners as brand "consumers," only a small number of critical studies have sought to theorize the impact of nation brands upon patterns of interaction between developed and developing countries (see e.g. Jansen 2008; Kaneva 2011a; Browning 2014; Pamment 2016c).

An implicit principle of the literature has been that under-development is connected to a bad image (e.g. Anholt 2007). Browning (2014) contends that such assertions abstract standard branding discourse from the experience of developed countries and transpose those assumptions to the conditions of developing countries. Thus, nation branding expertise becomes a vehicle to export Western knowledge and biases, which serves to naturalize a "market-based approach to development," and views the process of development "in terms of the monetised consumption of material goods and the relative ranking of a state's GDP" (ibid., p. 61). Nation brands appear to be viewed by their proponents as a means of socialization within the global economy, with the potential to integrate developing countries into a competitive marketplace. This fits well within the soft power and co-option thesis, reflecting a complex mixture of norms and interests converged upon the intent to socialize others in the techniques of branded market identities (Wolff and Spanger 2015). Through an examination of the UK's soft power strategy, for example, Pamment (2016d) argues that nation brands provide an "umbrella" for the influence techniques of wealthy donor countries in developing countries. As such, they may be positioned as "tools" of soft power that create and maintain a shared brand identity for activities that may be considered individually as aid, diplomacy, or public diplomacy.

Overview of the Volume

Chapter 2, by James Pamment, continues this theoretical discussion by delving into some of the similarities across concepts. Pamment argues that five principles demonstrate the common ground between fields: (i) an investment in resources to achieve an outcome according to a theory of change; (ii) a negotiation over the "common good"; (iii) collaboration with mediating actors; (iv) a linking of diplomatic issues and techniques to the everyday; and (v) the intention to "influence" thoughts, behavior, and/or communities. These similarities are not to be ignored if our knowledge of the commonalities between PD and Devcom is to develop.

In Chapter 3, Karin Gwinn Wilkins explores the bilateral branding of Organisation for Economic Co-operation and Development-Development Assistance Committee (OECD-DAC) donors. Donors promote their interests through branding their interventions in ways that are designed to attract public attention. Therefore, development branding needs to be situated within a public diplomacy framework in which strategic communication is used to convey positive sentiments toward aid programs. Wilkins analyses bilateral agencies' use of logos associated with their national agencies or aid programs in order to unpack the ways in which strategic campaigns are intended to foster good will that highlight the good deeds of development agencies. This furthermore explores the connection between development branding and business approaches, resonant with an emerging privatization in the field, considering the consequences of engaging effective and ethical development programs.

Chapter 4 takes the case study of Kosovo to explore how nation branding intersects with a neoliberal development agenda. Nadia Kaneva argues that Kosovo's "Young Europeans" campaign was an effort to legitimize the adoption of economic policies and ideologies that served the interests of global capital rather than of the local population. Furthermore, the campaign articulated a post-ethnic, cosmopolitan, entrepreneurial national subject, while disregarding real social divisions. By juxtaposing the campaign's messages with material indicators of life in

Kosovo, the analysis raises questions about the winners and losers of neoliberal development. The chapter ends with lessons for a broader understanding of the changing nature of the nation state under a neoliberal regime and suggests directions for future research at the intersection of public diplomacy and development communication.

In Chapter 5, Olga Lucia Sorzano and Toby Miller focus on the coastal city of Cartagena de Indias, Colombia's principal tourism destination and notorious site of sexual exploitation. Tracing the history of the Colombia–USA relationship through public diplomacy, development, and tourism branding, the authors explore the sexualization of the Colombian image in the US imaginary, leading to the creation of exploitative people-to-people relations ostensibly justified by the benefits of development.

Chapter 6, by Kyung Sun (Karen) Lee, provides a case study of South Korea's government-sponsored international volunteer program, World Friends Korea. The author explores Korean volunteers' experiences on the ground within the context of Korea's foreign policy narrative of being a former aid recipient which now has a social responsibility to develop a new role as an aid donor. Korean volunteers' experiences depict a hierarchical ordering of race, social status, and gender among development communities, which tend to prefer white males as providers of aid. The author argues that Korean volunteers struggle to find their place within this dominant imaginary of development, which often compels them to perform the cultural self in a way that satisfies the gaze of the host. She seeks to foreground race, gender, and culture as sites of intersection between public diplomacy and development communication, and calls for greater contestation of the pervasiveness of Western imaginaries of development by challenging the racialized and gendered development imaginaries.

In Chapter 7, Andreas Åkerlund moves beyond an analysis of the intellectual origins of PD and aid to show similarities in organizational practices and strategies. Through a historical study of education exchange programs at the Swedish Institute, Åkerlund demonstrates how foreign policy concerns have increasingly integrated PD with aid. Åkerlund explores the connection between values and knowledge as played out through strategic initiatives directed at the Baltic region. In doing so, he identifies an accelerated process of PD and aid merging with trade promotion as part of the Swedish response to the political transformation of Eastern Europe. This may be placed in a context in which education scholarships are increasingly focused on skilled migration and mobility, rather than development per se.

In Chapter 8, Senem Cevik, Efe Sevin and Banu Baybars-Hawks analyze the ways in which Turkey employs state and civil society resources in its development partnership with Somalia. Observing a strong ideological homogeneity between Erdoğan's AKP party, politically led government institutions, and religious civil society actors, the authors observe a loose network with little formal communication or leadership. Yet, a strong foreign policy direction, coupled with clear narratives about Turkey's role in the world, position these complex aid networks within an overarching brand identity that harkens back to discourses of the Ottoman Empire. The study demonstrates that Turkey uses a coherent communication *of* development rhetoric to promote its foreign aid in both domestic and international spheres, which reinforces an ideological view of Turkey's identity in the region.

In Chapter 9, Rebecka Villanueva Ulfgard provides a detailed explication of Mexico's international development strategy alongside its nascent connections to a national brand and public diplomacy. As it struggles with consolidating its internal organization and leadership, coupled with the lack of resources to carry out fully its mandate, these factors constitute a challenge for "branding" Mexico as an emerging economy with the capacity for undertaking global responsibility through its International Development Cooperation (IDC) programs and actions. This sees the Agency for International Development Cooperation acting as "translator" between different regions in the world and a "nodal point," using horizontal communication, multi-stakeholder communication, and communication through social media with domestic and foreign audiences. This agency also uses identity-building activities and the creation of narratives that seek to convey a new image and the soft power of Mexico.

In Chapter 10, Di Wu elaborates on some of the similarities and differences between the approaches to international developed employed by China and the USA in Afghanistan. Wu investigates the power relations in public diplomacy and development communication through network analysis and concludes that the US aid to Afghanistan empowers contractors, while Chinese aid gives power to state-owned enterprises.

In Chapter 11, Larisa Smirnova analyzes some of the Russian discourses around the Chinese "One Belt One Road." The chapter focuses on dominant media relevant to those with power in decision-making in the Russian government and seeks to interpret the discourses that come into play in this major geopolitical development project. The author identifies lack of trust as a central theme of Russian media discourse, particularly in relation to access to Central Asia. Development and PD overlap in a project that seeks to redefine the geography of the region, as the two major powers vie for influence over that process.

Finally, Chapter 12 provides some conclusions to the volume and suggestions for future research. We hope that our considerations of how to bridge central concepts and to work toward comparative research and strong evaluations will be helpful to other research scholars and practitioners engaged in development and diplomacy.

REFERENCES

Anholt, S. (1998). Nation-Brands of the Twenty-First Century. *The Journal of Brand Management, 5*(6), 395–406.

Anholt, S. (2007). *Competitive Identity: The New Brand Management for Nations, Cities and Regions.* Basingstoke: Palgrave Macmillan.

Aronczyk, M. (2008). "Living the Brand": Nationality, Globality and the Identity Strategies of Nation Branding Consultants. *International Journal of Communication, 2,* 41–65.

Aronczyk, M. (2013). *Branding the Nation: The Global Business of National Identity.* New York, NY: Oxford University Press.

Berridge, G. R. (2002). *Diplomacy: Theory and Practice.* Hampshire: Palgrave.

Boyd-Barrett, O. (1977). Media Imperialism: Towards an International Framework for the Analysis of Media Systems. In J. Curran, M. Gurevitch, & J. Woollacott (Eds.), *Mass Communication and Society* (pp. 116–135). London: Edward Arnold in Association with The Open University Press.

Boyd-Barrett, O. (2007). Cyberspace, Globalization and US Empire. In O. Boyd-Barrett (Ed.), *Communications Media, Globalization and Empire* (pp. 53–76). Eastleigh: John Libbey Publishing.

Browning, C. S. (2014). Nation Branding and Development: Poverty Panacea or Business as Usual. *Journal of International Relations and Development.* https://doi.org/10.1057/jird.2014.14.

Castells, M. (2008). The New Public Sphere: Global Civil Society, Communication Networks, and Global Governance. *The ANNALS of the American Academy of Political and Social Science, 616,* 78–93.

Comor, E., & Bean, H. (2012). America's 'Engagement' Delusion: Critiquing a Public Diplomacy Consensus. *International Communication Gazette, 74*(3), 203–220.

Cull, N. J. (2008). *The Cold War and the United States Information Agency: American Propaganda and Public Diplomacy.* Cambridge: Cambridge University Press.

Cull, N. J. (2009). Public Diplomacy before Gullion: The Evolution of a Phrase. In N. Snow & P. M. Taylor (Eds.), *Routledge Handbook of Public Diplomacy* (pp. 19–23). London and New York: Routledge.

Elwes, A. (1994). *Nations for Sale*. London: DBB Needham.

Entman, R. M. (2004). Theorizing Mediated Public Diplomacy: The U.S. Case. *Press/Politics, 13*(2), 87–102.

Gilboa, E. (2008). Searching for a Theory of Public Diplomacy. *The ANNALS of the American Academy of Political and Social Science, 616*(55), 55–77.

Hayden, C. (2012). *The Rhetoric of Soft Power: Public Diplomacy in Global Contexts*. New York: Lexington Books.

Hayden, C. (2013). Logics of Narrative and Networks in US Public Diplomacy: Communication Power and US Strategic Engagement. *The Journal of International Communication, 19*(2), 196–218.

Hayden, C. (2015). Scope, Mechanism, and Outcome: Arguing Soft Power in the Context of Public Diplomacy. *Journal of International Relations and Development, 20*, 331–357.

Hocking, B. (2005). Rethinking the "New" Public Diplomacy. In J. Melissen (Ed.), *The New Public Diplomacy: Soft Power in International Relations* (pp. 28–43). Hampshire: Palgrave Macmillan.

Hocking, B. (2006). Multistakeholder Diplomacy: Forms, Functions, and Frustrations. In J. Kurbalija & V. Katrandjiev (Eds.), *Multistakeholder Diplomacy: Challenges and Opportunities* (pp. 13–29). Malta and Geneva: DiploFoundation.

Hocking, B., Melissen, J., Riordan, S., & Sharp, P. (2012). *Futures for Diplomacy: Integrative Diplomacy in the 21st Century*. The Hague: Netherlands Institute of International Relations 'Clingendael'.

Jansen, S. C. (2008). Designer Nations: Neo-liberal Nation Branding—Brand Estonia. *Social Identities: Journal for the Study of Race, Nation and Culture, 14*(1), 121–142.

Kaneva, N. (2011a). Nation Branding: Toward an Agenda for Critical Research. *International Journal of Communication, 5*, 117–141.

Kaneva, N. (2011b). Who Can Play This Game? The Rise of Nation Branding in Bulgaria, 2001–2005. In N. Kaneva (Ed.), *Branding Post-communist Nations. Marketizing National Identities in the 'New' Europe* (pp. 99–123). London: Routledge.

Kaneva, N. (Ed.). (2012). *Branding Post-communist Nations: Marketizing National Identities in the 'New' Europe*. London: Routledge.

Kaneva, N. (2015). Nation Branding and Commercial Nationalism: Notes for a Materialist Critique. In Z. Volcic & M. Andrejevic (Eds.), *Commercial Nationalism: Selling the Nation and Nationalizing the Sell* (pp. 175–193). Basingstoke: Palgrave Macmillan.

Kelley, J. R. (2010). The New Diplomacy: Evolution of a Revolution. *Diplomacy & Statecraft, 21*(2), 286–305.

Kennedy, L., & Lucas, S. (2005). Enduring Freedom: Public Diplomacy and U.S. Foreign Policy. *American Quarterly, 57*(2), 309–333.

Keohane, R. O., & Nye, J. S. (1977). *Power and Interdependence: World Politics in Transition* (2nd ed.). Boston: Little, Brown and Company.

Keohane, R. O., & Nye, J. S. (1998). Power and Interdependence in the Information Age. *Foreign Affairs, 77*(5), 81–94.

Leonard, M. (1997). *Renewing Our Identity*. London: Demos.

Manheim, J. B. (1994). *Strategic Public Diplomacy and American Foreign Policy: The Evolution of Influence*. Oxford: Oxford University Press.

Mattelart, A. (1979). *Multinational Corporations & the Control of Culture: The Ideological Apparatuses of Imperialism* (M. Chanan, Trans.). Sussex: Harvester Press.

Mattelart, A. (2002). An Archaeology of the Global Era: Constructing a Belief. *Media, Culture and Society, 24*(5), 591–612.

Melissen, J. (Ed.). (2005). *The New Public Diplomacy: Soft Power in International Relations*. Hampshire, NY: Palgrave Macmillan.

Neumann, I. B. (2013). *Diplomatic Sites: A Critical Enquiry*. London, UK: Hurst & Company.

Nordenstreng, J. (1984). *The Mass Media Declaration of UNESCO*. Norwood, NJ: Ablex Publishing Corporation.

Nye, J. S. (1990). Soft Power. *Foreign Policy, 80*, 152–171.

Nye, J. S. (2004). *Soft Power: The Means to Success in World Politics*. New York, NY: Public Affairs.

Nye, J. S. (2008). Public Diplomacy and Soft Power. *The ANNALS of the American Academy of Political and Social Science, 616*, 94–109.

Pamment, J. (2013). *New Public Diplomacy in the 21st Century*. Oxon: Routledge.

Pamment, J. (2014). The Mediatization of Diplomacy. *The Hague Journal of Diplomacy, 9*(3), 253–280.

Pamment, J. (2015). Media Influence, Ontological Transformation & Social Change: Conceptual Overlaps Between Development Communication and Public Diplomacy. *Communication Theory, 25*(2), 188–207.

Pamment, J. (Ed.). (2016a). *Intersections Between Public Diplomacy & International Development: Case Studies in Converging Fields* (USC Center on Public Diplomacy Perspectives Series). Los Angeles, CA: Figueroa Press.

Pamment, J. (2016b). The International Aid Transparency Initiative: Communication for Development or Public Diplomacy? In J. Pamment (Ed.), *Intersections Between Public Diplomacy & International Development: Case Studies in Converging Fields* (USC Center on Public Diplomacy Perspectives Series). Los Angeles, CA: Figueroa Press.

Pamment, J. (2016c). Toward a New Conditionality? The Convergence of International Development, Nation Brands & Soft Power in the British

National Security Strategy. *Journal of International Relations & Development*, 1–16, Online first.

Pamment, J. (2016d). *British Public Diplomacy and Soft Power: Diplomatic Influence and Digital Disruption*. Basingstoke: Palgrave Macmillan.

Pamment, J., & Wilkins, K. G. (2016). Toward a 'Common Standard' for Aid Transparency: Discourses of Global Citizenship Surrounding the BRICS. *International Journal of Communication, 10,* 2989–3003.

Porter, M. E. (1990). *The Competitive Advantage of Nations*. New York: Free Press.

Schiller, H. I. [1969] 1992. *Mass Communications & American Empire* (2nd ed.). Boulder, CO: Westview.

Schiller, H. I. (1976). *Communication and Cultural Domination*. New York: International Arts and Sciences Press.

Sharp, P. (1999). For Diplomacy: Representation and the Study of International Relations. *International Studies Review, 1*(1), 33–57.

Ståhlberg, P., & Bolin, G. (2010). Between Community and Commodity: Nationalism and Nation Branding. In A. Roosvall & I. Salovaara-Moring (Eds.), *Communicating the Nation. National Topographies of Global Media Landscapes* (pp. 79–101). Göteborg: Nordicom.

Szondi, G. (2008). *Public Diplomacy and Nation Branding: Conceptual Similarities and Differences*. Discussion Papers in Diplomacy. Clingendael, Netherlands Institute of International Relations, The Hauge.

Thompson, J. B. (1995). *The Media & Modernity: A Social Theory of the Media*. Stanford, CA: Stanford University Press.

Thussu, D. K. (2013). *Communicating India's Soft Power: Buddha to Bollywood*. New York: Palgrave Macmillan.

Tomlinson, J. (1991). *Cultural Imperialism*. Baltimore: The Johns Hopkins University Press.

Tomlinson, J. (1997). Internationalism, Globalization and Cultural Imperialism. In K. Thompson (Ed.), *Media and Cultural Regulation* (pp. 117–162). London: Sage.

Tunstall, J. (1977). *The Media Are American: Anglo-American Media in the World*. London: Constable.

van Elteren, M. (2003). U.S. Cultural Imperialism Today: Only a Chimera? *SAIS Review, 23*(2), 169–188.

van Ham, P. (2002). Branding Territory: Inside the Wonderful Worlds of PR and IR Theory. *Millennium: Journal of International Studies, 32*(2), 249–269.

van Ham, P. (2010). *Social Power in International Politics*. Abingdon, UK: Routledge.

Volcic, Z., & Andrejevic, M. (2011). Nation Branding in the Era of Commercial Nationalism. *International Journal of Communication, 5,* 598–618.

Wilkins, K. G. (2016). *Communicating Gender and Advocating Accountability in Global Development*. Hampshire: Palgrave Macmillan.

Wilkins, K. G., & Mody, B. (2001). Reshaping Development Communication: Developing Communication and Communicating Development. *Communication Theory, 11*(4), 385–396.

Wolff, J., & Spanger, H. J. (2015). The Interaction of Interests and Norms in International Democracy Promotion. *Journal of International Relations and Development, 20*(1), 80–107.

CHAPTER 2

Communication at the Crossroads of Development, Public Diplomacy and Soft Power

James Pamment

The aim of this chapter is to develop a theoretical basis for better under-standing the intersections between public diplomacy (PD) and development communication (Devcom). Both fields involve theories of influence over social change in foreign countries, whether those changes are atti-tudinal, behavioral, or socio-political. Both involve a voluntary transfer of resources (e.g. money, knowledge, technology) from an actor pro-moting a specific cause or agenda to a group or organization in a for-eign country. Both seek to stimulate and deliver desired policy outcomes through an active civil society and private sector, and both ultimately support what is believed to represent the common good. Both are stra-tegic, planned, and intentional. Furthermore, both Devcom and PD could arguably be positioned as tools of soft power. What Joseph Nye describes as "co-optive power" involves one country influencing the cit-izens of another to "develop preferences or define their interests in ways

J. Pamment (✉)
Lund University, Lund, Sweden
e-mail: james.pamment@isk.lu.se

© The Author(s) 2018
J. Pamment and K. G. Wilkins (eds.), *Communicating National Image
through Development and Diplomacy*, Palgrave Studies in Communication
for Social Change, https://doi.org/10.1007/978-3-319-76759-8_2

23

consistent with its own" (Nye 1990, p. 168). The voluntary transfer of resources from a donor to a recipient country may have the primary objective of supporting economic or humanitarian development, but it can also offer secondary benefits to the donor country derived from patterns of interaction: a preference for a particular language, culture, values, and institutional structures, mirroring to a certain degree the patterns of colonialism (Schiller 1969/1992). These similarities are not to be ignored if our knowledge of the commonalities and overlaps between PD and Devcom is to develop.

The opening lines of a recent handbook on development communication for social change read, "The strategic use of communication and media as tools and processes to articulate and propel social, cultural, and political change has increased over the years" (Wilkins et al. 2014). Similarly, the editor's introduction to a major collection on public diplomacy notes that the concept of PD provides "a convenient framework for thinking about the impact of the 'communications revolution' on the practice of foreign policy" (Cowan and Cull 2008, p. 7). Thus, the shared interest in promoting social change through information and communication technologies is key. As Silvio Waisbord (2014) notes, the Devcom field has yet to explore fully the "theoretical insights, empirical findings, and implications" of more instrumentalist approaches to communication, despite their similar interests in "questions about suitable tactics and strategies to promote interpersonal communication, gain new knowledge, persuade others to participate, and to disseminate information" (p. 148). Public diplomacy, soft power, and development exist in similar circles and share similar theories of influence while holding contrasting perspectives on international power relations and how and why communicative power should be wielded.

Going back to the origins of the two fields, the similarities are pronounced. The seminal text in the field of development communication—Daniel Lerner's *The Passing of Traditional Society* (1958)—was based on research funded by the State Department to evaluate the effectiveness of PD initiatives in the Middle East (Lerner 1958; Shah 2011). The emergence of PD and Devcom in late 1950s and early 1960s US political science reflects a shared model of social change based around "awakening" foreign citizens with cosmopolitan values and ideas carried by mass media. PD and Devcom could be considered complementary tools of international influence premised on the same basic belief in the role of communication in shaping social change, drawn from a common Cold

War lens for shaping newly decolonized countries into liberal democracies; they are in essence "estranged siblings," viewing the same processes of social change from apparently irreconcilable perspectives (Pamment 2015). Amid the complex advocacy networks of the early twenty-first century, manifestations of PD and Devcom can together be considered the extension of contemporary diplomatic techniques into a public sphere buoyed by the potential power reconfigurations suggested by complex interconnectivity.

Concepts at the Crossroads

Jan Nederveen Pieterse (2010) defines *international development* as an "organized intervention in collective affairs according to a standard of improvement" (pp. 3–4). However, he argues that what constitutes improvement and "appropriate intervention" is a matter of "class, culture, historical context and relations of power" (pp. 3–4). Hence, the international development research field questions assumptions about what kinds of political, social, and cultural change are desirable, as well as what forms of knowledge can support this. The circulation of information is not considered neutral or objective, but rather a reflection of transnational power relations. *Development communication*, also known as *communication development* and *communication for social change*, brings into question these issues of class, culture, context, and power in order to explore the role of mediated knowledge in "strategic intervention toward social change initiated by institutions and communities" (Wilkins and Mody 2001, p. 385). Crucially, the field encompasses communication *for* development, *about* development, and *of* development, and hence traces the central issues of power and knowledge not just for the benefit of developing communities (communication *for* development), but also as discourses within the development community (communication *about* development), and as communication toward stakeholders and purse-holders (communication *of* development) (Pamment 2016a; Shah and Wilkins 2004; Wilkins and Mody 2001, pp. 385–386).

Public diplomacy has traditionally been considered state-based communication aimed at influencing well-connected individuals and organizations that are capable of impacting upon a foreign government's policy choices. As well as working through elites and experts, this also takes place through motivating groundswells of popular opinion, such as through news broadcasting. More recently, research has focused upon

challenges to boundary-spanning organizations' representational practices motivated by the broadening range of actors, communication technologies, and interests involved in quasi-diplomatic debates (Gregory
2011; Melissen 2005; Pamment 2013a; Sharp 1999). The term "soft
power," referring to the power of attraction emanating from liberal institutions, has been used in tandem with PD, particularly since 9/11, to
conceptualize the potential to exert influence through ideas and values
(Nye 1990). Consequently, definitions of PD have moved from the narrow idea of influencing public opinion in support of diplomatic objectives toward the efforts of a variety of transnational actors "to understand
cultures, attitudes and behavior; to build and manage relationships; and
to influence thoughts and mobilize actions to advance their interests and
values" (Gregory 2011, p. 353). It may therefore be observed that PD
research and practice has, generally speaking, assumed a functionalist perspective upon achieving desired policy outcomes, whereas Devcom has
focused on ethical and normative questions.

By way of zeroing in on these similarities, I wish to begin with a
definition of aid proposed by Carol Lancaster (2007), as a corrective
to the Organisation for Economic Co-operation and Development-
Development Assistance Committee's (OECD-DAC) definition:

> a voluntary transfer of public resources, from a government to another
> independent government, to an NGO, or to an international organization
> ... with at least a 25 percent grant element, one goal of which is to better
> the human condition in the country receiving the aid. (p. 9)

This is a useful intervention because it makes explicit some of the points
of overlap between Devcom and PD. For example, PD usually involves
a voluntary transfer of public resources. This may include funding for
scholarships, publications, or an event, or underwriting the costs of
research aimed at shifting perceptions of an issue. Generally speaking,
in PD somebody foots the bill in order to support one of their objectives. The role of NGOs and civil society is again emphasized, as is a general sense of the public good, which is implied in much contemporary
collaborative PD work. Usually, this takes shape in terms of one set of
interests aligning themselves with intermediaries with credibility among
public groups key to achieving specific goals. As such, PD often seeks
to become aligned with the general interest, such as in efforts to promote economic growth, health, democracy, and good governance in

collaboration with NGOs. Therefore, there appears to be enough common ground to establish a theory that encompasses the two fields and which can provide a basis for further analysis. It will be argued that PD and Devcom:

1. Imply an investment in and transfer of tangible or nontangible resources, including knowledge, best practice, and physical items according to a theory of change;
2. Intend to support, negotiate, and agree conceptions of common interests or common goals for the public good;
3. Involve relationship-building, engagement, and collaboration with civil society and private boundary-spanning actors;
4. Complement and extend diplomatic practice and objectives toward wider publics;
5. Seek to influence thoughts, behavior, and communities directly or indirectly.

In this chapter I will systematically interrogate these intersections across five divisions, each of which in turn focuses upon a point listed above. The final section also serves as a conclusion.

1. *Imply an investment in and transfer of tangible or nontangible resources, including knowledge, best practice, and physical items according to a theory of change*

Devcom and PD are predicated on a transfer of resources between actors, which is guided by an anticipated outcome. This simple proposition provides the first intersection between the two fields. In the case of international development, this resource transfer is predicated on the goal of promoting "human betterment in recipient countries" through a transfer aimed at producing "economic stabilization, long-term growth, and poverty reduction" (Lancaster 2007, p. 60). In public diplomacy, expectations are generally centered on the objectives of the communicating organization, which are linked to specific foreign policy goals. These goals are often commensurate with international development objectives, since both aid and PD may be expected to stem from overarching national policies. A major distinction, however, is that aid's ultimate outcomes are also defined by international membership organizations, such as the OECD-DAC and UN Sustainable Development Goals, rather than solely by each nation. In this sense, international development has a more overtly normative purpose, whereas PD might be considered to represent first and foremost the interests of the acting organization. However, as shall be discussed in the course of this chapter, there are a number of factors that complicate this picture.

Although the precise meanings and intentions of international development have changed over time, the principle of supporting societal and/or economic change through reform would appear to be endemic to the field. Thus, it may include a plurality of development purposes, theories, and practices across time and space that nonetheless appear to share the basic concern of producing positive change (Nederveen Pieterse 2010, pp. 5–8; Wilkins et al. 2014, pp. 1–3). That desired change may be viewed through the lens of distinct institutional objectives depending on the aims of the instigator of the aid programme, such as diplomatic, developmental, humanitarian, commercial, and cultural, it may also be analyzed through theoretical lenses which differ in their assumptions, epistemologies, and methodologies (Lancaster 2007, pp. 12–18; Nederveen Pieterse 2010, pp. 8–10). Nonetheless, the principle of investing in resources to produce a form of societal change would appear to be fundamental to the development field.

The procedural nature of that change is central to definitions of official development assistance (ODA). The OECD-DAC (2008) defines ODA through the key terms *flows*, *transfers*, and *transactions*. The resources in question are many and various, and can include loans, goods, subsidies, construction projects, education, training programmes, humanitarian assistance, personnel exchanges, research, media support, capacity building, collaborations, and even theatre productions (Lancaster 2007; OECD-DAC 2008; Wilkins et al. 2014). Together, these may be considered flows, transfers, or transactions in tangible and nontangible resources, broadly termed as knowledge, goods, and services. To qualify as ODA, these dealings must be of a concessional nature, and should produce—directly or indirectly—a "development impact" within the principle objectives of promoting welfare and economic development (OECD-DAC 2008, p. 3). In other words, international development requires "a voluntary transfer of public resources," which is anticipated to transform into specific desired outcomes (Lancaster 2007, p. 9).

This proposed transformational process is based on an often implied *theory of change*. It may be argued that any proposed link between an investment in resources and the achievement of a desired outcome is complex and contested, but essential to the most basic assumptions of both Devcom and PD (Coryn et al. 2011). Within the more specific remit of communication for development, these general principles are explicit. As Thomas argues (2014), Devcom is about "understanding the role played by information, communication, and the media in directed and nondirected social change" (p. 7). This has also been considered in terms of utilizing communication technologies in "strategic attempts to direct social processes" (Wilkins and Mody 2001, p. 394). Communication efforts *for* development are underpinned by discourses *about* development processes, which assume a theory of change for how an investment of resources can turn into a specific outcome. The communication *of* these activities to stakeholders uses aid data to justify the transformational process.

Theories of modernization from half a century ago held similar assumptions about the process. Early Devcom theories from the so-called dominant paradigm considered media technologies and the information they distributed to be instigators of transformation and modernization. Media could influence the attitudes and behavior of individual citizens in developing countries, enabling an ontological journey from traditional society to modernity; it was believed that "social change operates through persons and places ... We conceive [of] modernity as a participant style of life" (Lerner 1958, p. 78; Fair 1989). Schramm (1963) considered this in terms of awakening the political consciousness through information: a simple transformative experience of cosmopolitanism via communication technologies that could generate social change. This simplistic model was largely discredited by the 1970s (Fair 1989; Fair and Shah 1997; Huntington 1968; Lerner 1971; Schiller 1969/1992), but the underlying principle of strategically instigating social change did not change substantially.

For example, an alternative paradigm of participatory communication focused on the importance of meaning-making within social contexts to the developmental process (Huesca 2002; Rogers 1976). According to this model, social change should develop from the bottom-up, taking care to acknowledge the specific circumstances of each developing community (Freire 1983; Gumuci-Dagron 2001; Servaes et al. 1996; Waisbord 2001). This developed into a body of normative research into alternative outcomes in development, such as sustainability, equality of voice, self-realisation, human dignity, and social justice (Thomas 2014).

Such approaches provide both a more effective theory of change for transferring resources into outcomes, and new definitions of what those desirable outcomes might be. They do not, however, radically alter the underlying transformational process implied by strategic investments in producing change. Although the Devcom field is characterized by contestation between these two paradigms, both are underpinned by this same idea of transferring resources into outcomes; the contestation is best defined as tensions over what those outcomes should be and how resources should best be deployed to achieve them.

Like Devcom, PD has many definitions which are specific to certain cultures and time periods. Nonetheless, a common thread exists in the production of change through a strategic, and typically concessional, deployment of resources. Gilboa (2008, p. 57) notes that definitions of PD during the twentieth century "presented only general statements about goals," which invariably overstated and oversold its potentially transformative role. For example, the State Department defined PD in 1987 simply as "programs intended to inform or influence public opinion in other countries" (as cited in Waller 2007, p. 24). This would suggest that PD, like international development, is predicated on a purposive investment of resources anticipated to produce specific desired outcomes in a foreign society. The actual theory of change is typically implicit or buried in ambiguous terms such as *influence* and *engagement* (Comor and Bean 2012; Pamment 2013a).

More recently, Gregory (2011) shifts the definition of PD away from the narrow idea of influencing attitudes in foreign societies and toward the efforts of a variety of transnational actors to use media and communication technologies in order better to "understand cultures, attitudes and behavior; to build and manage relationships; and to influence thoughts and mobilize actions to advance their interests and values" (p. 353). In many respects, such a definition neatly encapsulates the principle themes of a "participatory turn" in PD research since 9/11, and begins the process of unpacking some of the ambiguous theories of change motivating these practices (Gilboa 2008; Melissen 2005; Pamment 2013a; Zaharna et al. 2013). Activities *for* social change have adapted to similar discourses *about* effective models for participation, and adapted a broader appreciation for how communication *of* these processes builds stakeholder confidence.

The key point is that PD may be defined not simply as attempts to generate desired outcomes in foreign societies, but also as concessional investments in resources that are anticipated to produce those desired outcomes according to often implicit theories of change. Gregory (2011) mentions cultural engagement, relationship-building, and mobilizing activities, which serves to provide some suggestions as to what those resources may include. Cull (2008) defines PD's components as listening, advocacy, cultural diplomacy, exchange diplomacy, and international broadcasting, each of which covers a cluster of resources allocated to producing desired outcomes. Just as ODA is defined by flows, transfers, or transactions of a concessional nature aiming to produce a direct or indirect development outcome, so PD involves an investment in knowledge, goods, and service resources in support of specific policy outcomes.

If this fundamentally "transformative" theory of change represents an intersection between PD and international development, how do the resources used and outcomes desired differ? The UK's Foreign and Commonwealth Office (FCO) has, since 2010, gradually extended ODA funding into core diplomatic and PD activities, with a particular focus on supporting economic development in middle income developing countries as a foreign policy priority. In 2015, some 40% of FCO spending could be budgeted as ODA, and this is anticipated to exceed 70% by 2020. Those activities that were traditionally called diplomacy and public diplomacy have in effect been reinterpreted as ODA-eligible efforts to promote economic development under a broader soft power strategy. The British Council, which classifies its work as cultural relations, receives approximately two-thirds of its financial support from the FCO as ODA. Although this was part of a new funding agreement made in 2010, the British Council has acted as a deliverer of aid programs for decades. The result of the latest reorganization has not been a substantial reformation of its work, but rather a new understanding of how existing programs simultaneously fit within a public diplomacy remit *and* meet ODA criteria (Pamment 2016b).

A second example may be seen in the overarching mission statement of the PD bureaus within the US State Department. Their objectives are to:

[S]upport the achievement of U.S. foreign policy goals and objectives, advance national interests, and enhance national security by informing and influencing foreign publics and by expanding and strengthening the relationship between the people and Government of the United States and citizens of the rest of the world.[1]

These objectives foreground desired outcomes as foreign policy goals defined by the national interest. The techniques used to achieve these goals include *informing*, *influencing*, and *strengthening relationships*. These techniques are subdivided into specific institutional resources, such as information programs, international broadcasting, public affairs, and cultural, exchange, and education programs. In other words, the programs represent an investment of knowledge, economic, and cultural resources into transfers, flows, and transactions which are anticipated to generate desired foreign policy outcomes. Some components overlap with aid activities more clearly than others, but the transformative process remains consistent.

Together, this lays the groundwork for interrogating convergences between Devcom and instrumentalist approaches to social change. Each of the fields involves an investment in and transfer of specific resources, with the aim of producing desired outcomes in a foreign society. Each follows implied theories of change, although such theories may be implicit or explicit, contested or taken for granted. Although the resources and outcomes may change depending on the context, the idea that social transformation may be instigated through these directed flows of knowledge, goods, and services, and empowered by communication technologies, remains consistent between the fields. Furthermore, these practices coalesce at the implementation level, with the increased integration of ODA-eligible funding into business-as-usual diplomatic programming. The next stage of the argument is to investigate more directly the processes of change implicit to this intersection between approaches. Through such an analysis, the aim is to understand better the principles underlying the transformational approach and the institutional grounds for their convergence.

2. Intend to support, negotiate, and agree conceptions of common interests or common goals for the public good

This section interrogates the underlying theories that have created an increasingly convergent field of practice. An important assumption since

---

[1] https://www.state.gov/r/.

the late 1990s is the importance of managing discourses of the common good, which might be further defined as those efforts to shape shared interests, definitions, solutions, and norms that are necessary to finding solutions to "wicked" global problems. This intersection is complicated by the fact that it is not one of simple causality, but relies upon claims about shaping systems in often intangible ways. In other words, theories of change are not limited to techniques for producing a desired outcome, but are full of intimations about influencing the rules of the game. This might be considered an aspect of diplomacy proper that has in turn shaped international development and PD practice, and that hence represents the expansion of "diplomatic thinking" into everyday social practices (Sharp 2009).

The characteristics of a "new diplomacy" have been long anticipated (Kelley 2010, pp. 289–293). Research has highlighted the impact of nonstate actors and digital technologies on diplomatic conduct, often in terms of the practical innovations such relationships entail (Murray 2008; Sharp 1999). In particular, scholars have emphasized the significance of new communication practices in supporting and enabling the collaborative participation of formal and informal actors in foreign policy areas. Through these practices, the state has adapted from a position of unquestioned authority to the role of "enabler" and "facilitator" of complex coalitions of interdependent actors, a shift which emphasizes changes to how, where, and with whom diplomacy is conducted (Roberts 2009, pp. 509–510). Recent debates have focused upon co-option techniques for drawing different actors with diverse interests into common agendas, including through intangible principles such as values, ideas, and norms. This is in many respects where increased interest in public diplomacy has come to the fore (Hayden 2012; Hocking et al. 2012; Melissen 2005; Nye 1990, 2004; Pamment 2013a; van Ham 2010).

This notion of *influence* is key to the second intersection between fields. The question of influence rests at the heart of many theories of change, implicitly or explicitly. The terms diplomacy and influence go hand in hand; indeed, the French refer to a *diplomatie d'influence*, and the British FCO refers to "core diplomatic skills in influencing" (FCO 2013; Pamment 2013b). The consensus is that the combination of the end of the geopolitical certainties of the Cold War, the emergence of digital communication technologies, the proliferation of nonstate actors involved in diplomacy, and the more general processes associated with globalization have highlighted the need for techniques which do not merely improve how actors play the game, but influence the rules and playing field (Hamilton and Langhorne 2011, pp. 229–254; Knutsen 1997, pp. 260–282). Concepts like soft power and new public diplomacy refer to those forms of communicative influence capable of eliciting cooperation in such a complex new international environment (Melissen 2005; Nye 1990, 2004, 2008; Pamment 2013a). Such perspectives would appear to displace the theory of change from the direct production of a desired outcome to influence over the sites at which common understandings are established. These sites are considered essential to producing desired outcomes at will, via the reproduction of norms. As Joseph Nye (1990) has argued:

> Co-optive power is the ability of a country to structure a situation so that other countries develop preferences or define their interests in ways consistent with its own. This power tends to arise from such resources as cultural and ideological attraction as well as rules and institutions of international regimes. (p. 168)

Peter van Ham (2010), developing upon Nye's soft power thesis, argues that contemporary power should be considered in terms of "the capacity to establish the norms and rules around which other actors' actions converge" (p. 8). Influence in this sense is about the "capacity to produce, shape, and influence the motives, attitudes, roles, and interests of actors in international politics" (p. 47). Such techniques draw on "non-material power resources, ranging from expertise, knowledge and information, credibility, respect and authenticity, to framing, representation, and discursive power" (p. 9). This sees diplomacy take a step back from its monitoring, negotiation, and advocacy functions to instead seek to influence the very structure, language, and norms of the environment in which diplomacy is supposed to take place, through a more participatory conceptualization of social practice (Castells 2008). In this context, the proliferation of *sites* for such engagement take on new significance, since they are in many respects the subject and stake of much twenty-first-century *public* diplomatic practice (Neumann 2013).

This expansion of diplomatic thinking is visible in Devcom theory. As Waisbord (2014) puts it, "social change reflects the activation of institutional and social networks to promote transformations at individual, community, and structural levels" (p. 156). The participatory paradigm of Devcom, with its emphasis upon empowering participants, shaping communities, and inspiring activism through values and ideas draws upon the same strategic toolset. Hence, twenty-first-century Devcom and PD may be situated as expressions of an expanded concept of diplomatic influence that increasingly sees its objectives as influencing the everyday social practices of actors outside of traditional diplomatic networks. In this comprehensive approach to securing desired outcomes, shaping discourses *of* and *about* development are as important as the actual communication *for* development.

The value ascribed to these principles by the likes of Nye and van Ham has practical value to the conduct of diplomacy. For example, France has long used an integrated approach to international development, diplomacy, public diplomacy, and soft power. Its *diplomatie d'influence* is premised on the idea that the "influence of France is based on the use of French in the world ... education and university cooperation, and the dissemination of French cultural products" (République Français 2012, p. 87). Diplomatic actors are encouraged to spread French standards and norms through the frameworks of partner governments and multilateral organizations by shaping the "political, normative, economic and administrative frameworks of our partners" (Duchêne and Lamouroux 2011, p. 3). According to this theory of change, influence cascades through the international system into the everyday social practices of foreign citizens:

> Providing expertise and advice to foreign governments and international organizations is therefore an essential vehicle for the distribution of French norms and standards, whether they be related to social, legal, health or environmental affairs. French international expertise also gives influence to our social organizational model and our values. (Duchêne and Lamouroux 2011, p. 3)

This suggests that sites of diplomacy, such as multilateral institutions, are the subject of efforts to influence rules, standards, norms, knowledge, frameworks, and ultimately the behavior that takes places in and through those sites. Adding the everyday social sites of PD and Devcom to the mix, and accounting for the range of actors now involved in shaping policy frameworks and content, it appears that influence over common ideas is now considered integral to producing foreign policy outcomes in their broadest sense. It is not a great leap from *diplomatie d'influence* to explanations of Devcom, such as the capacity to "help to mobilize support, create awareness, foster norms, encourage behavior change, influence policy makers, or even shift frames of social issues" (Wilkins and Mody 2001, p. 393). In other words, the theories of change discussed in the previous section would appear to be transformative in the sense that they have moved beyond the narrow world of diplomacy to the broader setting of the everyday, with the goal of shaping social practice via a generalization of what Paul Sharp (2009) refers to as "thinking diplomatically" (p. 10).

PD, soft power, and Devcom are manifestations of this new approach to diplomacy. They represent the harnessing of the participatory nature of a networked society and the shaping of consensus through dialogue, inclusion, shared values, and social practices. They support a form of persuasion based around strategic influence over knowledge, actors, technologies, norms, and rules. They seek to structure the rules of the game as much as they seek specific outcomes within the game. In doing so, they seek long-term structures of influence that exceed the simplistic cause and effect models of a singular objective. The principle of transferring resources according to a theory of change may therefore be augmented by a sense of establishing a *commonality* that is produced and reproduced through PD, soft power, and Devcom initiatives; whether we call them norms, values, or beliefs, they seek to structure social practice in a manner ultimately conducive to the realization of foreign policy goals. A sense of the common good, of cosmopolitan norms, and values viewed through the lens of institutional objectives and focused upon the everyday fuel these theories of change.

3. *Involve relationship-building, engagement, and collaboration with civil society and private boundary-spanning actors*

If everyday social practice is the explicit realm of both PD and Devcom, changes in diplomatic practice strongly underpin this approach. Iver Neumann's recent work on diplomatic sites paves the way for a critical reconsideration of the now standard argument about the proliferation of actors and agendas in international relations. For Neumann (2013), the core tasks of diplomacy remain what they always have been: information gathering, negotiation, and advocacy. What has changed is the social context in which diplomacy is conducted; in other words, the sites "where diplomacy is on display" (p. 3). The hybrid spaces of contemporary diplomacy situate its everyday in material and social conditions that necessarily have an impact upon its strategies and tactics. Whether through invite-only events, high level summits, multilateral fora, quiet discussions in a nondescript office, or high profile dinners with celebrities and politicians, the evolving linkages of digital components to the sites of diplomacy—such as webstreaming, live tweeting, publication of blogs and reports, and other forms of remote participation—play a role in shaping the sites' formats, channels, and contents of diplomatic practice (Neumann 2013, pp. 147–148; Pamment 2014). When further positioned within a context of multiple actors such as NGOs, local authorities, pressure groups, businesses, and multilateral organizations vying for their particular areas of interest to receive sufficient recognition on the agenda, it is clear that a complex interplay between actors, agendas, and sites of negotiation is occurring (Hocking et al. 2012).

The emergence of civil society during the 1990s has undoubtedly contributed to subtle changes to this picture. The proliferation of nongovernmental actors has made diplomatic policy networks increasingly complex and diffuse, with more players, more interests at work, and less predictable rules and norms. This may be considered in terms of a "fragmentation of rule sets and conflicts between agendas," which in turn provokes the assertion of common norms (Hocking et al. 2012). The traditional legitimacy of states is increasingly challenged by the credibility and expertise of multilateral organizations, local and grassroots movements, and specialist pressure groups; as such, no one actor can single-handedly set the terms, conditions, and solutions for engagement (Kelley 2010). The Paris Declaration shift towards recognizing aid recipients as *partners*, and the post-9/11 shift toward seeing public diplomacy as *engagement*, are cases in point, as former targets become reconfigured as equal participants.

Inclusive attitudes towards actors, and the shaping of common interests and goals, have emerged as a key technique of contemporary diplomacy that necessarily feeds into Devcom and PD practices. This involves mimicry: the FCO now refers to its foreign policy as "active and activist" (Pamment 2016b, p. 189). The core practice of producing common structures, agendas, and norms appears highly salient for further investigation, not least because the agency of NGOs involved in aid implementation is several steps removed from the instrumentalist objectives of foreign and aid policies. Yet PD techniques include engagement with civil society aimed at shaping conceptions of the common good via advocacy, collaborations, and partnerships. The layers of communication *of* and *about* development perform an essential socializing role.

However, such an analysis must be emplaced. Research into theatricality and symbolism in traditional diplomatic settings has noted the ways in which normative expectations attached to diplomatic negotiations can be asserted through architecture, seating arrangements, ceremonial rituals, dress codes, and seemingly innocuous decisions regarding the symbolism of colors and shapes. Such efforts seek to provide structure for "constructing and communicating meanings, managing and regulating inter-state relations, affecting collective feelings and motivating people" (Faizullaev 2013, p. 113). That the traditional sites for diplomacy are rife with techniques for asserting values is well-established. However, there is considerable merit to the argument that increased public and digital representations of diplomacy have "raised the use of state symbols and international symbolic interactions to a new level" (Faizullaev 2013, p. 97). Any potential for influence within the everyday sites of diplomacy should therefore be considered within the context of instrumentalist uses of technology and symbolism.

Research on mediatization is particularly useful for conceptualizing the interplay between communication technologies, the circulation of knowledge, and their impact upon social relations. According to Hjarvard (2013), mediatization refers to the ways in which communication technologies have become so fundamental to everyday activities that "social and cultural institutions and modes of interaction are changed as a consequence of the growth of the media's influence" (p. 19). Consequently, "social interaction—within the respective institutions, and in society at large—increasingly takes place via the media" (Hjarvard 2013, p. 17). Thus, mediatization underscores the ways in which social relations are continually affected by the existence of mediated knowledge. The impact of communication technologies upon the sites of diplomacy is one that potentially alters the epistemological and ontological grounds for representing diplomatic identities, and this in turn changes the ways in which diplomatic actors—and indeed members of the public—know and experience themselves as political entities (Pamment 2014). PD and Devcom are but two examples of how mediatization brings diplomatic thinking into the everyday.

This new context of the diplomatic quotidian may therefore be interpreted through what Der Derian (1987) referred to as the emergence of a *techno-diplomacy*, "in the sense of technical invention applied to social relations" (p. 203). For Der Derian, as for Foucault, the symbolic function of "normalization" is an example of how Western diplomacy has become dependent on bridging estrangement through technology (p. 204; Foucault 1997/2003, p. 38). Many of the new sites of every-day diplomacy are not just easily accessible material or digital spaces, but are simultaneously "well-groomed sites" that are deliberately planned and maintained by diplomatic actors to support the application of com-municative tools of influence (Neumann 2013, pp. 151–154). Indeed, as Pigman (2010) notes, multilateral actors such as the UN, NATO, and the WTO are both actors *and* venues, and their sites help define *what* they are as actors, interests, and processes (p. 29). Hence, it is important to study diplomatic representation through the context and emplacement—the materiality—of representational practices in this rapidly evolving con-text. The participation of actors and the development of agendas are in many respects contingent upon the affordances of the venue.

It may therefore be argued that the proliferation of actors has sup-ported a geopolitical environment in which Devcom, PD, and soft power represent a re-situation of diplomatic agendas in the everyday. The mon-itoring, negotiation, and advocacy functions of diplomacy have become structured into the very sites where this extended vision of diplomacy is supposed to take place. In a sense, Devcom and PD are intrinsically linked to strategic influence over quotidian spaces that exist outside of traditional policy environments, to the networks of actors that co-constitute them, to the flows of knowledge, and to the participatory affordances of the channels that sustain them (Neumann 2013). This clearly has implications for North–South relations, as partnership and participation suggest a new dynamic for asserting influence.

4. *Complement and extend diplomatic practice and objectives toward wider publics*

Devcom's participatory turn has been an important means of shifting debates away from "ahistorical, deterministic and functionalist" modern-ization theories (Fair 1989, pp. 133–134). These critiques have helped to shift the object of knowledge from how Western structures and ideas can be co-opted within developing countries toward the examination of "self-development strategies, horizontal and upward-flowing com-munication patterns, feedback mechanisms, and the impact of class on the ability of audiences to gain access to and use media messages" (Fair 1989, p. 132; Rogers 1976). Such approaches are heterogeneous and seek to establish a better understanding of the complex structures that impact upon the ability to shape change in a society. Social change may be considered a "diffused concept" referring to issues such as "changes in norms, attitudes, socioeconomic structures, policies, beliefs, information, behaviors, and so on" (Waisbord 2014, p. 155), and public participation is central to the credibility of communication *for* development.

> From a critical, participatory perspective, the selection of strategic goals is a political process by which stakeholders identify and choose objectives at multiple levels. Goals are not limited to information or persuasion. Certainly, they may include making individuals aware about issues and options, and/or convincing them about certain ideas, beliefs, and behaviors. But they also include promoting changes in social norms, policies, services, and organizational practices. (Waisbord 2014, p. 160)

The rejection of simplistic influence models reveals an ambiguity around foreign political influence. As discussed above, development actors seek to shape social change by investing resources according to a theory of change. The participatory paradigm suggests that the most appropriate theory of change is one that allows the participants in development to have a say in the methods and goals. The focus has fallen upon the idea of *participation* as the signifier of an inclusive approach. This emphasizes power structures within developing communities and creates stakeholder groups among what may be assumed to be elites or influencers within those communities. Social change according to the participatory paradigm is considered a process of collective action, choice, and involvement, but does not preclude structures of influence. The participatory paradigm is:

> primarily interested in understanding conditions that favor or discourage community dialogue, mutual learning, solidarity, and collective agency. It puts forth the notion that communication should contribute to openness, human agency, and criticism in development and social change. Consequently, it opposes understanding communication in terms of information, persuasion, and influence. (Waisbord 2014, p. 152)

In public diplomacy, the "participatory turn" has taken a similar path motivated by similar considerations. In the early 1990s, Public Relations theories were applied to Cold War-era PD to claim that exchanges and other forms of collaborative exercises provided the most symmetrical—and therefore persuasive—means of managing communication between actors, interest groups, and stakeholders (e.g. Signitzer and Coombs 1992, pp. 144–145). Inclusion was key to success. Public Relations tends to define itself in this benign way; for example, the Public Relations Society of America claims that PR contributes "to mutual understanding among groups and institutions,"[2] while a core textbook defines contemporary PR as "the management of mutually influential relationships within a web of stakeholder and organisational relationships" (Coombs and Holladay 2007). A number of influential lobbyists successfully advocated for a PR perspective on US public diplomacy post-9/11, for which PR standards like *relationship management* and *mutually beneficial relations* set the scene for a more inclusive style of communication. For example, Washington-based think tank the Council on Foreign Relations argued for "a new public diplomacy paradigm" based around normative principles such as *engagement, two-way dialogue, debate, collaboration,* and *relationship-building* (Peterson et al. 2002, p. 5).

In order to explain the difference between unidirectional and dialogical modes of communication, a number of categorizations of public diplomacy activities emerged, creating taxonomies that distinguished between the participatory affordances of "old" and "new" technologies and approaches (Pamment 2013a, b; see Evans and Steven 2008; Fisher and Bröckerhoff 2008; Gilboa 2008). Collaborative and participatory models have become the de facto best practice standard for practitioners and academics alike (Fitzpatrick 2010; Zaharna et al. 2013). However, the debate as a whole has struggled with the reality of PD programs, which often utilize the discourse of dialogue and engagement to justify activities which are often limited to persuading others to support their policy objectives. Critical scholars have thus argued that "engagement" approaches to PD merely conceal "a relatively participatory form of persuasion" (Comor and Bean 2012, p. 203; Hayden 2012; Pamment 2013a; Smyth 2001).

To build the theoretical case for this inclusive new form of public diplomacy, PD scholars turned to some strange bedfellows. *Noopolitik* (or *noöspolitik*) seeks to explain the potential of PD to shape a new

---

[2] http://www.prsa.org/aboutUs/officialStatement.html.

international society by postulating three informational spheres or domains that are of increasing importance in international affairs. First is the *noosphere*, developed from the work of controversial Jesuit theologian Pierre Teilhard de Chardin. This may be described rather abstractly as "a globe-circling realm of the mind," "a thinking circuit," a "stupendous thinking machine," a "planetary consciousness," or a "web of living thought" (Ronfeldt and Arquilla 2009). The other two spaces are *cyberspace*, which consists of the internet, databases, and other communication infrastructures, and the *infosphere*, which encompasses cyberspace and the entire output of all media and communication systems. The noosphere contains cyberspace and the infosphere, and may be considered a collective information processing and structuring system consisting of ideas, values, and norms. It implicitly links information to power (Ronfeldt and Arquilla 2009).

The noosphere develops the notion that public opinion has become a second superpower, a genuine alternative and counterweight to the dominance of state and market actors. This was seen for example in the Gulf War, in which the so-called "CNN Effect" intervened in decision-making cycles, forcing policy-makers into engagement with international satellite news channels which claimed to represent public opinion.

> When a person thinks "cyberspace," what typically comes to mind is a computer screen logged onto the Internet ... When a person thinks "infosphere," the image is likely a television showing something along the lines of a CNN broadcast conveyed by satellite. When a person thinks of the "noosphere," the image will not be of a technology, but probably of an idea floating in a cultural ether. (Ronfeldt and Arquilla 1999, p. 16)

Ronfeldt and Arquilla seek to differentiate the communicative aspects of globalization and assess the potential of what they call "information structuring" as a new form of power that is gradually phasing out realpolitik. They suggest that the totality of the communications revolution has in effect mirrored the mind, so that the noosphere—a kind of global consciousness—has been created through these systems. The actors doing the "information processing" and producing knowledge are individuals, groups, NGOs, governments, and market actors, each in their specific areas of activity. Hence, the new context for diplomacy is one of the emergence of information exchanges as a layer of thought beamed by satellites and connected by overlapping and intermingling networks across the earth.

Despite its pseudo-mystical and eschatological leanings, the concept of the noosphere gained credence through the work of Ronfeldt and Arquilla (1999) in a project for the RAND Corporation, in which they echoed McLuhan's conception of "a united, global village ... in the making," in this case joined by networks of boundary-spanning actors behaving diplomatically (pp. 18–19). Manuel Castells's limited observations on public diplomacy assume a similar stance, suggesting that PD is a means of establishing a common discourse around the definition of a problem in order to form consensus about how the international community should respond. Its purpose is "to induce a communication space in which a new, common language could emerge as a precondition for diplomacy" (Castells 2008, p. 91). Hence, this realm of ideas, as expressed through the notion of a global civil society, represents "the diplomacy of the public, that is, the projection in the international arena of the values and ideas of the public" (ibid.). By foregrounding the identities of publics as "world" citizens over national identities, such approaches reduce the role of states and emphasize the impact of norms, values, and ideas on the context for diplomacy. The view of an expanded, everyday diplomacy is clear, though it is remarkably devoid of the *interests* that have driven these developments and indeed are so fundamental to the practice of diplomacy.

A more recent explication of these principles may be seen in the concept of *relational public diplomacy* (Zaharna et al. 2013). This approach emphasizes the role of building relationships, earning trust, and shaping cooperation between actors. Terming this a "connective mindshift," Zaharna et al. (2013) argue that "the communication dynamics of the contemporary international arena thrive on complex and multidirectional networks. This operational landscape requires cooperative approaches and international collaboration involving nonstate or non-geographically located actors" (p. 7). Observing strong currents within contemporary PD research relating to dialogue, engagement, networks, and collaboration, this approach foregrounds the importance of "the complex architecture of the multi-hub, multi-directional networks" used in contemporary diplomacy, and the inherent power of interconnected publics (p. 1). Hence, building strong, lasting relationships with the inhabitants of these networks is of far greater use to public diplomacy outcomes than messaging, since it helps to structure the architecture of the networks.

This leaves PD debates about participatory communication in a similar position to debates in the field of Devcom. The sense of a shift in global power relations toward interconnected citizens is persuasive, as is the call to empower further such groups by emphasizing their *actor-ness*: their ability to further their own interests and to shape their own communities through the strength of their ideas. This fits with some of the key intersections outlined earlier in the chapter: namely, (2) the sense of a common public good; and (3) the collaboration with civil society. But it loses the key principles of the first intersection, which rests upon the interests of those most powerful and influential actors who seek to shape the behavior of others across borders by committing resources to the production of desired social change. It would seem that the prevalence of theories of change centered on encouraging participation may at times obfuscate the underlying political interests foregrounded in intersection (1), at the expense of appreciating the power modalities that have preferred the participatory as their modus operandi. This therefore represents a shared challenge for critical researchers interested in convergence within Devcom and more instrumentalist approaches.

5. *Seek to influence thoughts, behavior, and communities directly or indirectly*

Perhaps the most important questions emerging from these thematic intersections between fields relate to the nature and modality of the influence that is produced. Many different forms of influence have been alluded to in this chapter, but their actual impact is a problem to be analyzed through empirical studies, using a careful analysis of where local contexts meet global networks. The collection of essays in this book is one small contribution to that end. Key to making sense of these initiatives, however, is an understanding of the extent to which publics are prepared for dealing with these new power configurations. In particular, these fields reveal the difficult balance between empowering citizens to shape their own development and social realities, and the exigencies of institutions whose sole purpose is to shape the world—and its rules, norms, and common beliefs—according to their preferred vision and values. While citizens can be active players in foreign affairs, scholars and practitioners should be wary of theories that postulate a meeting of equals between institutions controlling vast amounts of tangible and intangible resources, and a network of engaged individuals. From the perspective of civil society, participation is an effective way to shape change, but it is also an effective way for powerful institutions to manage challenges to their leadership and to promote buy-into their ideas. It does not resolve power inequality, and at times appears to obfuscate it. Hence, the extension of diplomatic thinking into the realm of the everyday juxtaposes the deployment of resources by powerful institutions with the capacity of these newly empowered public groups to exert their will in an effective manner.

The "problem of influence" (Pamment 2013a) remains at the crux of Devcom, PD, and soft power enterprises, and consequently establishes a central problematic for the future of the communication of the development and social change research field. Activities created *for* development are so dependent on complex networks of actors that influence via communications *about* and *of* development have become essential both to twenty-first-century statecraft and to the craft of civil society and the private sector. The strategic ambiguities of investing resources in specific outcomes, shaping a sense of the common good, working through influential and well-intentioned actors, and extending diplomatic objectives to the quotidian, draw upon the three levels of communication *for*, *about*, and *of* development because any single level cannot exist in a vacuum. However uncomfortable Devcom scholars might feel about including instrumentalist approaches within their area of study, to deny the convergence of Devcom with PD and soft power via these exigencies is in certain respects to misrepresent the realities of the international development sector. This chapter is therefore a call for theoretical convergence, on the basis that we cannot truly claim to understand the nature of influence over social change in communities without a greater appreciation for how these strategies and actors intersect in practice.

REFERENCES

Castells, M. (2008). The New Public Sphere: Global Civil Society, Communication Networks, and Global Governance. *The Annals of the American Academy of Political and Social Science, 616,* 78–93.

Comor, E., & Bean, H. (2012). America's 'Engagement' Delusion: Critiquing a Public Diplomacy Consensus. *International Communication Gazette, 74,* 203–220.

Coombs, W. T., & Holladay, S. J. (2007). *It's Not Just PR: Public Relations in Society.* Oxford: Blackwell.

Coryn, C., Noakes, L. A., Westine, C. D., & Schröter, D. C. (2011). A Systematic Review of Theory-Driven Evaluation Practice from 1990 to 2009. *American Journal of Evaluation, 32*(2), 199–226.

Cull, N. J. (2008). *The Cold War and the United States Information Agency: American Propaganda and Public Diplomacy*. Cambridge: Cambridge University Press.

Der Derian, J. (1987). *On Diplomacy: A Genealogy of Western Estrangement*. Oxford: Basil Blackwell.

Duchêne, H., & Lamouroux, E. (2011). *Promoting French Expertise Internationally*. Paris, France: Directorate-General of Global Affairs, Development and Partnerships, French Ministry of Foreign and European Affairs.

Evans, A., & Steven, D. (2008). Towards a Theory of Influence for Twenty-First Century Foreign Policy: Public Diplomacy in a Globalised World. In J. Welsh & D. Fearn (Eds.), *Engagement: Public Diplomacy in a Globalised World* (pp. 44–61). London: Foreign & Commonwealth Office.

Fair, J. E. (1989). 29 years of Theory and Research on Media and Development: The Dominant Paradigm Impact. *International Communication Gazette, 44*, 129–150.

Fair, J. E., & Shah, H. (1997). Continuities and Discontinuities in Communication and Development Research Since 1958. *Journal of International Communication, 4*(2), 3–23.

Faizullaev, A. (2013). Diplomacy and Symbolism. *The Hague Journal of Diplomacy, 8*(2), 91–114.

FCO. (2013, October). *Diplomatic Excellence MFA Briefing*.

Fisher, A., & Bröckerhoff, A. (2008). *Options for Influence: Global Campaigns of Persuasion in the New Worlds of Public Diplomacy*. London: Counterpoint.

Fitzpatrick, K. R. (2010). *The Future of U.S. Public Diplomacy: An Uncertain Fate*. Leiden, the Netherlands: Martinus Nijhoff Publishers.

Foucault, M. (1997/2003). *Society Must Be Defended: Lectures at the Collège de France, 1975–1976*. New York: Picador.

Freire, P. (1983). *Pedagogy of the Oppressed* (M. B. Ramos, Trans.). New York, NY: Continuum.

Gilboa, E. (2008). Searching for a Theory of Public Diplomacy. *The Annals of the American Academy of Political and Social Science, 616*, 55–77.

Gregory, B. (2011). American Public Diplomacy: Enduring Characteristics, Elusive Transformation. *The Hague Journal of Diplomacy, 6*, 351–372.

Gumuci-Dagron, A. (2001). *Making Waves: Stories of Participatory Communication for Social Change*. New York, NY: Rockefeller Foundation.

Hamilton, K., & Langhorne, R. (2011). *The Practice of Diplomacy: Its Evolution, Theory and Administration* (2nd ed.). London: Routledge.

Hayden, C. (2012). *The Rhetoric of Soft Power: Public Diplomacy in Global Contexts*. Lanham, MD: Lexington Books.

Hjarvard, S. (2013). *The Mediatization of Culture and Society*. New York, NY and London: Routledge.

Hocking, B., Melissen, J., Riordan, S., & Sharp, P. (2012). *Futures for Diplomacy: Integrative Diplomacy in the 21st Century*. Netherlands Institute of International Relations 'Clingendael'.

Huesca, R. (2002). Participatory Approaches to Communication and Development. In W. B. Gudykunst & B. Mody (Eds.), *Handbook of International and Intercultural Communication* (pp. 499–518). Thousand Oaks: Sage.

Huntington, S. P. (1968). *Political Order in Changing Societies*. New Haven & London: Yale University Press.

Kelley, J. R. (2010). The New Diplomacy: Evolution of a Revolution. *Diplomacy & Statecraft, 21*(2), 286–305.

Knutsen, T. L. (1997). *A History of International Relations Theory* (2nd ed.). Manchester: Manchester University Press.

Lancaster, C. (2007). *Foreign Aid: Diplomacy, Development, Domestic Politics*. Chicago, IL: Chicago University Press.

Lerner, D. (1958). *The Passing of Traditional Society*. Glencoe, IL: Free Press.

Lerner, D. (1971). Is International Persuasion Sociologically Feasible? *The ANNALS of the American Academy of Political and Social Science, 398*, 44.

Melissen, J. (Ed.). (2005). *The New Public Diplomacy: Soft Power in International Relations*. Basingstoke, UK: Palgrave Macmillan.

Murray, S. (2008). Consolidating the Gains Made in Diplomacy Studies: A Taxonomy. *International Studies Perspectives, 9*, 22–39.

Nederveen Pieterse, J. (2010). *Development Theory: Deconstructions/ Reconstructions* (2nd ed.). Los Angeles: Sage.

Neumann, I. B. (2013). *Diplomatic Sites: A Critical Enquiry*. London, UK: Hurst & Company.

Nye, J. S. (1990). Soft Power. *Foreign Policy, 80*, 152–171.

Nye, J. S. (2004). *Soft Power: The Means to Success in World Politics*. New York, NY: Public Affairs.

Nye, J. S. (2008). Public Diplomacy and Soft Power. *The Annals of the American Academy of Political and Social Science, 616*, 94–109.

OECD-DAC. (2008, November). *Is it ODA? Factsheet*. www.oecd.org/dac/stats.

Pamment, J. (2013a). *New Public Diplomacy in the 21st Century*. Oxon: Routledge.

Pamment, J. (2013b). West European Public Diplomacy. In M. K. Davis Cross & J. Melissen (Eds.), *European Public Diplomacy: Soft Power at Work*. New York, NY: Palgrave.

Pamment, J. (2014). The Mediatization of Diplomacy. *The Hague Journal of Diplomacy, 9*(3), 253–280.

Pamment, J. (2015). Media Influence, Ontological Transformation & Social Change: Conceptual Overlaps Between Development Communication and Public Diplomacy. *Communication Theory, 25*(2), 188–207.

48   J. PAMMENT

Pamment, J. (Ed.). (2016a). *Intersections Between Public Diplomacy &*
International Development: Case Studies in Converging Fields (USC Center on
Public Diplomacy Perspectives Series). Los Angeles, CA: Figueroa Press.

Pamment, J. (2016b). *British Public Diplomacy and Soft Power: Diplomatic
Influence and Digital Disruption.* Basingstoke, UK: Palgrave Macmillan.

Peterson, P. G., Sieg, J., Bloomgarden, K., Grunwald, H., Morey, D. E., &
Telhami, S. (2002). *Public Diplomacy: A Strategy for Reform: A Report of
an Independent Task Force on Public Diplomacy Sponsored by the Council on
Foreign Relations.* Washington, DC: Council on Foreign Relations.

Pigman, G. (2010). *Contemporary Diplomacy.* Cambridge: Cambridge University
Press.

République Français. (2012). *Document de politique transversal projet de loi
finances pour action extérieure de l'état* [Interdepartmental Policy and Finances
for External Action]. Paris, France: République Français.

Roberts, I. (Ed.). (2009). *Satow's Diplomatic Practice.* Oxford: Oxford
University Press.

Rogers, E. (1976). Communication and Development: The Passing of the
Dominant Paradigm. *Communication Research, 3*(2), 213–240.

Ronfeldt, D., & Arquilla, J. (1999). *The Emergence of Noopolitik: Toward an
American Information Strategy.* Santa Monica, CA: RAND, MR-1033-OSD.

Ronfeldt, D., & Arquilla, J. (2009). Noopolitik: A New Paradigm for Public
Diplomacy. In N. Snow & P. M. Taylor (Eds.), *Routledge Handbook of Public
Diplomacy* (pp. 352–366). London and New York: Routledge.

Schiller, H. I. (1969/1992). *Mass Communications & American Empire* (2nd
ed.). Boulder, CO: Westview.

Schramm, W. (1963). Communication Development and the Development
Process. In L. Pye (Ed.), *Communications and Political Development.*
Princeton: Princeton University Press.

Servaes, J., Jacobson, T. L., & White, S. A. (1996). *Participatory
Communication for Social Change.* New Delhi, India: Sage.

Shah, M. (2011). *The Production of Modernization: Daniel Lerner, Mass Media,
and the Passing of Traditional Society.* Philadelphia, PA: Temple University
Press.

Shah, M., & Wilkins, K. G. (2004). Reconsidering Geometries of Development.
Perspectives on Global Development and Technology, 3(4), 395–416.

Sharp, P. (1999). For Diplomacy: Representation and the Study of International
Relations. *International Studies Review, 1*(1), 33–57.

Sharp, P. (2009). *Diplomatic Theory of International Relations.* Cambridge, UK:
Cambridge University Press.

Signitzer, B. H., & Coombs, T. (1992). Public Relations & Public Diplomacy:
Conceptual Convergences. *Public Relations Review, 18*(2), 144–145.

Smyth, R. (2001). Mapping U.S. Public Diplomacy in the 21st Century. *Australian Journal of International Affairs, 55*(3), 421–444.

Thomas, P. N. (2014). Development Communication and Social Change in Historical Context. In K. G. Wilkins, T. Tufte, & R. Obregon (Eds.), *The Handbook of Development Communication and Social Change* (pp. 7–19). Chichester, UK: Wiley.

van Ham, P. (2010). *Social Power in International Politics*. Abingdon, UK: Routledge.

Waisbord, S. (2001). *Family Tree of Theories, Methodologies and Strategies in Development Communication*. New York, NY: The Rockefeller Foundation.

Waisbord, S. (2014). The Strategic Politics of Participatory Communication. In K. G. Wilkins, T. Tufte, & R. Obregon (Eds.), *The Handbook of Development Communication and Social Change* (pp. 147–167). Chichester, UK: Wiley.

Waller, J. M. (Ed.). (2007). *The Public Diplomacy Reader*. Washington, DC: The Institute of World Politics Press.

Wilkins, K. G., & Mody, B. (2001). Reshaping Development Communication: Developing Communication and Communicating Development. *Communication Theory, 11*(4), 1–11.

Wilkins, K., Tufte, T., & Obregon, R. (Eds.). (2014). *The Handbook of Development Communication and Social Change*. Chichester, UK: Wiley.

Zaharna, R. S., Fisher, A., & Arsenault, A. (2013). *Relational, Networking and Collaborative Approaches to Public Diplomacy: The Connective Mindshift*. New York: Taylor & Francis.

CHAPTER 3

The Business of Bilateral Branding

Karin Gwinn Wilkins

The mission of global development intervention is to benefit donor and recipient communities through strategic and constructive social change. Recipient communities expect to improve social and political conditions, while donor communities expect to be recognized and appreciated for their resource allocation. Donors promote their interests through branding their interventions in ways that are designed to attract public attention.

This argument builds on Pamment's (2016b) articulation of nation branding as a way of engaging in soft power through publicized aid programs, raising potential concerns with the process, and outcomes of development. I situate bilateral branding as a product of development intervention through a targeted analysis of dominant bilateral agencies' use of logos associated with their national agencies or aid programs. I explore the connection between development branding and business approaches, resonant with an emerging privatization in the field, considering the consequences of engaging effective and ethical development programs.

K. G. Wilkins (✉)
University of Texas at Austin, Austin, TX, USA
e-mail: karin.wilkins@austin.utexas.edu

51
J. Pamment and K. G. Wilkins (eds.), *Communicating National Image through Development and Diplomacy*, Palgrave Studies in Communication for Social Change, https://doi.org/10.1007/978-3-319-76759-8_3

While the field of development has grown in scope to consider the intentional and constructive collective acts of social movements and civic organizations (Wilkins et al. 2014), in this study I focus on implications of bilateral branding by wealthy donor agencies, foregrounding the significance of power dynamics in situated development practice in order to underscore the importance of politics in development communication. The underlying feature of this dynamic lies in the difference in resources that contribute to asymmetrical power relationships across donor and recipient countries and agencies (Shah and Wilkins 2004). Even within the development enterprise the very conceptualizations of development range widely, from historically bound attention to gross national product guiding modernization approaches, to more comprehensive frameworks that include human welfare and social justice (Kremer et al. 2009).

The work of global development is in intervention, or the *doing* of development. It is the very idea that defined problems may be solved through strategic intervention that unites the extremely divergent collectives that drive social change. While we witness a spectrum of approaches to intervention, from hierarchical modernization employing external approaches to more dialogic processes building from indigenous engagement (Huesca 2002; Nederveen Pieterse 2009a), the decision to engage in intervention at all builds on a determination that a condition should be seen as a problem, and that problem can and should be solved. But in the course of *doing*, intended to be *good*, without solid assessment we have little idea if what has been done has been done *well*, which is necessary for meeting accountability, not to donor interests but to the global community (Wilkins 2016). An interest in doing well through intervention is at the heart of development work.

The advent of bilateral branding as a more serious strategy has evolved along with an emerging privatization sensibility within the development industry, in a post-Washington consensus world. Originally introduced by Washington DC-based economists as a set of specific financial policies promoting trade, privatization, and deregulation, over time the term "Washington Consensus" came to signify free market approaches to development more broadly, justified through neoliberal narratives. The current global market of development agencies includes many more players who lack consensus on how to engage in global development (Kremer et al. 2009; Nederveen Pieterse 2009b). In the next section I characterize the increasingly privatized landscape of formal development agencies engaged in this global industry. In this study, I focus on the branding strategies of bilateral agencies as one manifestation of this broader political process steeped in privatization.

DEVELOPMENT PRIVATIZATION

Although the development industry encompasses a wide spectrum of organizations and communities mobilizing and distributing resources, this group of donors is becoming more privatized in terms of agencies engaged as well as the frameworks followed. Development donors constitute varied organizations, movements, and communities that allocate resources through strategic programs implemented across national and cultural communities. Their significance can be witnessed in the asymmetrical power dynamics that contribute to an ability to dominate which problems gain attention as well as which solutions are deemed worthy of funding.

Although privatization of development is indeed a contemporary and significant trend, the development industry is largely dominated by public agencies, in what is referred to as "official development assistance" or ODA (Wilkins and Lee 2016). The Development Assistance Committee (DAC) defines ODA as "those flows to countries and territories on the DAC list of ODA recipients and to multilateral institutions which are provided by official agencies" (OECD 2016a). Although still a dominant group of donors in terms of spending (contributing collectively US$134.4 billion spent in 2014; OECD 2015), bilateral development assistance has been gradually reducing its proportionate contribution to development. The number of bilateral agencies operating in the development industry has been increasing, notably among those operating outside of DAC, who are estimated to contribute up to 20% of total development assistance (Tomlinson 2014).

Not only has the number of bilateral agencies devoted to development increased, but so has the number of private agencies and individuals in the enterprise (Kremer et al. 2009). Riddell (2009) describes this period of foreign aid as "on track to be the period of the most rapid expansion of aid ever, notwithstanding a brief downturn in 2006 and 2007" (p. 47). The growth of private sector contributions to development is significant, though quite varied, including individual remittances to families across national boundaries as well as individual financial transfers through trade and migration (Kremer et al. 2009, p. 21). Overall development aid emanating from private sources appears to have been "increasing in both absolute and relative terms at a time when official ODA is static or declining" (Edwards 2009, p. 241).

This trend toward privatization, while significant as an aggregate inclination, needs also to be considered along the lines of the incredibly divergent groups devoted to profit, whether as corporations or individuals, distinct from others working as non-governmental organizations (NGOs), civil society organizations, and social movements. Even the category of philanthropy includes organizations quite varied in terms of their visions of social change, whether complementary or oppositional to the status quo, as well as in terms of size and financial structure. It is the assumed intent toward public interest that is used to justify the tax incentives that are meant to stimulate individual and agency investment in philanthropy. Some distinguish "old" from "new" philanthropy, marking contemporary approaches as more driven by "use of the market as a vehicle for reducing poverty, protecting the environment, and achieving social objectives" (Edwards 2009, p. 244), while others suggest that business strategies have dominated US approaches to private foundations all along (McGoey 2015). Some point to significant concerns raised with the integration of business approaches in interventions designed toward public benefit (such as Dutta 2011; Escobar 1995; Hawkins 2012).

The development industry landscape has shifted over time toward a more populated architecture, with more players from an increasingly diverse set of territories and with more varied funding structures. The reigning bilateral and multilateral donors of a half-century ago must now share the stage and the direction of foreign aid. It is not just the political-economic structure that must be considered, but also the sensibility that privatization brings to the industry, contributing to the way that public agencies engage in the process of social change. Dutta (2011), Li (2007), and others (such as Chakravartty 2008; Edwards 2009; Mitchell 1999; Peck 2008; Wilkins 2016) have considered the ways in which neoliberal ideologies guide development intervention.

DEVELOPMENT PRACTICE

The projected paradox pits the profit incentive of business against the targeted public benefit of development intervention. Despite the considerable variations in structures and missions of the increasingly populated field of development donors, their overarching purpose is dedicated to improving social conditions. It is this commitment to change, in a defined beneficial direction, for the greater good that unites the work of public development and philanthropic agencies. Without an explicit articulation of public interest, institutional programs could not be seen as doing development work. The goal of the work matters, but so does the act of intervention, organized and implemented through institutions, as *doing* the *good* that institutional missions envision.

While the articulated missions of development agencies allow us to identify the discourse in which institutions believe they can do *good*, this does not answer the question of whether development strategies are doing particularly *well*. Evaluations of strategic interventions, necessary for understanding how interventions may have done well, or not, tend to exclude the work of private agencies and NGOs, as well as emergency humanitarian work, collectively accounting for a growing proportion of development work (Riddell 2009). Edwards cites the field of philanthro-capitalism as being particularly "plagued" by having too few evaluations, and therefore little accountability (2009, p. 248). While many wealthy individuals and private agencies appreciate the celebratory praise that they excite in Davos and other global venues, and may genuinely believe in their own importance and impact, the nature of positioning resource transfers as "gifts" implies a generosity not needing assessment to gain currency (McGoey 2015). NGOs and other private organizations could be encouraged or compelled to engage in serious assessment contingent upon collaborations with other partners or approvals from national and other public agencies. Development donors could be more transparent through longer-term and more comprehensive evaluations that are shared and discussed in public. This type of accountability would require assessment of social problems in context over time, in order to contribute toward social justice (Wilkins 2016). But an interest in doing well may be jeopardized by a need to promote a particular appearance, looking good, in the process.

DEVELOPMENT DISCOURSE

The public image of development intervention can be construed through analysis of discourse, situating communication as a way of looking at constructions of development rather than as a tool for development (Pamment 2015; Wilkins and Mody 2001; Wilkins 2016). Studies of communication about development have tended to explore the implicit narratives engaged in the selection and articulation of problems, characterizations of targeted communities, and assertions of institutional solutions as interventions. Population programs, for example, might be suggesting that women are responsible for fertility decisions, thus justifying programs directed toward women alone, rather than understanding the complex gendered dynamics within which people connect sexually and decide on contraception, and social norms that guide decisions about relationships and families. This approach to development as a discourse situates these narratives within implicit political ideologies. With this work, I expand this attention on discourse to highlight the explicit articulation of political interests through public communication.

Studies of celebrities acting as philanthropists highlight the importance of public appearance, whether they are being featured visually in public relations, attending fundraising events, actively visiting politicians and policy-makers, or initiating their own foundations (Cooper 2008; Kapoor 2013; Tsaliki et al. 2011). The attention given to celebrities in this discourse risks elevating the status of donors against an artificial portrait of poverty, obscuring the conditions that give rise to extreme inequities in wealth (Richey and Ponte 2011; Wilkins 2015). The wealthiest among the global elite benefit from profits in global industry, which then allow them to act as named and celebrated individual donors.

Development donors, whether as private individual or agencies, public agencies, or corporate donors, wish to project the appearance of doing good in the world, justifying their work and their funding. In 2013 the Gates Foundation hosted a number of "strategic media partners," such as the *New York Times*, NBC, and NPR, in an effort to "improve the narrative" of development, focusing on "good news stories." The profitable public relations agency Ogilvy was granted US$100,000 to "tell the world" that "aid is working" (McGoey 2015). This same corporate agency was also hired by the UN to tell its story of development success (Monllos 2015).

Development donors want to project an image of *doing good* in the world and to dedicate resources toward strategic communication campaigns to *look good* in the process. They justify this investment as a way to convince others of their legitimacy and their value, to attract resources, particularly when public opinion indicates declining support for foreign aid. This public relations approach has been articulated more recently in the development industry as branding.

Development Branding

Building on business models of branding, development organizations now invest in strategic public communication campaigns meant to build an image of their work as beneficial and as effective. As Hoogeveen (2016) remarks, "branding is everywhere, and development agencies are no stranger to it." Pamment (2016b) positions "nation brands as a key component of contemporary soft power strategies," which may be used to leverage economic growth and political influence. In what he describes as an era of "post-conditionality," programs that promote development may inscribe less tangible benefits to donors, such as encouraging recipient adoption of donor language, values, and processes (Pamment 2016b).

Branding of one country's image as a directed campaign to appear in a particular way to other countries is part of strategic public diplomacy. Pamment defines public diplomacy as "state-based communication aimed at influencing well-connected individuals and organisations that are capable of impacting upon a foreign government's policy choices" (2016a, p. 9). Both public diplomacy and development branding may target foreign citizens in their communication approaches.

Relatively recent attention to branding in the development industry has emerged in concert with privatization, as wealthy individuals and private organizations have become more involved in global development. Business models underscore some of the dominant approaches to social change among the wealthiest private foundations, encouraging consumption as a way to direct interests in solving global problems (Peck 2008; Richey and Ponte 2011; Wilkins and Enghel 2013). In their seminal analysis of Project Red, Richey and Ponte (2011) differentiate the ways that branding can accentuate the images of celebrities and private organizations through the shading of red corporate logos. Promoting a brand for charitable organizations is deemed important in creating "the right impression," of the foundations' "inherent beliefs and values" (Saxton 2006).

Bilateral agencies share this interest with multilateral agencies in wanting to appear to be doing good work, strategically characterizing their programs as positively contributing to social change. The United States Agency for International Development (USAID 2016b) asserts that "American aid is clearly one of the 'good-news stories' overseas and yet too little attention has been paid to making that story visible." Although recent explanations of USAID branding point to a 1961 Foreign Assistance Act (Section 641) as the official authorization for explicit identification as "American Aid" (USAID 2015), more visible and highly regulated recognition of USAID as a "brand" intensified along with post 9/11 attention to global security and increased foreign assistance budgets (Kremer et al. 2009).

On another level though it is not just awareness that matters. These public communication campaigns are meant to inspire positive opinions of donor countries among those citizens living outside them. One case cited across documents clearly asserts US interests in promoting its good character on a global stage: the USA credits its new "brand identity" used in the "U.S. tsunami relief effort" (USAID 2016b) with raising favorability ratings of the USA by citizens in Muslim countries from "record lows" in 2004 to much higher rates in 2005 following US assistance. They cite a State Department study that shows Indonesian public opinion in favor of the USA increasing from 37 to 66% in this time period, suggesting that this is "thanks to the massive delivery of—for the first time "well branded"—U.S. foreign assistance" (it should be noted though that Pew research indicates more modest rates rising from 15 to 38% according to Balive 2012).

Branding campaigns are designed to manage agency reputations building from commercial practices. As a communication strategy, branding relates to classic social marketing models (Kotler et al. 2002), in which commercial approaches targeting individual behavior change guide interventions. What does distinguish social marketing from public relations strategies is its attention to behavior change instead of monitoring presence and awareness. The USAID-supported Health Communication Capacity Collaborative offers guides supporting social and behavioral change communication strategies, in which they define "branding" as "a marketing technique that has been successfully used in the commercial sector for years to sell products and services" (Health ComPass 2016).

Branding appears to be built on an adulation of corporate approaches to persuasion. In explaining the branding process, Health ComPass (2016) references "Coca-Cola® and Apple®" as "globally successful commercial companies" with "the most recognized and respected brands." A business mentality also informs these approaches in their constructions of audiences as consumers and not citizens (see Evans et al. 2008; Health ComPass 2016).

While public guidelines on branding suggest that decision processes should include marketing professionals, key stakeholders, and representatives of targeted consumers, it is not clear how this works within big development agencies when determining their logos. Are target audiences considered to be the foreign citizens articulated in public diplomacy approaches, or the citizens of donor countries needed to justify legitimacy and funding of bilateral organizations? Or, are these campaigns meant to appeal to an elite? With this study, I offer an introduction to a broader and significant line of inquiry concerning the political agendas communicated through official public communication in the development industry.

BILATERAL BRANDING

Branding involves a comprehensive communication strategy meant to project an image of *looking good* while *doing good*. USAID (2015) identifies "branding" as "how a program or project is named and positioned, who it is from; it identifies the sponsor of the work," through "marking" or "applying graphic identities or logos to program materials or project signage to visibly acknowledge contributors." Part of this strategy includes determining an official visual logo that connects the image to the sponsoring organization. In this work, I focus on these official logos as particular manifestations of broader branding strategies. Official logos incorporate visual elements with verbal statements through taglines, with dictated colors and sizes.

In concentrating on logos, we must recognize the limitations of narrowing this study to these subjects. In USAID's own terms, their "brand is more than a logo ... it represents the goodwill of the American people in providing assistance to those in need" (2016c). Narrowing the unit of analysis to the logos themselves, however, gives us an opportunity to explore comparable articulations of public images across agencies. Considering how these are explained in official documentation may also add needed context to our consideration of these as communication strategies.

The pool of logos considered are among those projected by the set of wealthy DAC member states. This includes 29 wealthy bilateral donors[1] who engage in "overseas development assistance," but not all assert logos in public digital spaces. Although there are many other development agencies, even bilateral agencies, operating outside of DAC, this sample includes the wealthiest of the bilateral group. In absolute terms, the bilateral agencies distributing the most funding include the USA (US$30.8 billion), Germany (US$20.9 billion), the UK (US$19.9 billion), France (US$10.9 billion), and Japan (US$10.4 billion, though for a brief period during better economic times had led this pack) in 2015. However, if considering donor contributions in relation to capacity to give, as a proportion of their gross national income, we recognize the top bilateral donors as Sweden (1.4%), Norway (1.05%), Luxembourg (0.9%), Denmark (0.9%), and the Netherlands (0.8%). Although the USA may be the largest donor in terms of absolute amount given, its percentage of resources devoted to development is only 0.17%, placing it 20th in rank among all 29 DAC members (OECD 2016b).

Although other development agencies deserve critical attention as well, in this analysis I focus on the branding of dominant bilateral agencies, defined earlier as those within OECD. Next I explore the visual representation of these logos, official policies regulating their practice, stated objectives and justifications, along with potential consequences of posted logos as material artifacts.

OFFICIAL LOGOS

What do these logos indicate about the brand of bilateral agencies? First I consider how the colors, symbols, and taglines articulate development missions. I am particularly interested in how they might reference national patriotism toward home countries, cross-cultural collaboration, or interest in host countries.

Among the 29 members of OECD, 86% ($n = 25$) have specific logos associated with their development assistance agencies, either referring

---

[1] The members of DAC are comprised of Australia, Austria, Belgium, Canada, Czech Republic, Denmark, the European Union, Finland, France, Germany, Greece, Iceland, Ireland, Italy, Japan, Korea, Luxembourg, the Netherlands, New Zealand, Norway, Poland, Portugal, Slovak Republic, Slovenia, Spain, Sweden, Switzerland, the United Kingdom, and the United States.

to aid as a whole from the country or to specific agencies. These logos were accessed through public websites. Canada, the European Union, Finland, and the Netherlands then are the few with no official symbol associated with their foreign aid separate from national images, such as the Canadian maple leaf. How foreign aid is positioned within national agencies does not clearly predict whether logos are used. It is important to note that some of these refer to their countries' aid in general (such as logos from Australia, Ireland, and Norway among others), but most reference development agencies specifically; moreover, this distinction does not predict other patterns considered, such as colors, language, and symbols portrayed.

About two-thirds of those who do engage in bilateral branding directly reference the national flags of donor countries, either through specific inclusion of the flag itself or through reliance on flag colors (Australia, Austria, the Czech Republic, France, Iceland, Italy, Japan, Poland, Portugal, Slovak Republic, Spain, Switzerland, the UK, and the USA). Referencing patriotism differently, Denmark integrates a royal crest image into its foreign aid logo. Other bilateral branding hints at national colors but less directly. For example, Germany relies on only red rather than the black, red, and gold of their flag, and Greece blends grey with the blue of their flag. Those using colors other than shadings in their flags include: Belgium, Ireland, Korea, Luxembourg, New Zealand, and Norway, which may suggest more distance from the donor nation and more independence of the aid agency from national agendas.

In addition to considering the colors invoked, the most prominent symbol shared across these logos focuses on hands. Representations of hands offer creative ways to express emotion, as in the sculpture of Rodin, or through the political iconography of protest (Kraidy 2016). Slovenia's logo for foreign aid presents five shades between blue and green in a figure of a hand, quite distinct from its red/white/blue flag (see Fig. 3.1). What might be interpreted as four sets of hands connected in the Swedish logo relies on sets of blue and yellow as in their flag, but adding in green and red. Hands are also featured in the USAID logo (see Fig. 3.2). Although not identified as clearly as a brand until after 2004, this agency's predecessor, the Mutual Security Agency, did invest in creating a logo featuring clasped hands as long ago as 1953, later adapted from a previously deemed "masculine" grasp to a more "gender neutral" touch in 2004 (Balive 2012). Insertion of hands connecting may be seen as indicating human collaboration across cultural and national boundaries.

**MEDNARODNO RAZVOJNO
SODELOVANJE SLOVENIJE**
SLOVENIA'S DEVELOPMENT
COOPERATION

Fig. 3.1 Slovenia's International Development Cooperation and Humanitarian
Assistance logo (*Source* http://www.mzz.gov.si)

Fig. 3.2 United States Agency for International Development (USAID) logo
(*Source* http://www.usaid.gov/)

Most of the taglines read in English; and while it is not surprising to
see English used in branding from Australia, Ireland, New Zealand, the
UK, and the USA, witnessing the use of English in logos from Austria,
Belgium, the Czech Republic, Denmark, Iceland, Italy, Luxemburg,
Poland, and the Slovak Republic demonstrates a targeting toward a
global economic and cultural elite. Japan (see Fig. 3.3), Korea, and
Slovenia use both English and their own languages, signaling a dual
targeting of global and donor audiences, while France, Germany (see
Fig. 3.4), Portugal, and Switzerland rely on their own national languages
in taglines, with Switzerland using four languages. Norway and Spain
avoid this issue by using only the acronyms of their agencies.

Fig. 3.3 Japan International Cooperation Agency logo (*Source* https://www.jica.go.jp/)

Fig. 3.4 German Corporation for International Cooperation logo (*Source* https://www.giz.de/en/worldwide/germany.html)

The rhetoric of business is employed as the "USAID Standard Graphic Identity" and is specified as "the trademark, by commercial usage, of the United States Agency for International Development." Although this is clearly a public agency, with annual allocations determined through the US Congress, USAID intends its "graphic identity" to be "as recognizable as McDonald's and the Golden Arches or Nike and the SWOOSH" (Balive 2012). Similarly, the UK's Department for International Development (DFID) explicitly describes its "corporate logo" as enabling them to explain "who we are as an organisation, the UK government department with responsibility for the UK development budget and policy. It is consistent with the corporate branding of all UK government departments" (2014, p. 3).

Along with this reverence toward successful corporate branding, bilateral development branding asserts both a patriotism to donor nationalities, along with recognition of an Anglo global elite operating in English. Those logos that do not connect explicitly with official or national symbols are more in concert then with global or foreign audiences than concerned with home donor citizens. The few that reference cross-cultural collaboration share in their use of hands as a connecting gesture. These logos do not, however, adapt to languages of host countries, but rely on the universal use of approved logos.

GUIDELINES FOR USE

While most wealthy bilateral donors project public logos, very few offer detailed, public guidelines on their use. Only four member states have specific rules and restrictions posted on public electronic sites regarding appropriate use of these brands: Australia, Ireland, the United Kingdom, and the United States. For example, USAID sports three officially approved logos in color, in black, and in white, with the blue color in the first option, along with the fonts, symbols, and taglines being mandated through carefully defined policy (USAID 2016a). Taglines must read: "This assistance is from the American people." The USAID logo is used instead of the US flag, asserted by the US Department of State in its official promotions (USAID 2015). The Irish government (2016) also offers detailed examples of acceptable logos in its official documentation.

For these four agencies, guidelines are detailed and their use compulsory. Official documentation explains: "Failure to brand violates U.S. law and USAID policy, regulations, and guidance, creates audit vulnerability, and perhaps most importantly, deprives beneficiaries of U.S. Government foreign aid programs from understanding the source of the assistance and deprives U.S. taxpayers and USAID from receiving credit for the important work that USAID performs across the globe" (USAID 2016a). The UK foreign aid program DFID similarly pushes its own logo on to the work of development. This logo includes the union flag, the term "UK," the word "aid," and the tagline "from the British people" through the colors officially recognized in the UK flag (DFID 2014) (Fig. 3.5). These components contribute to an assertion of a national identity as well as a reinforcement of donor citizens as responsible for the foreign assistance.

Similar to policies among other bilateral agencies, DFID branding should appear on program artifacts such as infrastructure (e.g. buildings, roads, and signs) and on public communications (e.g. publications, websites, and posters). USAID similarly details the importance of branding in host country infrastructure projects, as well as public communication,

Fig. 3.5 Department
for International
Development, UK
aidlogo (*Source* https://
www.gov.uk/govern-
ment/organisations/
department-for-interna-
tional-development)

such as press statements, "media interviews, site visits, success stories, beneficiary testimonials, professional photography, PSAs, videos, webcasts" (USAID 2015). The Irish government (Irish Aid 2016) briefly states that the "Irish Aid logo (together with an acknowledgement of Irish Aid support) should be used on all documentation (both hard copy and electronic) and signage produced in respect of programmes funded, in whole or in part, by Irish Aid." Whereas USAID, DFID, and Irish Aid are quite explicit in terms of wanting to consider exceptions only to the rule of logo positioning, the Australian government suggests that its aid logo, featuring a red kangaroo on a blue background, be used "wherever practical, the previous (AusAID) Australian Aid Identifier should be replaced progressively and sensibly" (Australian Government 2016).

JUSTIFICATIONS

Bilateral agencies justify these investments in official logos as part of broader branding strategies, designed to raise visibility, assert credit, and take responsibility. USAID (2015) explains the purpose of positioning logos on public communications as "intended for distribution to audiences external to the recipient's organization" (USAID 2015, p. 28). USAID (2015) intends its campaign to "generate awareness … from American people," through "showcas(ing) publications or other materials, research findings, or program success." Sharing "America's good-news story" may also be seen as a way to "symbolically stake out a space like flags planted in the sand" to be noticed by citizens in host countries (Balive 2012). Groups funded by these bilateral agencies are required to use official logos and acknowledge their sources of funding (DFID 2014, p. 5). British and American agencies suggest that this visibility is significant in terms of transparency, clarifying to their own citizens as to how their taxes are being allocated toward global development (DFID 2014; USAID 2015), yet they are positioned in places outside of donor territories.

Another level of justification, beyond visibility and transparency, is to assert credit for development intervention. An official DFID announcement (Vaishnav 2012) states that their newly designed logo "will help to drive home the message that Britain deserves credit for the results that UK aid delivers, for example in vaccinating millions of children and getting millions more into school over the past two years." British International Development Secretary Andrew Mitchell reportedly determined that "for too long, Britain has not received the credit it deserves for the amazing results we achieve in tackling global poverty … I believe it is important that aid funded by the British people should be easily and clearly identified as coming from the UK … from now on, Britain will not shy away from celebrating and taking credit." Vaishnav's (2012) discussion of this official strategy suggests an irony in which Britain's "brand value" may be gained through *not* "seeking credit for its good work." The assumption that governments will receive credit for their public investments in other countries is designed to motivate citizens in host countries to have favorable opinions of donor governments.

Some bilateral agency justifications add another layer to the assertion of transparency, reasoning that branding strengthens their accountability. It is not just being visible that matters, or gaining credit, but agencies may want to take public responsibility. The Australian Government (2016) credits branding as "a key mechanism for enhancing the visibility of the Australian Government's international development and aid initiatives," in order to increase "the accountability and transparency of Australia's aid program." Similarly, the Swedish International Development Cooperation Agency explains that their "new badge is expected to boost openness and accountability of the Swedish aid program" (Mungcal 2012), while the Irish Government (2016) declares that it "places accountability at the heart of its development cooperation programme. It is more important than ever that the Irish Government and its partners clearly demonstrate to the public the results which are achieved through the Irish Aid support." These justifications argue that logos assert the visibility bilateral agencies need to gain credit they feel they deserve for their good work.

THE BUSINESS OF LOOKING GOOD

Bilateral development agencies project positive images of their work in attempting to take credit for what they hope to be seen as beneficial acts. Although looking good could be seen as an outcome by itself, these communication strategies may encompass multiple goals, from raising legitimacy and encouraging financial support among donor citizens toward inspiring appreciation from those in recipient communities. But beyond these more explicit goals, we need to consider the potential consequences of these branding strategies to donor–recipient relationships, given the structuring of business approaches engaged.

Bilateral agencies use their logos as part of broader branding strategies in which they promote their nations as benefactors. These are complicated processes, as evidenced through Pamment's (2016b) analysis of the UK's "GREAT" campaign, building toward a contested yet asserted national identity meant to be more unified than fragmented. Many donors unite cultural programs with economic incentives in their public diplomacy strategies. Integrating these programs further strengthens the potential for donors to engage soft power, structuring their relationships with recipients through the lens of commercial models of interaction.

The problem here is that by considering the project of development, meant to find success through public benefit, through a business model, we are privileging individual consumption and material conditions. A more participatory approach might instead consider social and political benefits, and when highlighting economic factors, focus more on issues of equity than growth. This would resonate with a social justice understanding of global development.

The potential to work toward social justice on a global scale is challenged when we allow business models to influence the work of public agencies. Just as we might raise concerns that consumption contributing to corporate profit might not be the best response to global inequity, we need to question how corporate strategies in public development agencies assume rather than question the importance of markets (McGoey 2015; Richey and Ponte 2011). Instead of legitimizing the extreme wealth of those who then get to determine global agendas, we might consider how best to articulate strategies that build toward advocacy for global social justice. We need to stop selling development as spectacle and invest in people as citizens with rights to dignity and respect.

REFERENCES

Australian Government. (2016, May). *Branding Aid Projects and Initiatives*. Department of Foreign Affairs and Trade. Retrieved September 1, 2016, from http://dfat.gov.au/about-us/corporate/Pages/branding-aid-projects-and-initiatives.aspx.

Balive, T. (2012, April 24). *The Branding of U.S. Development Aid: Territorial Masquerades*. Retrieved September 1, 2016, from http://territorialmasquerades.net/the-branding-of-u-s-development-aid/.

Chakravartty P. (2008, October). Modernization Redux? Cultural Studies & Development Communication. *Television & New Media*. Retrieved September 27, 2016, from http://tvn.sagepub.com/content/early/2008/10/07/1527 476408325730.

Cooper, A. F. (2008). *Celebrity Diplomacy*. Boulder: Paradigm.

DFID. (2014, June). *UK Aid Branding Guidance*. DFID. Retrieved September 1, 2016, from https://www.gov.uk/government/uploads/system/uploads/attachment_data/file/326391/UK_aid_branding_guidance_June_2014.pdf.

Dutta, M. (2011). *Communicating Social Change: Structure, Culture, Agency*. New York: Routledge.

Edwards, M. (2009). Why 'Philanthrocapitalism' Is Not the Answer: Private Initiatives and International Development. In M. Kremer, P. van Lieshout, & R. Went (Eds.), *Doing Good or Doing Better: Development Policies in a Globalizing World* (pp. 237–254). Amsterdam: Amsterdam University Press.

Escobar, A. (1995). *Encountering Development: The Making and Unmaking of the Third World*. Princeton: Princeton University Press.

Evans, W. D., Blitsetin, J., Hersey, J. C., Renaud, J., & Yaroch, A. L. (2008). *Systematic Review of Public Health Branding*. Retrieved September 22, 2016, from www.comminit/com/global/content/systematic-review-public-health-branding.

Hawkins, R. (2012). A New Frontier in Development? The Use of Cause-Related Marketing by International Development Organization. *Third World Quarterly, 10*, 1783–1801.

Health ComPass. (2016). *How to Create a Brand Strategy. How-to Guide*. Retrieved September 22, 2016, from www.healthcompass.org/how-to-guides/how-create-brand-strategy-part-1-using-audience-insight-drive-your-brand, www.healthcompass.org/how-to-guides/how-create-brand-strategy-part-2-developing-positioning-brand-product-or-service-or-behavior, www.healthcompass.org/how-to-guides/how-create-brand-strategy-part-3-developing-personality-and-look-brand.

Hoogeveen, J. (2016). *Branding Development? World Bank.* Retrieved September 1, 2016, from http://blogs.worldbank.org/africacan/branding-development.
Huesca, R. (2002). Participatory Approaches to Communication and Development. In W. B. Gudykunst & B. Mody (Eds.), *Handbook of International and Intercultural Communication* (pp. 499–518). Thousand Oaks: Sage.
Irish Aid. (2016, June). *Guidelines: Irish Aid Logo for Partners.* Retrieved October 1, 2016, from https://www.irishaid.ie/media/irishaid/allwebsitemedia/20newsandpublications/irish-aid-logo-guidelines-partners-june-2016.pdf.
Kapoor, I. (2013). *Celebrity Humanitarianism: The Ideology of Global Charity.* New York: Routledge.
Kotler, P., Roberto, N., & Lee, N. (2002). *Social Marketing: Improving the Quality of Life* (2nd ed.). Thousand Oaks: Sage.
Kraidy, M. (2016). *The Naked Blogger of Cairo: Creative Insurgency in the Arab World.* Cambridge: Harvard University Press.
Kremer, M., van Lieshout, P., & Went, R. (2009). *Doing Good or Doing Better: Development Policies in a Globalizing World.* Amsterdam: Amsterdam University Press.
Li, T. M. (2007). *The Will to Improve: Governmentality, Development, and the Practice of Politics.* Durham: Duke University Press.
McGoey, L. (2015). *No Such Thing as a Free Gift.* London: Verso.
Mitchell, T. (1999). No Factories, No Problems: The Logic of Neo-liberalism in Egypt. *Review of African Political Economy, 26*(82), 455–468.
Monllos, K. (2015, May 4). *The United Nations is Working on the 'World's Largest Advertising Campaign' with the Goal of Tackling Society's Greatest Challenges in 15 years. Adweek.* Retrieved September 1, 2016, from http://www.adweek.com/brand-marketing/united-nations-working-worlds-largest-advertising-campaign-164497/.
Mungcal, I. (2012, July 30). *Sweden Redesigns Aid Brand. Inside Development.* Retrieved September 1, 2016, from https://www.devex.com/news/sweden-redesigns-aid-brand-78801.
Nederveen Pieterse, J. (2009a). *Development Theory: Deconstructions/ Reconstructions.* London: Sage.
Nederveen Pieterse, J. (2009b). Twenty-First Century Globalization, Paradigm Shifts in Development. In M. Kremer, P. van Lieshout, & R. Went (Eds.), *Doing Good or Doing Better: Development Policies in a Globalizing World* (pp. 27–46). Amsterdam: Amsterdam University Press.
OECD. (2015). *Development Aid Stable in 2014 but Flows to Poorest Countries still Falling.* OECD. Retrieved April 27, 2015, from http://www.oecd.org/dac/stats/development-aid-stable-in-2014-but-flows-to-poorest-countries-still-falling.htm.
OECD. (2016a). *Official Development Assistance—Definition and Coverage.* Retrieved April 27, 2015, from http://www.oecd.org/dac/stats/officialdevelopmentassistancedefinitionandcoverage.htm.

OECD. (2016b). *Table 1: Net Official Development Assistance from DAC and Other Donors in 2015.* Retrieved October 17, 2016, from https://www.oecd.org/dac/stats/ODA-2015-complete-data-tables.pdf.

Pamment, J. (2015). Media Influence, Ontological Transformation, and Social Change: Conceptual Overlaps between Development Communication and Public Diplomacy. *Communication Theory, 25*(2), 188–207.

Pamment, J. (2016a). *British Public Diplomacy and Soft Power: Diplomatic Influence and the Digital Revolution.* New York: Springer.

Pamment, J. (2016b). Towards a New Conditionality? The Convergence of International Development, Nation Brands and Soft Power in the British National Security Strategy. *Journal of International Relations and Development.* https://doi.org/10.1057/s41268-016-0074-9.

Peck, J. (2008). *The Age of Oprah: Cultural Icon for the Neoliberal Era.* Boulder: Paradigm.

Richey, L., & Ponte, S. (2011). *Brand Aid: Shopping Well to Save the World.* Minneapolis: University of Minnesota Press.

Riddell, R. C. (2009). Does Foreign Aid Work? In M. Kremer, P. van Lieshout, & R. Went (Eds.), *Doing Good or Doing Better: Development Policies in a Globalizing World* (pp. 47–80). Amsterdam: Amsterdam University Press.

Saxton, J. (2006). *Polishing the Diamond: Values, Image and Brand as a Source of Strength for Charities.* Retrieved September 1, 2016, from www.comminit/com/global/content/polishing-diamonds-value-image-and-brand-source-strength-charities.

Shah, H., & Wilkins, K. (2004). Reconsidering Geometries of Development. *Perspectives on Global Development and Technology, 3*(4), 395–416.

Tomlinson, B. (2014). *Reality of Aid 2014 Report: Rethinking Partnerships in a Post-2015 World: Towards Equitable, Inclusive and Sustainable Development.* Quezon City, Phillippines: IBON International.

Tsaliki, L., Franonikolopoulos, C., & Huliaras, A. (2011). Making Sense of Transnational Celebrity Activism: Causes, Methods and Consequences. In L. Tsaliki, C. A. Frangonikilopoulos, & A. Huliaras (Eds.), *Transnational Celebrity Activism in Global Politics: Changing the World?* (pp. 297–311). Bristol, UK: Intellect.

USAID. (2015). *ADS Chapter 320: Branding and Marking.* File Name: 320_010215. Responsible Office: LPA. Partial Revision Date: 01/02/2015. Retrieved September 1, 2016, from https://www.usaid.gov/sites/default/files/documents/1868/320.pdf.

USAID. (2016a). *USAID Branding: Frequently Asked Questions.* Retrieved September 1, 2016, from https://www.usaid.gov/branding.faqs.

USAID. (2016b). *Branding.* Retrieved September 1, 2016, from https://www.usaid.gov/branding.

USAID. (2016c). *USAID Graphic Standards Manual and Partner Co-branding Guide*. Retrieved September 1, 2016, from https://www.usaid.gov/branding/gsm.

Vaishnav, M. (2012, June 26). *Will Branding Hurt the "Brand Value" of the UK's Aid Agency? Center for Global Development*. Retrieved September 1, 2016, from https://www.cgdev.org/blog/will-branding-hurt-"brand-value"-uk's-aid-agency.

Wilkins, K. (2015). Celebrity as Celebration of Privatization in Global Development: A Critical Feminist Analysis of Oprah, Madonna, and Angelina. *Communication, Culture & Critique, 8*(2), 163–181.

Wilkins, K. (2016). *Communicating Gender and Advocating Accountability in Global Development*. Hampshire: Palgrave Macmillan.

Wilkins, K., & Enghel, F. (2013). The Privatization of Development Through Global Communication Industries: Living Proof? *Media, Culture and Society, 35*(2), 165–181.

Wilkins, K., & Lee, K. S. (2016). Political Economy of Development. In O. Hemer (Ed.), *Voice & Matter* (pp. 71–86). Hampshire: Palgrave Macmillan.

Wilkins, K., & Mody, B. (Eds.). (2001). Communication, Development, Social Change, and Global Disparity [Special Issue]. *Communication Theory, 11*(4).

Wilkins, K., Tufte, T., & Obregon, R. (Eds.). (2014). *Handbook of Development Communication and Social Change*. IAMCR Series. Oxford: Wiley.

CHAPTER 4

Nation Branding, Neoliberal Development, and the Remaking of the Nation-State: Lessons from Post-war Kosovo

Nadia Kaneva

Rediscovering the Nation-State in Development

In the 1990s the World Bank (WB), considered by some "the most influential purveyor of development theory and strategy" (Sandbrook 2000, p. 1073), introduced a shift in its conceptual framework for development. The "new paradigm," elaborated in various documents and public speeches by WB President James Wolfensohn, augmented the Bank's almost exclusive previous focus on macroeconomic growth policies and called, instead, for greater integration of political and social factors with economic goals as part of a "Comprehensive Development Framework" (Wolfensohn 2005 [1999]). To be sure, the WB's overall approach to development remained firmly rooted in market-based strategies. However, the new framework emphasized that market mechanisms and

N. Kaneva (✉)
University of Denver, Denver, CO, USA
e-mail: Nadia.Kaneva@du.edu

© The Author(s) 2018
J. Pamment and K. G. Wilkins (eds.), *Communicating National Image through Development and Diplomacy*, Palgrave Studies in Communication for Social Change, https://doi.org/10.1007/978-3-319-76759-8_4

reforms required active support from national governments in order to be successful in advancing development goals (Sandbrook 2000). This "rediscovery" of the nation-state as an important actor in development has been largely overlooked or, in some cases, flatly dismissed by scholars of development communication. Waisbord (2003) has noted that inattention to the role of the state has characterized this field of study for decades. As he puts it, "the state remained a blindspot in the modernization literature in the 1950s and 1960s. In subsequent studies, the state is present, but has rarely been at the forefront of the analysis" (p. 148). Grounded in a critique of globalization, critical approaches to development communication have focused more on the role of non-governmental organizations, social movements, and transnational actors in implementing development programs, while depicting the state as either irrelevant or downright detrimental to development goals (p. 159).

Critical voices in the field of development communication have decried the erosion of the public sector under the onslaught of neoliberalism and have portrayed transnational organizations and multinational corporations as the chief "villains" of neoliberal globalization. Mohan Dutta sums up the typical charges leveled against neoliberal development as follows:

> Erstwhile development agencies such as the United States Agency for International Development (USAID) and the Department for International Development (DfID) and international financial institutions such as the International Monetary Fund (IMF) and the World Bank (WB) that established the development agenda within the purviews of capitalist transformations of newly independent nation states evolved rapidly and massively into conduits for market promotion, utilizing development as the strategy for the promotion of a global market for transnational corporations (TNCs) geographically centered in the United States and in the United Kingdom. (Dutta 2015, p. 124)

Informed by post-colonial critiques, this view of development portrays "newly independent nation states" as captured in a global system of dependency through a combination of aid and loans administered by transnational organizations under Western control (Dutta 2011, 2015; Servaes 1999). While such claims correctly highlight the inequitable distribution of economic and political power in the system of international relations, they tend to obscure the role of national elites and of state institutions in development.

In contrast to such approaches, in this chapter I focus on the engagement of national and extra-national actors within the context of development in an effort to highlight the ways in which the nation-state is reconstituted under a neoliberal regime. My premise is that when transnational purveyors of neoliberal development, such as the WB, seek a greater engagement with the state, they are, in fact, interested in a particular type of state, which can best advance the neoliberal agenda. In that sense, they are not merely seeking to rediscover the state, but rather to *remake* it anew according to market principles. This process, I would argue, can best be observed in nation-building efforts in post-conflict societies, such as Afghanistan, Kosovo, or South Africa. In light of this, my empirical focus in this chapter is on post-war Kosovo—a recently independent and still contested state in the Western Balkans where development, nation building, and nation branding have unfolded simultaneously. As I will elaborate later, the case of Kosovo allows us to examine the ways in which the neoliberal nation-state employs nation branding as communication *for*, *about*, and *of* development (Wilkins and Mody 2001; Pamment 2016a). Although the case of Kosovo is unique in some ways, it also reveals key characteristics of the paradigmatic "neoliberal nation-state."[1]

A central goal of this chapter is to invite a renewed analytical focus on how the nation-state factors in development communication and in public diplomacy, especially (but not exclusively) as these fields intersect in the praxis of nation branding. My arguments build upon and extend a critical, interdisciplinary perspective on nation branding as a neoliberal tool of governance (Aronczyk 2013; Browning 2016; Cánepa 2013; Jansen 2008; Kaneva 2011a; Volcic and Andrejevic 2011). In previous work, I have advocated the need to develop empirically grounded and historically situated examinations of the practices and discourses of nation branding (Kaneva 2011b, 2015). In this chapter, I adopt a similar grounded analytical approach and focus on nation branding in post-war Kosovo as a way to get at two larger theoretical questions: What are some key characteristics of the neoliberal nation-state? And how does the ideological discourse of nation branding articulate the agenda of neoliberal development with the project of producing national subjects within the parameters of a reconstituted, neoliberal nation-state?

NATION BRANDING AND DEVELOPMENT COMMUNICATION

In order to address these questions, it is necessary to outline a few theoretical coordinates. To start, I propose that the practices and discourses of nation branding are located at the intersection of public diplomacy and development communication, although this conceptual junction has been understudied to date. Since the late 1990s, nation branding—a commercialized and media-centric variant of public diplomacy—has become a standard tool in the implementation and legitimization of neoliberal development (Browning 2016; Dinnie 2008). There is an ongoing debate about the nature, boundaries, and effectiveness of nation branding (Anholt 2010; Aronczyk 2013; Kaneva 2011a; Szondi 2008), suggesting the need to define briefly my own understanding of this phenomenon. For the purposes of this study, I view nation branding as an area of practice *and* an ideological discourse whereby the agendas of neoliberal development and of nation building converge. What this means in practice is that nation branding is often deployed simultaneously as a tool for economic development *and* as a tool for collective identity making, and these two objectives cannot be neatly separated from each other.

Along with other critical scholars (Volcic and Andrejevic 2011; Aronczyk 2013), I argue that the discursive construction of nations *as brands* constitutes a distinct regime of nationhood, within which nation-states are reimagined as having to play an *entrepreneurial* role within a global marketplace. As brands, nation-states are expected to bear the main responsibility for their own development by attracting foreign capital investment, securing international goodwill, and mobilizing citizens at home and in the diaspora to "live the brand" (Aronczyk 2008). In that respect, the praxis of nation branding bridges the categories of "communication *for* development" and "communication *about* development" as these have been defined by Wilkins and Mody (2001). On the one hand, nation-branding programs are introduced and justified as interventions that can produce tangible economic outcomes, such as increasing foreign direct investment or tourism flows—that is, communication *for* development. On the other hand, in articulating national goals through a market-oriented paradigm, the ideology of nation branding, as it begins to circulate within the institutions of government, serves as a structuring discourse about what the nation is and what it aspires to be—that is, communication *about* development. In this latter manifestation, nation branding shapes long-term national development goals and frames them in capital-friendly, economistic ways (Browning 2016; Jansen 2008; Kaneva 2011b; Varga 2013).

More recently, James Pamment (2016a) has proposed adding a third dimension to the theorization of the relationships between communication and development. In addition to communication *for* and *about* development, he argues that it is necessary to consider how development actors deploy what he calls "communication *of* development." In Pamment's formulation, communication *of* development refers to the "branding, marketing, and promotion of aid activities to foreign citizens and domestic stakeholders in a manner that supports the actor's reputation and image" (2016a, p. 11). In other words, this third dimension highlights how the adoption of promotional practices in public diplomacy contributes to the instrumentalization of development communication.

The normalization of promotion as part of public diplomacy establishes a transactional relationship between aid givers and aid recipients in which the putative "benefactors" of development aim to extract reputational added value from their allegedly philanthropic actions. Pamment's distinction between communication *for*, *about*, and *of* development adds important nuance to our understanding of the way development communication operates under a neoliberal regime. However, he describes these dynamics only from the point of view of aid-giving actors—that is, the benefactors of development. He points out that, in some cases, these actors use branded aid as part of comprehensive nation-branding programs (Pamment 2016b). By contrast, my analysis in this chapter focuses on a nation that is heavily reliant on receiving aid while, at the same time, deploying a comprehensive nation-branding program. This reversal of perspectives may reveal new insights about the ways in which development communication and public diplomacy intersect through nation branding.

As the preceding discussion indicates, the praxis of nation branding should be of significant interest to scholars from the fields of development communication and public diplomacy. At the same time, a focus on nation branding allows for a productive, conceptual juxtaposition of these two fields, specifically in relation to their engagement with the concept of the nation-state. In certain respects, both fields tend to take the nation-state for granted. As noted earlier, critical perspectives within development communication have treated the nation-state mainly as a container of populations that become targets (or even victims) of development programs. By contrast, public diplomacy is traditionally defined as "state-based communication aimed at influencing well-connected individuals and organizations that are capable of impacting upon a foreign government's policy choices" (Pamment 2015a, p. 190). In that sense, public diplomacy is a function of national governance to the extent that it is perceived as advancing the legitimate interests of a nation-state. However, neither of the two fields problematizes the structural and ideological foundations of the nation-state as a political entity.

Much of the existing literature on public diplomacy views the nation-state as a more or less coherent and legitimate source of policy goals, while rarely questioning the political justifications and sources of legitimacy for these goals (although see Pamment 2015b). For public diplomacy scholars and practitioners, communication—including nation branding, which is often reduced to a type of strategic communication—is a *tool* of advancing and supporting national interests abroad. In that regard, public diplomacy and development communication share an interventionist approach (Pamment 2015a). What both fields lack, however, is a clear account and theorization of the ways in which power flows between transnational, national, and subnational actors and institutions as these become entangled in struggles over the making, enforcement, and legitimization of national and development goals in the first place. While the scope of my study in this chapter is limited, I hope that it begins to outline a framework and a methodological approach for filling this gap in the literature.

The remaining part of this chapter is organized as follows. First, I examine the ways in which state building in Kosovo unfolded within a neoliberal framework for development. I highlight the types of accommodations made between Western and local power elites in this process. Next, I discuss how nation branding was used to advance and legitimize the structural and ideological framework of the neoliberal nation-state by modeling a particular type of national subject. Third, I briefly juxtapose the branded articulations of the nation with the material conditions of life in Kosovo in order to raise questions about the winners and losers of neoliberal development. I argue that, while local and transnational elites benefited from the creation of a neoliberal nation-state in Kosovo, the welfare of the majority of the population has failed to improve. In conclusion, I summarize some general propositions that emerge from this case and offer directions for future critical research at the intersection of development communication and public diplomacy.

The Making of a Neoliberal Nation-State in Kosovo

Kosovo's declaration of independence on February 17, 2008 came nearly a decade after the end of NATO's bombing campaign in Serbia in 1999. While the declaration was presented to the world as a unilateral act of self-determination, in reality it was the carefully orchestrated outcome of a protracted and complicated process.[2] As Serbian forces pulled out of Kosovo in June 1999, the soldiers of the NATO-led Kosovo Force (KFOR) entered the territory and were welcomed as liberators by the local Albanian population. A UN Mission to Kosovo (UNMIK) was established and put in charge of developing and rebuilding the reconstruction efforts in the region. However, the legal status of Kosovo remained unclear with no definite timeline in place for its settlement. Ultimately, this led to growing frustration among Kosovo Albanians and an eruption of violent riots in March 2004, five years after the end of the war. The riots, which left 19 people dead and thousands displaced, succeeded in elevating the question of Kosovo's status to the level of top priority for international peace-builders (Ernst 2011, pp. 131–133; Judah 2000).

Subsequently, in November 2005, Finnish diplomat Martti Ahtisaari was appointed by the UN Secretary General to serve as Special Envoy and conduct status negotiations between Serbia and the provisional Kosovo government in Pristina. The brief negotiations took place in Vienna in 2006, but failed to produce a mutually agreeable outcome. Consequently, in March 2007, Ahtisaari recommended to the UN Security Council that "the only viable option" for settling Kosovo's status was "independence with international supervision" (Ahtisaari 2007a, p. 3). The report was accompanied by a "Comprehensive Proposal for the Kosovo Status Settlement" (Ahtisaari 2007b), widely known as the Ahtisaari Plan, which specified a set of provisions with which Kosovo had to comply in order to earn "supervised independence." The provisions in this document became the basis for the Constitution adopted by independent Kosovo in 2008.[3]

Article 1 of the Ahtisaari Plan outlines 11 general principles which set up the overall framework for state building in Kosovo. Two of these are of particular relevance to my analysis here: Section 1.1 of Article 1 specifies that "Kosovo shall be a multi-ethnic society, which shall govern itself democratically," and Section 1.4 of the same article mandates that "Kosovo shall have an open market economy with free competition"

(Ahtisaari 2007b, p. 3). Both of these statements were included—almost verbatim—in Chapter I of the Constitution of the Republic of Kosovo, which lays out the "Basic Provisions" for the new state entity (Constitution of the Republic of Kosovo, n.d.).

The principles of multiculturalism and free markets are key for understanding the structural parameters of the kind of nation-state that was being built in Kosovo under international supervision. On the one hand, multiculturalism was supposed to replace the principle of ethnic identification, which had been a major source of conflict in the past, and become the main source of legitimacy for the nation-state. On the other hand, an "open market" economy would ensure that foreign capital would have ready access to the natural and human resources on the territory of Kosovo, leading to a neoliberal model of economic development that relies heavily on foreign capital investment.

David Harvey (2005) notes that, according to neoliberal theory, "the elimination of poverty (both domestically and worldwide) can best be secured through free markets and free trade" (p. 65). This logic and its associated policies of privatization and deregulation are commonly deployed in developing countries by the IMF and the WB. The same formula was followed in Kosovo. However, what was unusual in Kosovo's case, was that the dogma of an "open market" economy was not only enforced through outside supervision by lenders and investors, but was written directly into the text of the new country's Constitution.[4]

In practice, the mandated emphasis on open markets and trade provided the justification for a number of development policies that opened up Kosovo's fledgling economy to transnational capital while providing minimal social safety nets. As documented on the website of the Kosovo Investment and Enterprise Support Agency (KIESA), a government agency under the Ministry of Trade and Industry, these policies include: adoption of the euro as the national currency, despite the fact that Kosovo is not a member of the European Union; membership of the Central European Free Trade Agreement and customs-free exports to the EU; and duty-free trade to the US market (KIESA n.d.). In addition, Kosovo boasts a flat corporate tax of 10% and offers exemptions on value added taxation (VAT) for new exporters (U.S. Department of State 2014). KIESA's website also emphasizes the low costs of labor in Kosovo and the low average age of the local population. At the same time, Kosovo has maintained low levels of government spending, following recommendations by the IMF, and has invested very little in building a welfare system to support vulnerable groups of the population (Gashi 2012; Stambolieva 2012). In light of this, it appears that the enshrinement of market competition as a constitutional principle, and the subsequent adoption of capital-friendly policies, configured the new nation-state in Kosovo, from its very inception, to function as a guarantor of neoliberal economic principles.

The second important mandate of the Ahtisaari Plan was that Kosovo would be a multi-ethnic democracy. This was supposed to provide the necessary antidote to ethnic nationalism that had led to the Kosovo conflict in the first place. An emphasis on multiculturalism was, at least in part, also an effort to demonstrate to the rest of the world that the intervention by Western powers in the Kosovo War had been truly motivated by human rights concerns, rather than by a political agenda, and that all ethnic groups on the territory of Kosovo were entitled to the same rights and protections. In reality, post-war Kosovo is a highly homogeneous society, with ethnic Albanians comprising close to 93% of the population (CIA, n.d.), and tensions between Albanians and Serbs living in Kosovo continue.

Nevertheless, multiculturalism has been publicly enacted through the adoption of a new national flag and anthem, both of which were chosen through a tightly managed process that invited proposals from citizens in a show of democratic participation. The selection process took place in 2007, in the months leading up to the declaration of independence. The conditions for participation stipulated that flag designs could not use the colors or symbols of either the Serbian or the Albanian national flags (Wander 2008). The result was a flag that uses the colors of the European Union—it displays a golden-colored map of Kosovo, crowned by six white stars, intended to represent the major ethnic groups within the population, against a solid blue background. Similarly, the national anthem, approved by the Kosovo Parliament in June 2008, is a composition entitled "Europe" which has no lyrics. This choice was made in order to avoid tensions related to the use of the Albanian or Serbian language in the national anthem (Pavkovic and Kelen 2016).[5] While both languages have the status of official languages in Kosovo, the vast majority of the population speaks Albanian.

These symbolic acts have been insufficient as a means of quelling ethnic tensions in Kosovo and building enthusiasm for multiculturalism among the population. Some scholars have suggested that an emphasis on multiculturalism may have, in fact, led to the institutionalization of ethnic divisions within governance structures. Hehir (2010b) argues that key institutions—including parliament, the police, and the judiciary—were manipulated to reflect "ethnic plurality" in post-war Kosovo and that this hindered the development of a "new shared identity" (p. 191). Rather than promoting a sense of inclusion, the creation of political structures that were "superficially multi-ethnic" served to reproduce the difference between Serbs and Albanians and made "ethnicity a basis for administrative and political delegation, and therefore social divisions were formally incorporated into the new polity" (p. 191).

Be that as it may, the mandates of the Ahtisaari Plan were not subject to negotiation. Their adoption was the price that post-war Kosovo elites had to agree to pay in order to secure Western support for their right to govern on the territory of Kosovo. In exchange for enforcing the neoliberal agenda of its sponsors, the local ruling elite, drawn from the ranks of the former Kosovo Liberation Army, has enjoyed certain protections despite allegations of corruption, war crimes, and links to organized crime (Hehir 2016). At the same time, it guaranteed stability on the ground and committed to a dialogue towards normalizing relations with Serbia, both of which were important to Western powers (Bytyci 2011; Ernst 2011). In short, the functionaries of the new nation-state in Kosovo have benefited from establishing a clientelistic relationship with Western actors while agreeing to enforce an agenda of neoliberal development for Kosovo.

NATION BRANDING AND THE PRODUCTION OF NEOLIBERAL NATIONAL SUBJECTS

In this context, nation branding was deployed in two directions. First, it was used to demonstrate to the outside world, and especially to Kosovo's Western supporters, that the new state had truly embraced the directives of multiculturalism and open markets, which had been set as key preconditions for its independence. In that respect, the projection of branded messages through transnational media offered a highly visible way for Kosovo's governing elite to perform compliance with the neoliberal agenda. In other words, Kosovo's government used nation branding to advertise *itself* as an obedient pupil of neoliberal development and, therefore, worthy of continued foreign support in the form of economic aid, as well as military and diplomatic protections. This can be seen as an inverse application of Pamment's notion of "communication *of* development" (2016a). In this case, branding was deployed to establish a favorable reputation for Kosovo among its development benefactors who could, in turn, use this favorable reputation to justify their continued support of Kosovo to their own populations.

The use of nation branding also had to be justified domestically and this was done through a public discourse about the need to transform Kosovo's international "image." As early as November 2008—only nine months after the declaration of independence—the Kosovar Stability Initiative (IKS), a Pristina-based think tank funded by Western donors, published a report titled, *Image Matters!*, which urged Kosovo's government to make use of nation branding in order to deal with the key challenges the country was facing. The report argued that:

> To increase the number of countries recognizing Kosovo, to sway public opinion in Europe and to operate effectively on the international stage, Kosovo's government and civil society need to better understand its image problem and develop a new "national brand." (IKS 2008, p. 8)

The report also claimed that a successful national brand would enhance Kosovo's ability "to turn around its economy, to be granted membership in international institutions and to realize its Euro-Atlantic aspirations" (IKS 2008, p. 7).[6] In other words, a better international image was expected to deliver both political and economic benefits.

Second, nation branding was also touted domestically as a way for Kosovo's citizens to unite around a post-conflict narrative of belonging to a young and optimistic nation with a shared sense of identity and a common future. Importantly, the two projects—of outward image projection and of inward identity building—were seen as closely intertwined. As a 2009 government press release put it:

> Branding [Kosovo] is not merely a commercial advertisement nor is it a political campaign. Branding is a comprehensive national effort to bring the new image of the country to the world. In this effort every citizen is an ambassador and each public institution a stakeholder. By becoming familiar with and supporting this endeavor, the people of Kosovo will succeed in amplifying the effect of the campaign many times over. (quoted in Wählisch and Xharra 2010, p. 13)

In short, nation branding was presented as a tool that would serve simultaneously the nation-state's goals of economic development, international recognition and support, and nation building. In that sense, nation branding was deployed as communication *for* development in terms of its expected economic impact; as communication *about* development insofar as it articulated the ideological foundations of a market-based national identity at home; and as communication *of* development because it aimed to enhance the country's reputation among its economic and political benefactors abroad.

Against this backdrop, in 2009, Kosovo's government allocated €5.7 million (approximately $6.3 million) from its otherwise scant budget to a comprehensive nation-branding campaign and issued a call for proposals. The contract was awarded to Israeli advertising agency BBR Saatchi & Saatchi Tel Aviv, which developed and implemented an international multi-platform campaign with the tagline: "Kosovo: The Young Europeans." The campaign aimed to reach a wide range of domestic and international audiences through video and print advertisements, posters, billboards, branded events, stakeholder relations, and social media outreach.[7] Importantly, the messages of the "Young Europeans" campaign were circulated both internationally and domestically (Ströhle 2012). In that sense, they constituted a unified ideological narrative about Kosovo as a nation. This narrative was structured according to the logic of commercial media and constituted what some communication scholars have described as "commercial nationalism" (Volcic and Andrejevic 2011, 2015). Graeme Turner (2015, p. 25) argues that "in commercial nationalism, the aim is to build a market, not a polity." In other words, commercial nationalism—as expressed through nation branding—fits the needs of the neoliberal nation-state which, as discussed above, prioritizes the establishment of favorable conditions for business over the delivery of public services and the provision of social supports to citizens.

To maintain its legitimacy, the neoliberal nation-state must also produce a particular type of national subject. That is where commercial nationalism, expressed through nation branding, is particularly useful. Two central themes emerge in the messages of the "Young Europeans" campaign: *youth* and *creative self-expression*.[8] The emphasis on youth was based, in part, on the statistical fact that Kosovo had the youngest population in Europe with an average age of only 27. According to executives from BBR Saatchi & Saatchi, the positive emotions associated with youth formed the key strategic insight that gave focus to the entire campaign (Wählisch and Xharra 2010). This insight informed the campaign's tagline as well as the creative executions of all communication materials, which featured young, attractive Kosovars as the faces of their country. The decision to focus on youth also had a local precedent—an earlier branding exercise that had been conceived by Kosovo's own advertising minds with a keen awareness of global media. During the declaration of independence ceremony in 2008, the government unveiled a typographic monument on Pristina's main square, which spelled the word NEWBORN (in English) in giant, yellow-colored, capital letters. The monument was created just days before the public ceremony by Pristina-based advertising agency Ogilvy Karrota, headed by Creative Director Fisnik Ismaili (Sopi 2008). On the night of the event, illuminated by projectors, the yellow letters of NEWBORN presented a compelling visual, which was captured by media cameras and featured in transnational media, including CNN, the BBC, and *The New York Times*.[9] This turned NEWBORN into an instantaneous iconic symbol for post-war Kosovo and garnered a number of international industry awards for Ogilvy Karrota (Karrota n.d.). In 2009, the agency was among those who responded to the government's call for proposals for a nation-branding program, but the contract was ultimately awarded to the Israeli firm BBR Saatchi & Saatchi Tel Aviv. Nevertheless, "The Young Europeans" campaign extended the metaphor that had already been established by NEWBORN. Indeed, Ströhle (2012, p. 228) argues that the NEWBORN monument and "The Young Europeans" campaign are the two key symbols that "embody the desire to reinvent Kosovar society in terms of self-understanding and outside perception."

The decision of Kosovo's branders to focus on youth taps into the symbolic repertoire of a secular, consumer-oriented, media-driven, and youth-obsessed global popular culture. The tropes of this culture are familiar to Western audiences who have seen them replayed in numerous entertainment media and advertising messages. Katja Valaskivi (2016) argues that an association with popular culture and, particularly, with the idea of "cool" is endemic to the global discourse of nation branding, which urges nations to join the global competition and "to become innovative, creative, attractive, youthful, entrepreneurial and authentic" (p. 15). Kosovo's nation branding efforts were clearly in line with this trend. This is particularly evident in a series of posters and billboards unveiled in the second phase of the "Young Europeans" campaign, which were displayed prominently throughout Pristina. They featured

ten real youths, between the ages of 17 and 25. The group included students in acting, graphic design, costume design, and computer science;
a student in economics who was an avid soccer player; an aspiring DJ;
a guitar player; and a winner of a modeling competition. The interests
of these youths included art, photography, skateboarding, animals, reading, and writing. All had Albanian names, although their ethnic identities were not discussed in the messaging, and all were physically attractive
(Wählisch and Xharra 2010, p. 16).

These youths were selected to represent the face of the Kosovo
nation—its aspirations and its potential. It is noteworthy, therefore, that
their personal pursuits were almost exclusively in the creative fields. In
this way, the campaign modeled a particular type of subjectivity that
was supposed to represent the future of Kosovo. It valorized creativity,
self-expression, an entrepreneurial mindset, and the pursuit of "free"
professions that are not typically associated with poor, war-ravaged societies. In addition, by portraying attractive youth, dressed in trendy cloth-
ing, whose interests were overwhelmingly related to entertainment and
sports, the campaign was positioning them as members of a "cool," cosmopolitan, media-savvy generation who were not defined by their ethnicity or socio-economic status. In essence, the youth in the "Young
Europeans" posters were model neoliberal subjects who embraced indi-
vidualism, personal choice, and a focus on the entrepreneurial cultivation
of one's self.

Many scholars have identified similar themes in examining how mediated discourses contribute to the production of neoliberal subjectivities
in a variety of national contexts (e.g., Gill 2008; Kaneva and Popescu
2014; Salmenniemi and Adamson 2015; Türken et al. 2016; Volcic and
Erjavec 2015; Yurchak 2003). In that regard, Kosovo's branders were
hardly breaking new ground. Rather, they were reproducing a well established, globalized, neoliberal ideology and delivering it via commercial
media channels through a blitz of promotional messages. This ideology
supported the legitimacy needs of the neoliberal nation-state in Kosovo
because it placed the responsibility for one's success on the individual,
rather than on state policies or systemic factors. One might say that, by
embracing nation branding, Kosovo was learning to express its national
identity through the tropes of the global hegemonic discourse of neoliberalism. However, as I will discuss in the next section, the lived experiences of the vast majority of the population, and especially of Kosovo's

youth, were significantly at odds with the messages of the campaign and that has fueled an ongoing crisis of identity in Kosovo.

"LIVING THE BRAND" VS. LIFE ON THE GROUND

Based on in-depth interviews with Western brand consultants, Melissa Aronczyk (2008) describes the ways in which they envision the role of citizens in nation branding. She explains that branders place the responsibility for the success of a national brand on the citizens of the nation, whose "key function is to 'live the brand'—that is, to perform attitudes and behaviors that are compatible with the brand strategy" (p. 54). Based on the preceding discussion, we might conclude that the "brand-appropriate" attitudes for Kosovo's citizens would include optimism, cosmopolitanism, and creative entrepreneurialism. However, seven years after declaring independence, the mood on the ground in Kosovo is much darker. The country's economy is still highly dependent on aid and half of the gross domestic product, approximately €600 million annually, comes from remittances from the diaspora (Hehir 2016). According to WB statistics, 80% of the population lives on less than $5 per day (World Bank 2015, p. 6). In 2015, unemployment among 15–24 year olds, roughly the same age group that was featured in the "Young Europeans" campaign, was above 55%, and, based on a 2013 survey, 35.3% of the same age group were neither employed nor studying or in training (World Bank 2015, p. 7). Overall unemployment hovers around 35%, compared to a 10% average for the EU. In addition, Kosovo's citizens are among the most isolated in the world as they can travel without a visa to only six countries—Albania, Turkey, Macedonia, Montenegro, Serbia, and the Maldives—none of which are part of the EU. All of this means that, although capital can flow freely between the EU and Kosovo, and the euro is the country's official currency, the mobility of Kosovo's citizens is extremely limited and the economic circumstances they face at home are dire. In response, scores of young Kosovars are migrating illegally to EU countries to seek asylum. According to statistics compiled by the Pew Research Center, in 2015 alone, Kosovars filed 68,000 new applications for asylum in EU countries, but the vast majority of these cases have been denied (Connor 2016).[10]

Political recognition of Kosovo's statehood has also stalled. Although the majority of countries in the world have recognized its status as an independent state, Russia, China, and Serbia continue to reject

Kosovo's legitimacy, as do five countries in the EU and four in NATO (Hehir 2016). This prevents Kosovo from being able to join the United Nations and makes its ambitions of EU membership highly problematic. In the mean time, ethnic nationalist sentiments have reasserted themselves in Kosovo's domestic politics, channeled by the opposition party Vetëvendosje [Albanians for "self-determination"]. In 2010, Vetëvendosje participated for the first time in Kosovo's parliamentary elections winning 14 seats, and in 2013 the movement made significant gains in local elections, winning the mayoral race in the capital Pristina. Importantly, the messages of the "Young Europeans" campaign served as highly visible ideological targets for the Vetëvendosje movement in its early days. In 2009, activists launched a counter-campaign using graffiti to subvert the messages of the original "Young Europeans" billboards by spray-painting on them words such as "isolated," "unemployed," and "poor" (Wählisch and Xharra 2010, p. 25).

Despite such signs of trouble, the neoliberal model of development that was established in Kosovo appears to have produced real results for transnational capital, enabling a kind of predatory capitalism that extracts short-term profit without long-term benefits for the local population. One highly publicized and politicized example was the construction of the Ibrahim Rugova Highway (aka the Kosovo Highway or R7), which was built by the American-Turkish consortium Bechtel-Enka. Bechtel, the largest contractor in the USA and third largest in the world, secured the contract from the Kosovo government in 2010 with the help of American lobbyists and the US Ambassador to Kosovo, Christopher Dell (Brunwasser 2012, 2015). Construction was completed in 2013 at a cost of $1.3 billion, or roughly $25 million per mile (Brunwasser 2015). A report on Kosovo's investment climate, issued by the U.S. Department of State, lists the highway's completion as one of the most successful investment projects in Kosovo, noting that the cost was "paid entirely by [Kosovo] Government funds without incurring any debt" (U.S. Department of State 2014, p. 2). Kosovo's government praised the highway as a major infrastructural project that would boost trade, tourism, and regional ties (Brunwasser 2015).

Notwithstanding such glowing accounts, the highway remains largely underused and is seen by many in Kosovo as a waste of public money that could have been spent on other, much more needed, public projects (Brunwasser 2015). Notably, the IMF shared this unfavorable view, criticizing the highway project as putting "considerable pressure" on

Kosovo's budget and leading to "higher deficits financed by drawing down cash buffers" (IMF 2012, p. 15). Following his diplomatic tenure in Kosovo, Ambassador Christopher Dell was hired as a consultant by the Bechtel Corporation, raising further questions about the collusion between corporate and political interests (Lewis 2014). In short, the Kosovo Highway represents a particular outcome of the model of neoliberal development that was set in motion in Kosovo with the adoption of the Ahtisaari Plan. Its construction delivered substantial profits to a transnational corporation, with pressure from US officials and the consent of the governing Kosovo elite, yet it provided dubious benefits to the citizens of Kosovo.

Lessons Learned and Questions for Future Interventions

I began this exploration with the goal of mapping out some of the parameters of the neoliberal nation-state and problematizing the role of nation branding in legitimizing an agenda of neoliberal development. In this effort, I am also responding to the critical call by Karin Gwinn Wilkins (2015) who argues that scholars need to "consider how political conditions within and across countries contribute to the rise of private global capital and the intensity of poverty" (p. 121). What then are some lessons that emerge from the case of post-war Kosovo? Based on my analysis, I offer three general propositions that may have implications beyond the Kosovo case.

First, the ability of the neoliberal nation-state to implement a capital-friendly development agenda is dependent on the collusion between national and extra-national political and economic elites. In the case of Kosovo, this collusion has manifested in structural ways, such as the establishment of particular economic and constitutional frameworks, as well as in symbolic ways, which include the government's sizable investment in nation branding. As I have argued above, one essential purpose of nation branding for Kosovo has been to serve as a platform for performing compliance with the values and expectations of its Western benefactors. In that way, Kosovo has tried to parlay its reputation as a good pupil of neoliberalism into assurances of continued foreign aid and political support.

At the same time, when analyzing the messages of Kosovo's branding program, it is evident that nation branding cultivates and projects particular types of national images and subjectivities. Specifically, the neoliberal discourse of nation branding imagines Kosovo—and, by extension, other aid-receiving nations—as young, entrepreneurial, and eager to join the rest of the "developed" world. The historical roots and structural explanations for poverty, underdevelopment, and other social problems are entirely obscured in this way of reinventing the nation. Importantly, this allows Western benefactors to reframe aid as a form of "new business investment," rather than as a humanitarian act that aims to correct global inequalities. This shift, in turn, justifies the expectation of a certain "return on investment." In Kosovo's case, the results of this transactional quid pro quo logic are exemplified by the ill-fated Kosovo Highway—a grossly overpriced piece of infrastructure, which was built by an American corporation at a significant profit and was simultaneously touted as a positive sign of development. In light of this, I would argue that the neoliberal nation-state is, by design, prone to corruption and cronyism—not only as a path to personal enrichment for individual functionaries, but also as a matter of its systemic survival. This has important implications for future development efforts and aid mechanisms within a neoliberal policy environment.

Second, while more research is needed, Kosovo's case suggests that the neoliberal nation-state is ultimately a politically weak state because it must continually satisfy the interests of its transnational "patrons" while finding ways to pacify and control domestic populations. The ways in which the state accomplishes this control may vary based on its political system of government. Nevertheless, the state's legitimacy is constantly in question, creating the need for ongoing legitimization efforts through various ideological programs, including nation-branding campaigns. While the "Young Europeans" campaign is probably the best-known example of nation branding on behalf of Kosovo, it was not the first or last initiative of this kind. The government has funded various other branding projects and the structure of the Ministry of Foreign Affairs includes a Deputy Minister of Public Diplomacy (see e.g., Brentin and Tregoures 2016; Wählisch and Xharra 2012). Beyond the example of Kosovo, many aid-receiving nations, especially on the African continent, have established government-backed institutions charged with nation branding (e.g., Browning 2016; Papadopoulos and Hamzaoui-Essoussi 2015). This indicates a growing recognition among national elites that there is a need to mediate continually the relationships between the state, its foreign benefactors, and its domestic constituents.

Third, in conditions of prevailing commercial mediatization of global proportions, nation branding provides a particularly appealing and expedient avenue for the state's legitimization efforts, although its effectiveness remains highly problematic. One of the advantages of nation branding is that it offers a vision of the nation that does not need to be rooted in ethno-nationalist symbols, and this signals compliance with the neoliberal global order, which is largely indifferent to culture as long as it does not stand in the way of capital. Importantly, even when particular nation-branding messages are rejected by some groups of the population, the structuring discourse of nation branding endures as a generic form of constructing narratives and counter-narratives about the nation and its subjects. This is illustrated in Kosovo by the engagement of the Vetëvendosje movement with the "Young Europeans" campaign.

Additional empirical research is needed to confirm how well these propositions hold in other contemporary cases of post-conflict state building and restructuring. This kind of research can help us gain new perspectives on the role of the nation-state in development and, potentially, it can shift policy agendas as well. As I suggested in the beginning of this chapter, the nation-state has remained a sort of "black box" within the literature on public diplomacy and development communication. It is either taken for granted in the public diplomacy literature, or dismissed as less relevant because of globalization in the development communication literature. Its agency is either assumed, as in claims that it is the source of "soft power," or disregarded, as in accounts of the state's powerlessness in the face of transnational corporations and development organizations. Such ways of thinking about the nation-state may be accurate under certain conditions, but there may be more nuanced ways to account for the complex role of the nation-state in development, and this is what I have tried to illustrate in this study.

Finally, the "rediscovery" of the nation-state opens new avenues for critical research at the intersection of public diplomacy and development communication. The broad questions I propose in closing are far from exhaustive but offer a starting point. First, if we accept the propositions I have outlined above, where can we begin to locate the institutional bases for development interventions that can actually benefit vulnerable segments of national populations? Second, if neoliberalism has spawned a new form of "commercial nationalism," is the only recourse for political mobilization a return to forms of nationalism that are based on ethnicity, religion, or race, or are there other, less divisive, bases for political empowerment? And lastly, how can we move our analyses beyond purely theoretical critiques of neoliberal development and use them to articulate alternative paths to poverty reduction and social justice?

Acknowledgements I owe special thanks to Bujar Aruqaj for his invaluable research assistance in the early stages of this project.

NOTES

1. My position is in line with international studies scholars who have argued that Kosovo "has served as something of a microcosm of broader international trends and also, in many respects, a guinea pig upon which new ideas and policies have been tested" (Hehir 2010b, p. 185; see also Van Ham and Medvedev 2002).

2. The process of state building in Kosovo is described here in rather incomplete terms, focusing predominantly on events and actions that relate to the notion of establishing the parameters of a neoliberal state. For a fuller account of the history of Kosovo's post-war status, see Hehir (2010a) and Ernst (2011).

3. In the course of conducting research for this study I was jokingly told by some Kosovars that Ahtisaari is one of the "founding fathers" of Kosovo.

4. By way of comparison, although the USA has been a leading exporter of free market ideology around the world, there is no language in the US Constitution that mandates that the USA must have a free market economy. In fact, the words "market," "economy," or "competition" do not appear anywhere in the US Constitution's text. In contrast, Kosovo's Constitution mentions both the phrase "market economy" and the word "competition" three times.

5. Notably, the anthem that was used in the official declaration of independence on February 17, 2008 was Beethoven's "Ode to Joy," which has been adopted as the EU's anthem (Pavkovic and Kelen 2016, p. 162).

6. The IKS was founded in 2004 and is supported by the Open Society Foundation and others (http://www.iksweb.org/en-us/partners). Its stated goal is to provide "policy-relevant research with the aim of initiating debates on issues of importance for Kosovo's future" (http://www.iksweb.org/en-us/about-us). In light of this, it could be argued that the choice of nation branding as the most appropriate solution to the problem of Kosovo's international recognition and its development was not a home-grown idea, but an accommodation between transnational and domestic elite interests.

7. For a detailed description of the campaign, see Wählisch and Xharra (2010).
8. For more comprehensive discussions of the messages in the "Young Europeans" campaign and reactions to them, see Ströhle (2012) and Wählisch and Xharra (2010).
9. After the unveiling, Kosovo's leaders signed their names on the monument and were then spontaneously joined by citizens attending the ceremony. In subsequent years, the monument has become a physical site of contestation, upon which different ideas about the nation's identity and aspirations have been projected (see Marku 2014).
10. This was a significant increase from 2014, when the reported number of asylum seekers from Kosovo was 35,000. Kosovo's total population was estimated to be close to 1.9 million in 2016 (CIA, n.d.).

References

Ahtisaari, M. (2007a). *Report of the Special Envoy of the Secretary-General on Kosovo's Future Status.* Retrieved October 23, 2016, from www.esiweb.org/pdf/kosovo_Ahtisaari%20Proposal%20.pdf.

Ahtisaari, M. (2007b). *Comprehensive Proposal for the Kosovo Status Settlement.* Retrieved October 23, 2016, from www.esiweb.org/pdf/kosovo_Ahtisaari%20Proposal%20.pdf.

Anholt, S. (2010). *Places: Identity, Image and Reputation.* New York: Palgrave Macmillan.

Aronczyk, M. (2008). "Living the Brand": Nationality, Globality, and the Identity Strategies of Nation Branding Consultants. *International Journal of Communication, 2,* 41–65. Retrieved October 20, 2016, from http://ijoc.org/index.php/ijoc/article/view/218.

Aronczyk, M. (2013). *Branding the Nation: The Global Business of National Identity.* Oxford and New York: Oxford University Press.

Brentin, D., & Tregoures, L. (2016). Entering Through the Sport's Door? Kosovo's Sport Diplomatic Endeavours Towards International Recognition, *Diplomacy & Statecraft, 27*(2), 360–378.

Browning, C. S. (2016). Nation Branding and Development: Poverty Panacea or Business as Usual? *Journal of International Relations and Development, 19*(1), 50–75.

Brunwasser, M. (2012, December 11). That Crush at Kosovo's Business Door? The Return of U.S. Heroes. *The New York Times.* Retrieved October 10, 2016, from http://www.nytimes.com/2012/12/12/world/europe/americans-who-helped-free-kosovo-return-as-entrepreneurs.html?_r=0.

Brunwasser, M. (2015). Steamrolled: A Special Investigation into the Diplomacy of Doing Business Abroad. *Foreign Policy.* Retrieved October 1, 2016, from http://foreignpolicy.com/2015/01/30/steamrolled-investigation-bechtel-highway-business-kosovo.

Bytyci, F. (2011). Merkel Urges Serbia, Kosovo to Normalize Relations. *Reuters*. Retrieved October 20, 2016, from http://www.reuters.com/article/us-germany-merkel-kosovo-idUSTRE7BI1HM20111219.

Cánepa, G. K. (2013). Nation Branding: The Re-foundation of Community, Citizenship and the State in the Context of Neoliberalism in Peru. *Medien Journal, 37*(3), 7–18.

CIA. (n.d.). Kosovo. *The World Fact Book*. Retrieved October 22, 2016, from https://www.cia.gov/library/publications/the-world-factbook/geos/kv.html.

Connor, P. (2016). *Number of Refugees to Europe Surges to Record 1.3 Million in 2015*. Pew Research Center. Retrieved October 20, 2016, from http://www.pewglobal.org/2016/08/02/number-of-refugees-to-europe-surges-to-record-1-3-million-in-2015.

Constitution of the Republic of Kosovo. (n.d.). Retrieved October 20, 2016, from http://www.assembly-kosova.org/common/docs/Constitution1%20of%20the%20Republic%20of%20Kosovo.pdf.

Dinnie, K. (2008). *Nation Branding: Concepts, Issues, Practice*. New York: Butterworth-Heinemann.

Dutta, M. (2011). *Communicating Social Change: Structure, Culture, Agency*. New York: Routledge.

Dutta, M. (2015). Decolonizing Communication for Social Change: A Culture-Centered Approach. *Communication Theory, 25*(2), 123–143.

Ernst, A. (2011). Fuzzy Governance: State-Building in Kosovo since 1999 as Interaction Between International and Local Actors. *Democracy and Security, 7*(2), 123–139.

Gashi, K. (2012). Kosovo. In *Nations in Transit 2012: Democratization from Central Europe to Eurasia* (pp. 279–295). Washington, DC and New York: Freedom House. Retrieved October 23, 2016. https://www.freedomhouse.org/sites/default/files/NIT2012Kosovo_final.pdf.

Gill, R. (2008). Culture and Subjectivity in Neoliberal and Postfeminist Times. *Subjectivity, 25*(1), 432–445.

Harvey, D. (2005). *A Brief History of Neoliberalism*. Oxford and New York: Oxford University Press.

Hehir, A. (Ed.). (2010a). *Kosovo, Intervention and Statebuilding: The International Community and the Transition to Independence*. New York: Routledge.

Hehir, A. (2010b). Microcosm, guinea pig or *sui generis*? Assessing International Engagement with Kosovo. In A. Hehir (Ed.), *Kosovo, Intervention and Statebuilding: The International Community and the Transition to Independence* (pp. 185–196). New York: Routledge.

Hehir, A. (2016, August 31). How the West Built a Failed State in Kosovo. *The National Interest*. Retrieved October 20, 2016, from http://nationalinterest.org/feature/how-the-west-built-failed-state-kosovo-17539.

IKS. (2008). *IMAGE MATTERS! Deconstructing Kosovo's Image Problem.* Pristina, Kosovo: Kosovar Stability Initiative. Retrieved September 10, 2016, from http://kfos.org/wp-content/uploads/2011/10/Image-Matters-ENG.pdf.

IMF. (2012). *Republic of Kosovo: Second Review under the Stand-by Arrangement, Request for Rephrasing of Purchases and Modification of Performance Criterion.* Washington, DC: International Monetary Fund. Retrieved October 20, 2016, from https://www.imf.org/external/pubs/ft/scr/2012/cr12345.pdf.

Jansen, S. C. (2008). Designer Nations: Neo-liberal Nation Branding—Brand Estonia. *Social Identities, 14*(1), 121–142.

Judah, T. (2000). *Kosovo: War and Revenge.* New Haven, CT: Yale University Press.

Kaneva, N. (2011a). Nation Branding: Toward an Agenda for Critical Research. *International Journal of Communication, 5,* 117–141. Retrieved October 20, 2016, from http://ijoc.org/index.php/ijoc/article/view/704.

Kaneva, N. (2011b). *Branding Post-communist Nations: Marketizing National Identities in the "New" Europe.* New York: Routledge.

Kaneva, N. (2015). Nation Branding and Commercial Nationalism: A Critical Perspective. In Z. Volcic & M. Andrejevic (Eds.), *Commercial Nationalism: Selling the Nation and Nationalizing the Sell* (pp. 175–189). New York and London: Palgrave Macmillan.

Kaneva, N., & Popescu, D. (2014). "We are Romanian, not Roma": Nation Branding and Post-socialist Discourses of Alterity. *Communication, Culture and Critique, 7*(4), 506–523.

Karrota. (n.d.). Awards. *Karrota.net.* Retrieved March 10, 2016, from http://www.karrota.net/awards.

KIESA. (n.d.). Invest in Kosovo. Retrieved October 10, 2016, from http://www.invest-ks.org/en/Why-Kosovo.

Lewis, P. (2014). US Ambassador to Kosovo Hired by Construction Firm He Lobbied for. *The Guardian.* Retreived October 20, 2016, from https://www.theguardian.com/world/2014/apr/14/us-ambassador-kosovo-construction-contract-firm-highway.

Marku, H. (2014). Newborn: Private, Public, or Somewhere in Between? *Kosovo 2.0.* Retrieved October 24, 2016, from http://archive.kosovotwopointzero.com/en/article/1015/newborn-private-public-or-somewhere-in-between.

Pamment, J. (2015a). Media Influence, Ontological Transformation, and Social Change: Conceptual Overlaps Between *Development Communication* and *Public Diplomacy. Communication Theory, 25*(2), 188–207.

Pamment, J. (2015b). "Putting the GREAT Back into Britain:" National Identity, Public–Private Collaboration and Transfers of Brand Equity in 2012's Global Promotional Campaign. *The British Journal of Politics and International Relations, 17*(2), 260–283.

Pamment, J. (2016a). "Introduction." In J. Pamment (Ed.), *Intersections Between Public Diplomacy & International Development: Case Studies in Converging Fields* (pp. 8–18). Los Angeles: Figueroa Press. Retrieved January 15, 2017, from http://uscpublicdiplomacy.org/sites/uscpublicdiplomacy. org/files/useruploads/u35361/Intersections%20Between%20PD%20 International%20Development_final.pdf.

Pamment, J. (2016b). Toward a New Conditionality? The Convergence of International Development, Nation Brands and Soft Power in the British National Security Strategy. *Journal of International Relations and Development*. https://doi.org/10.1057/s41268-016-0074-9.

Papadopoulos, N., & Hamzaoui-Essoussi, L. (2015). Place Images and Nation Branding in the African Context: Challenges, Opportunities, and Questions for Policy and Research. *Africa Journal of Management, 1*(1), 54–77.

Pavkovic, A., & Kelen, C. (2016). *Anthems and the Making of Nation States: Identity and Nationalism in the Balkans*. New York: I.B. Tauris.

Salmenniemi, S., & Adamson, M. (2015). New Heroines of Labour: Domesticating Post-feminism and Neoliberal Capitalism in Russia. *Sociology, 49*(1), 88–105.

Sandbrook, R. (2000). Globalization and the Limits of Neoliberal Development Doctrine. *Third World Quarterly, 21*(6), 1071–1080.

Servaes, J. (1999). *Communication for Development: One World, Multiple Cultures*. Cresskill, NJ: Hampton Press.

Sopi, V. (2008). Newborn: In More Ways Than One. *Under Consideration*. Retrieved October 20, 2016, from http://www.underconsideration.com/ speakup/archives/004483.html.

Stambolieva, M. (2012, October 12–13). *Kosovo—From State of Welfare Emergency to Welfare State?* Paper presented at the Conference "Economic Development and Political Transition in Kosovo," American University in Kosovo, Pristina, Kosovo. Retrieved October 23, 2016, from https://papers. ssrn.com/sol3/papers.cfm?abstract_id=2687677.

Ströhle, I. (2012). Reinventing Kosovo: Newborn and the Young Europeans. In D. Suber & S. Karamanic (Eds.), *Retracing Images: Visual Culture after Yugoslavia* (pp. 223–250). Leiden, The Netherlands: Brill.

Szondi, G. (2008). *Public Diplomacy and Nation Branding: Conceptual Similarities and Differences*. The Hague: Netherlands Institute for International Relations "Glingendael." Retrieved October 16, 2016, from https://www.clingendael.nl/sites/default/files/20081022_pap_in_dip_ nation_branding.pdf.

The World Bank Group in Kosovo. (2015). *Country Snapshot, April 2015*. Retrieved March 26, 2018, from http://www.worldbank.org/content/dam/ Worldbank/document/eca/Kosovo-Snapshot.pdf.

Türken, S., Nafstad, H. E., Blakar, R. M., & Roen, K. (2016). Making Sense of Neoliberal Subjectivity: A Discourse Analysis of Media Language on Self-Development. *Globalizations, 13*(1), 32–46.

Turner, G. (2015). Setting the Stage for Commercial Nationalism: The Nation, the Market, and the Media. In Z. Volcic & M. Andrejevic (Eds.), *Commercial Nationalism: Selling the Nation and Nationalizing the Sell* (pp. 14–26). New York and London: Palgrave Macmillan.

U.S. Department of State. (2014). Investment Climate Statement—Kosovo. Retrieved October 20, 2016, from https://www.state.gov/documents/organization/229098.pdf.

Valaskivi, K. (2016). *Cool Nations: Media and the Social Imaginary of the Branded Country.* New York and London: Routledge.

Van Ham, P., & Medvedev, S. (Eds.). (2002). *Mapping European Security after Kosovo.* Manchester, UK: Manchester University Press.

Varga, S. (2013). The Politics of Nation Branding: Collective Identity and Public Sphere in the Neoliberal State. *Philosophy and Social Criticism, 39*(8), 825–845.

Volcic, Z., & Andrejevic, M. (2011). Nation Branding in the Era of Commercial Nationalism. *International Journal of Communication, 5,* 598–618. Retrieved October 20, 2016, from http://ijoc.org/index.php/ijoc/article/view/849.

Volcic, Z., & Andrejevic, M. (Eds.). (2015). *Commercial Nationalism: Selling the Nation and Nationalizing the Sell.* New York and London: Palgrave Macmillan.

Volcic, Z., & Erjavec, K. (2015). Watching Pink Reality TV. *Feminist Media Studies, 15*(1), 74–91.

Wählisch, M., & Xharra, B. (2010). *Public Diplomacy of Kosovo: Status Quo, Challenges and Options.* Pristina: Friedrich-Ebert-Foundation. Retrieved October 20, 2016, from http://library.fes.de/pdf-files/bueros/kosovo/07845.pdf.

Wählisch, M., & Xharra, B. (2012). *Beyond Remittances: Public Diplomacy and Kosovo's Diaspora.* Pristina: Foreign Policy Club. Retrieved October 23, 2016, from http://papers.ssrn.com/sol3/papers.cfm?abstract_id=2108317.

Waisbord, S. (2003). State, Development, and Communication. In B. Mody (Ed.), *International and Development Communication: A 21st-Century Perspective.* Thousand Oaks, CA: Sage.

Wander, A. (2008, February 8). With Independence Looming, Kosovo to Pick a Flag. *The Christian Science Monitor.* Retrieved October 20, 2016, from http://www.csmonitor.com/World/Europe/2008/0208/p25s04-woeu.html.

Wilkins, K. G. (2015). Editorial. *Communication Theory, 25*(2), 117–122.

Wilkins, K. G., & Mody, B. (2001). Reshaping Development Communication: Developing Communication and Communicating Development. *Communication Theory, 11*(4), 385–396.

Wolfensohn, J. D. (2005 [1999]). A Proposal for a Comprehensive Development Framework. In J. D. Wolfensohn (Ed.), *Voice for the World's Poor: Selected Speeches and Writings of World Bank President James D. Wolfensohn, 1995–2005.* Washington, DC: World Bank.

Yurchak, A. (2003). Russian Neoliberal: The Entrepreneurial Ethic and the Spirit of "True Careerism". *The Russian Review, 62*(1), 72–90.

CHAPTER 5

Odd Bedfellows? US Pub(l)ic Diplomacy, Colombian Industry Policy, and Sex Tourism in Cartagena

Olga Lucía Sorzano and Toby Miller

INTRODUCTION

"Explotación sexual commercial de niños, niñas, y adolescentes (ESCNNA)" (The commercial sexual exploitation of boys, girls, and adolescents)[1] in Colombia is one of the principal issues confronting the nation's tourism industry, social movements, and government, with numerous agencies and resources dedicated to opposing it. But in doing so, they are, ironically, opposed to some of their own actions, for there is a link between these crimes, official national branding, and policies for economic development. That connection derives from: decades of imagery sexualizing young women to attract visitors as part of nation branding; the role of the USA in particular in the Colombian imaginary as a desired source of

O. L. Sorzano (✉)
City, University of London, London, UK

T. Miller
Universidad del Norte, Barranquilla, Colombia
e-mail: tobym69@icloud.com

© The Author(s) 2018   99
J. Pamment and K. G. Wilkins (eds.), *Communicating National Image through Development and Diplomacy*, Palgrave Studies in Communication for Social Change, https://doi.org/10.1007/978-3-319-76759-8_5

men and money; and Washington's public diplomacy and military inter-ventions in the region. The mixture of these forces and tensions makes the country a key site in the global crisis created by masculine desires to commit statutory rape.

The backdrop to this is a nation emerging from extraordinary tur-moil and with a strong economy. The 2016 peace accord signed with the Fuerzas Armadas Revolucionarias de Colombia (Armed Revolutionary Forces of Colombia) may put a stop to half a century of violence that has claimed hundreds of thousands of lives and dislocated millions. With a large, educated middle class and significant resources suitable for sec-ondary accumulation, the country is supposedly poised to open a newly secure, bountiful territory to increased foreign investment, extraction, construction, and natural and human exploitation via international tour-ism. Hence the slogan adopted by the federal government in 2012, "La Respuesta es Colombia" (The Answer is Colombia), displacing the idea of the nation as a problem with the conceit that it is instead a solution—rebranding the country as enduringly appealing and newly safe. The desire for economic development has been twinned with a wish to improve the nation's standing internationally and to generate ideal con-ditions for tourism based on an extraordinary climate, ecology, and herit-age. Such possibilities encourage bourgeois boosters and carpet-bagging consultants alike.

Our contention in this chapter is that the informal economy, pub-lic diplomacy, sexualized national imagery, and efforts to dynamize the nation's tourism industry through rebranding are synchronizing in an accidental (but far from incidental) misogynistic, exploitative cocktail of promotional campaigns and child sex-trafficking. This odious mix-ture needs critique and reform. For while its structural inequalities and destructive impact are widely recognized (Büscher and Fletcher 2017; Browning and Ferraz de Oliviera 2017), many analysts and people in power continue to perpetuate a sunny mythology of the benefits of tour-ism (Niesing 2013; Echeverri et al. 2017).

We focus on the coastal Caribbean city of Cartagena de Indias, Colombia's principal tourism destination and site of sexual exploita-tion, as well as a key figure in its history, symbolism, and diplomacy (Mosquera and Bozzi 2005). Our methods include textual and policy analysis, political economy, gender and ethnic studies, and ethnography. We begin by examining the USA and its prevailing mythology of pub-lic diplomacy, then consider Colombia's social structure, tourism history and policy, national imagery and gender, the links between these topics and sexual exploitation, and implications for the future.

THE USA AND PUBLIC POLICY

We write in the early days of an unprecedentedly chaotic and incompetent US presidential administration, which appears to misunderstand the light and dark arts of international relations in equal measure. It is difficult to speak with confidence about US public diplomacy or foreign policy towards Latin America, and Colombia in particular, given the complete ignorance exhibited by Tiberius (currently trading as Donald Trump) in his presidential meeting with Juan Manuel Santos (Alsema 2017) and tendentious saber-rattling towards Venezuela (Sancho 2017). Tiberius' vows to diminish the role of the State Department and embellish yet further the trillions of the Pentagon appear to bode ill both in terms of diplomacy more generally and the region in particular; but that is speculation. We can, however, provide some historical perspective. This must begin with public diplomacy's archeological and contemporary doctrine of imperialism at a distance, as opposed to classic colonial occupation and settlement.

Yanqui imperialism has always differed from the classic nineteenth-century model. As a consequence, it has proven even harder for dependent, client, or invaded states to gain independence from the USA than was the case with European colonists. This is because Yanqui imperialism began at a well-developed stage of industrial capitalism and led into the post-industrial age, breaking down conventional European colonialism in order to control labor and consumption on a global scale. This contradictory heritage poses complexities for opponents, analysts, and fellow travelers alike. It has involved invasion and seizure (in the case of the Philippines and Cuba); temporary occupation and permanent militarization (Japan); naked ideological imperialism (Latin America and Theodore Roosevelt); and a cloak of anti-imperialism (Franklin Delano Roosevelt and Barack Hussein Obama II).

As part of Yanqui imperialism, Latin America is subject to the USA's Monroe Doctrine, adopted in the 1820s under the eponymous President James Monroe in opposition to European intervention in the western hemisphere. It holds that all activities taking place in the Americas are the business of the USA. Over two centuries, no administration has resiled from regional intervention as a legitimate pastime, to be indulged in as desired. For example, the last twenty years have seen the federal government seeking to interdict and divert drug trafficking via Plan Colombia. Under the Plan, the repressive state apparatus of the USA has generally operated at arm's length—drawing on, reinforcing, and sustaining the Colombian military, rather than participating directly. Planning for post-conflict national reconstruction has seen a proliferation of opportunities for the USA to appear as a benign partner rather than a continental overlord (Lindsay-Poland and Tickner 2016).

This loose model of control has suited Washington. And the free markets that had been undermined by more classic European imperialism were firmly re-established by the 1990s as rhetorical tropes in ways that confirmed the drive towards a largely informal model of domination, with economic power underwritten by militarism but not settlement. The exploitation of a regional division of labor saw governmentality without government, as it were. As a consequence, today's Yanqui imperialism is as much a discursive formation as a military struggle.

It is fitting that the exchange of people, from artists to everyday travelers, has long been part of US foreign policy, initially directed against Nazism and Sovietism; in the case of the Americas, FDR's bipartisan Good Neighbor Program was a classic instance (Miller and Yúdice 2004). When the Republican Party took control of Congress in the mid-1990s, it came close to ending official US propaganda, dramatically diminishing funding and staffing for culture in line with its supporters' contempt for expertise, art, and intellection, and in response to the end of anti-Sovietism (Miller 2000).

But the demise of Ronald Reagan's Cold War II was soon followed by September 11, 2001. The newly modish term "public diplomacy" suddenly appealed to the federal government, which sought an answer to the plaintive cry of "Why do they hate us?" uttered by a desperate survivor of the attack. The White House Office of Global Communications and a Policy Coordinating Committee on Strategic Communications were created to build trust in the USA overseas, stress common interests and ideologies, and influence elites.

Almost simultaneously, the former National Intelligence Council chair and international relations scholar Joseph Nye promulgated the embarrassingly penile metaphor "soft power" to describe the use of US culture as propaganda (2002) by contrast with the "hard power" of military and financial dominance. Soft power, as per the new public diplomacy, is now supposed to transcend the material impact of US foreign policy and corporate expropriation by fostering communication at a civil-society level, directly linking citizens across borders to "influence opinions and mobilize foreign publics" by "engaging, informing, and influencing key international audiences" (Council on Foreign Relations 2003, p. 15; Gilboa 1998; Brown 2004). The idea is to work in the interests of the USA, but avoid that connotation.

By 2003, the State Department's cultural budget amounted to US$600 million. Under the Bush Minor and Obama Administrations, initiatives were launched across a wide array of governmental agencies: the State Department itself, the U.S. Agency for International Development, the Broadcasting Board of Governors, the Pentagon, and the Open Source Center (Advisory Committee on Cultural Diplomacy to the Department of State 2005; Government Accountability Office 2007). The State Department Office of International Media Engagement created "regional media hubs" in the name of *Leading Through Civilian Power* (2010, pp. 60–61).

Some optimistic analysts discern the potential to transcend the use of such diplomacy as a cloak for national interests via more cosmopolitan third-sector possibilities (Ang et al. 2015). But for many of us, this is just modish rhetoric about a use of culture as propaganda that has long been crucial to imperial ideology and practice. For example, the State Department's Media Hub of the Americas pushes US perspectives across the hemisphere.[2]

Within the sphere of public diplomacy, tourism holds a special place in the era of Colombian reconstruction: its emphasis on visitation and civil society incarnates the idea of an organic understanding between peoples, *sans* state interference (Dinnie 2016). Tourism also suits plans to expand service industries and animate ecological tourism as putatively post-smokestack, green exemplars of economic development. To appreciate the real impact of such a strategy on the nation, one must understand Colombia's structure of gender and race, which produces its own desires for just such an industry policy.

GENDER AND RACE IN COLOMBIA

Violence against women is more common in Latin America than the rest of the world, as are female deaths from firearms (Small Arms Survey 2016). The Instituto Colombiano de Medicina Legal (Colombian Legal Institute of Medicine) reported 21,115 cases of sexual violence in 2014, with 85.05% of victims being women (2015). As in many countries, over 90% of Colombia's homicide victims are men, but, unlike women, generally not as a consequence of violence undertaken at home, or with a sexual element (De la Hoz Bohórquez and Romero Quevedo 2016; Wonder Women and Macho Men 2015). A spate of acid attacks by men on women over the last five years has affected thousands (Alarma y repudio en Colombia por ataques con ácido 2014; Guerrero 2013; Gaviria-Castellanos et al. 2015). Meanwhile, public-health experts argue that a failure to consider historical patterns of violence produces discounted statistics (Bello-Urrego 2013). At the same time, there has been a wave of US-inspired Evangelical-Protestant opposition to women's and queer rights, culminating in the defeat of the nation's 2016 peace plebiscite: the process had dared to guarantee rights to such groups (Marcos 2016).

Women's health and participation in the workforce, education, and politics saw Colombia ranked 42nd of 145 countries in 2015, descending from the 22nd spot it attained in 2006 (World Economic Forum 2015); and this during a period of significant economic growth and virtually zero inflation (Organización para la Cooperación y el Desarrollo Económico 2015, p. 8). The Human Development Report's index of gender inequality reveals that Colombian women encounter serious difficulties in securing positions of leadership (Programa de las Naciones Unidas para el Desarrollo 2015) and the United Nations notes a stark gendered difference in the unemployment rate: 11.5% for women as opposed to 6.9% for men (2010). Women are more likely to be stuck in the informal sector and secondary labor markets, especially if they are indigenous or black (Organización para la Cooperación y el Desarrollo Económico 2015, p. 34; Perazzi and Merli 2016; Cabezas Cortés 2016).

Colombian women have formed various social movements to define and defend their rights over the past two centuries (Lamus 2008; Villarreal Méndez 1994; Solano 2003). But state policies designed to alleviate systematic gender discrimination and inequality have been inconsistently applied and largely ineffective, as these figures illustrate (Gómez Cano et al. 2015).

Of course, daily life in Colombia is subject to additional forms of social stratification (La Furcia 2016). Ethnicity/race is defined differently from the norms of the Global North. The state counts most of the population as mixed race—a single group that would be disaggregated as indigenous, black, Asian, and so on in Western Europe and its white-settler colonies. The majority is therefore defined as one despite being a blend of indigenous, Afro-Colombian, Asian, European, Sephardim, and Arabic heritage, with 37% considered white and 49% *mestiz@*—a distinction that is itself not always clear (Hudson 2010, p. 10). The latest Colombian census (2005) identifies three minorities, comprising about a sixth of the population via 87 national indigenous groups, amounting to 1.4 million people who live communally and use their original languages (3.4% of the overall population); 4.3 million purely Afro-Colombian descendants of slaves (10.6%); and 5000 Gitano (Roma) (0.01%) (Departamento Administrativo Nacional de Estadística 2007, p. 33). Discrimination and inequality based on skin color are rampant, with whites and *mestiz@s* dominating political, economic, and social life.

Cartagena

Founded in 1533 by the Spanish, Cartagena declared independence in 1811. It is called La Heroica [the Heroic One] because of its history of withstanding naval assaults during colonialism and independence, the two most prominent being brutal blockades by the British and Spanish Empires (McNeill 2010). The city is filled with streets, statues, and neighborhoods named to celebrate and commemorate Spanish conquistadores and rulers. Pedro de Heredia, who founded the city, and Blas de Lezo, who defended it for Spain against the British, are among the most prominent. The recent mayoral administration of Dionisio Trujillo (2013–2015) sought to legitimize Cartagena's colonial past by returning the city's logo (a celebration of the eradication of slavery and independence from Spain) to the old emblem of the Spanish colony (Abello 2016) and appealing to latter-day little-Englander imperialists by glorifying their country's eighteenth-century attempt to starve Cartageneros into submission (Hernández-Mora 2014).

Today's population is well over a million (Cartagena Cómo Vamos 2017). Approximately 63% of residents are defined as *mestiz@* (with mixed heritage from native peoples, Africans, Spaniards, and the Arab world) and 36% as Afro-Colombian. There are small numbers of indigenous people.[3] Lighter-skinned *mestizo* oligarchs dominate finance, business, education, and politics, and largely deny the structure and causes of racial inequality (Valle 2017). A third of the population lives below the poverty line. As per the national situation, women suffer disproportionately from unemployment, while the informal sector, which includes sex work, accounts for well over half the city's jobs (Cartagena Cómo Vamos 2017).

The decades-long conflict in Colombia has seen many internal exiles flee the center of the country for the Caribbean, where the guerrilla and *narcotraficantes* (narcotraffickers) rarely focused their efforts, but death has still come easily due to the violence of *paramilitares* (the paramilitary forces), state proxies of the right. Now that major steps have been taken towards peace, there are equivalent movements towards economic development through tourism that draw on past and present gender stereotypes to create a new-yet-aged image of the nation. But those steps are radically disarticulated from the real material needs of the local population. Systematic inequality and violence continue as the image of the domestic nation is decoupled from the one projected abroad, with little or no regard for the impact that international imagery has on the local population, despite drawing on elements of identity that it values in order to sell the country via an ode to ecology, peace, and pleasure that belies the country's history.

Tourism and Cartagena

Domestic tourism in Colombia, much of it dedicated to returning to places of origin or pilgrimages to such holy sites as Popayán and Mompox, has been a feature of national life for decades (Escovar 2012), but is rarely foregrounded in federal policies and programs. Instead, resources and images alike focus on attracting foreigners, especially from the USA, which generally provides many more tourists than any other country (Oficina de Estudio Económicos 2017).

Even before the nation's great conflict began seven decades ago, international tourism was regarded as a future panacea, and was linked to stereotypical femininity. The formulation of tourism policy in Colombia and the creation of a Comité de Turismo (National Tourism Board) coincided with the first Concurso Nacional de Belleza de Colombia (Colombian National Beauty Contest) in 1934 (Nasser 2012). The Concurso has played a crucial role ever since in constructing gender, articulating it to national identity, and promoting Colombia through its annual coronation. The Concurso is celebrated in Cartagena. It captures the attention of the wider population and commemorates the city's status as the first province to free itself from the Spanish Crown. Tourism promotion highlights it as an emblematic event that brings all the regions of the country together around the beauty of Colombian women, linked in turn to its natural resources (CO 2017).

David Letterman distinguished himself on network television by saying that the 2001 Queen, Andrea Noceti, included among her special skills the capacity to swallow 50 kg of heroin (Miss Colombia to Sue Letterman 2001). Such stereotyping perfectly captures both the arrogance of US public figures towards the region, and the way that Colombia is portrayed in dominant discourse—as a place of sex and risk. That particularly applies to Cartagena's image.

Named the Distrito Turístico y Cultural de Cartagena de Indias (Tourism and Culture District of Cartagena) in 1991, this world heritage city is well known for beautiful colonial architecture, varied international colloquia, racialized social inequality, and child-sex tourism. Cartagena's world heritage status derives from its place in the annals of military and religious history. At almost 200 hectares, the fortifications are the largest in South America and one of the most intact examples from the Spanish era. The city's monuments pay remarkable testimony to faith and craft alike, and zones within the Old Town correspond to areas once occupied by slaves, merchants, artisans, and the occupying elite. UNESCO values these qualities both because they illuminate the history of maritime trade routes and are imperiled by tourism's impact on the natural and built environments.[4] A fortified history and a contemporary dependence on tourism based in colonial architecture characterize a racially divided city in a fractured nation, torn apart by conflict.

Some date the exploitation of the local population through tourism as far back as a century (Caraballo 2014). In any event, by the mid-1950s, Cartagena was designated as the nation's major tourist destination, combining its architecture, history, and myth with a reputation as a "*ciudad turística con un ambiente alegre y múltiples diversiones para los turistas*" (a tourist city with a relaxed environment and many pleasurable activities for visitors). The first National Conference on Tourism, held in Bogotá in 1952, recommended promotions to attract visitors from the USA and western Europe and the construction of "*un elegante casino internacional con todo el lujo posible, como hoteles con aire acondicionado, piscinas olímpicas, salones de bailes con shows internacionales, festivales, carreras de lanchas y de caballos*" (an elegant international casino with every imaginable luxury, such as air-conditioned hotels, Olympic swimming pools, dance halls featuring international acts, festivals, marinas, and stables) (PCNT 1952, p. 20).

Two decades later, a World Bank economic commission studying Colombia proposed a strategy for generating foreign exchange and diversifying the economy through tourism. As per the 1950s, the Bank favored a Caribbean economic-development zone, drawing on the region's comparative advantages: proximity to the USA, reverse climatic seasons, and warm-water beaches (World Bank 1972, p. 4). Cartagena would convert itself into a paradise of "*sol y playa*" (sun and sand), a playground for North Americans, in keeping with what have been called the four Ss sought by US visitors: sea, sand, sun, and sex (Boyer 2002). We might rewrite these as citizen-to-citizen exchanges by the beach or bed.

In response to the Bank's report, and various studies produced by the tourism industry, the Centro de Investigación Económica y Social (Fedesarrollo) (Center for Economic and Social Research) argued that mass tourism would produce benefits across society following the provision of "*exenciones e incentivos claros y atractivos*" (clear and attractive tax exemptions and incentives). Fedesarrollo acknowledged that this would not necessarily be a boon for low-income segments of the population. Mass expansion of the industry could produce "*una distorsión social de consecuencias imprevisibles*" (social disruption through unforeseen consequences) (Fedesarrollo 1972, p. 140). The report expressed anxiety that a service class of workers, poor and poorly treated, would arise in order to meet the needs created by an influx of tourists, and ordinary people would be displaced from their traditional homes.

Those predictions proved to be prescient. The sector's growth has been accompanied by intense income and social inequality, unemployment, under-employment, social clearances, and sex tourism—in the cause of economic growth, a fresh national image, and relations with the USA, inter alios (Bernal-Camargo et al. 2013; Mosquera and Bozzi 2005; Londoño et al. 2014).[5]

The city prioritizes the interests of tourists above those of its own people. Because public services are stagnating, violent crime increasing, teen pregnancy cresting, and education faltering, local residents have extremely negative views of the quality of their daily lives by contrast with most other Colombian city dwellers (Cartagena Cómo Vamos 2017).[6] Meanwhile, tourism mavens work assiduously with chorine academics to negate bad news, lest potential visitors turn away (González et al. 2010; Xiang and Gretzel 2010; Pan et al. 2011).

National Imagery and Gender

Tourism campaigns have long placed great emphasis on Colombian women, as per the Concurso Nacional de Belleza. Promotional campaigns have included: "*Turista satisfecho trae más turista*" (A Satisfied

Tourist Brings More Tourists) (1970); *"Enamórese de su Colombia"* (Fall in Love with Your Colombia) (1975); *"Por las rutas de Colombia"* (To the Pathways of Colombia) (1985); *"Colombia: Para amarla, hay que andarla"* (Colombia: To Love Her, You Must Wander) (1994). Aimed at national and international visitors, they highlighted the country's diverse regions and peoples as essential components of national identity and displayed beauty queens alongside products, places, and objects such as fruit, landscape, and religious centers (Escovar 2012). With the neoliberal opening of the economy in the 1990s came increased violence; the new century brought a reaction from the tourism establishment about reclaiming the nation: *"Vive Colombia Viaja por Ella"* (Colombia Lives; Walk with Her) (2001) (Criscione and Vignolo 2014). This may have been a cry of desperation from a nation dominated by armed conflict (Toro 2013), but it presaged a different future that would draw upon the association of beauty, nature, and light-skinned femininity.

The nation's 2005 branding exercise took *"Colombia es Pasión"* (Colombia is Passion) as its motto.[7] It linked women with orchids, coffee, gems, and geography, feminizing the image of Colombia as a country loaded with ardor to distance it from a male image of drug trafficking and violence. The campaign's signature feminine silhouette constructed women's bodies as visitor sites (Echeverri et al. 2010; Bolívar 2007; Nasser 2012, 2013). Its heart logo, red color, floral design, and silhouette, designed by the US firm Visual Marketing Associates, were alternately celebrated and denounced by public opinion. Advocates saw this as an opportunity for sensual experience and emotional connection (Echeverri et al. 2010). Critics likened the logo and its representation of *passion* to "a curvaceous woman's midsection" (Nasser 2013, p. 7).

The official video of "Colombia is Passion" stressed "the true face of the country," accompanied by the image of a beauty queen (Mejia 2007—minute 1:06), while *"El riesgo es que te quieras quedar"* (2008) (The One Risk is You'll Want to Stay) profiled Colombia as a land of sea, with the central scene an image of a woman walking sensually from the ocean to the beach (Visitcolombia 2008—0:47 minute). The recent toursim slogan *"Realismo Mágico"* (Magical Realism) associated images of nature and femininity with the Nobel Laureate Gabriel García Márquez.[8] The type of woman celebrated is not representative of Colombia's racial and ethnic diversity, but rather of people connected to the country's historic and contemporary elite (Bolívar 2007).

The most recent brand, "The Answer is Colombia," focused on a broader economic and investment strategy (La nueva Marca País, ¿mejor que las anteriores? 2012). Colombia presents itself as a modern and flexible country with an unparalleled natural and cultural wealth. Its people were promoted as entrepreneurs "propelled into the future" (Wickcreativo 2012) who stood ready to be exploited by the international market. Passion and the color red remained present, indices of that putative human entrepreneurial resource. Despite being postulated as innovative and breaking with previous efforts of image of country, this campaign was not so distant from its predecessor. Although the image of women as an export product was less prominent, because minerals and biodiversity became the principal actors, Colombian women continued to be the chief human protagonists. A recent example included the promotion of Cali, "city of salsa and fun," where "visitors will feel welcomed by the local charm and hospitality, by beautiful women and salsa music" (Procolombia 2015). For many in the Colombian establishment, there is no better campaign than one that articulates human and natural beauty to tourism. They draw no connection between such campaigns and the thousands of US visitors arriving each year in search of illegal citizen-to-citizen engagement—sexual components of development and national imagery (Torres 2011).

Again and again, Cartagena in particular is presented as an object of casual scopophilic pleasure for tourists, who are addressed in ways that obfuscate and fetishize history, race, gender, and beauty into just so many street names or topographic formations, viewed *en passant* and photographed or forgotten all too easily (Cunin and Rinaudo 2008; Carbonell 2006).

The USA and Sexual Tourism

Throughout these transformations, one factor has remained constant: the symbolic and monetary dominance of the USA, the *coloso del norte* (the giant of the north), in daily Colombian life.[9] After the loss of the Panama Canal and subsequent betrayal by the USA, Colombia adopted a timid, isolationist foreign policy (Tokatlian 1997). Under extreme pressure from Washington, Bogotá reasserted itself in the international community by combating *narcotraficantes* over the last decade and a half (ibid). Once the drug cartels and terrorist guerrillas were dispensed with, it was said, the nation would enter a new golden age. Following such stereotypes as being considered the Tibet Suramericano (the Tibet of South America) in the 1980s and a *narcodemocracia* (narcodemocracy) in the 1990s, Colombia now seeks to define itself as *una estrella que brilla* (a shining star) and the new *tigre de Latinoamérica* (tiger of Latin America), troping the booming South Asian economies of the 1980s, ready and able to help meet the world's economic needs.

Less conventionally, glamorously, legally, and legitimately, those demands include the development of child-sex tourism for US nationals, which has accelerated since its first spike from soldiers involved in the American War in Vietnam (Boyer 2002). The reality is known to all, but subtly recoded through informal tourism strategies that sexualize young but legal-age women as part of the landscape in much the same way as flora and fauna.

Sexual tourism and exploitation are a blight on many tourist destinations (George and Panko 2011). But studies conducted by the Renacer Foundation, the Instituto Colombiano de Bienestar Familiar (Colombian Institute of Family Welfare), and numerous academics demonstrate the seriousness of the problem in Cartagena (Granados-Díaz and Rodríguez-Cruz 2006; Bernal-Camargo et al. 2013; Mosquera and Bozzi 2005; Londoño et al. 2014).[10] Their research suggests that between 30,000 and 40,000 Colombian children and adolescents have been victims of commercial sexual exploitation since the expansion of tourism:

> *en Cartagena la ESCNNA está principalmente relacionada con la actividad turística, existe una red que trabaja en la negociación de los servicios sexuales de los menores, se encuentran vinculadas a esto personas que desempeñan labores relacionadas directa e indirectamente con el turismo, el valor de la oferta comercial de los NNA depende de la edad de éstos y del lugar de procedencia del turista. Las víctimas de ESC son generalmente de género femenino, entre los 14 y 17 años. Los factores propiciatorios descritos son: situación de pobreza y hambre, descuido o complicidad de familiares, y falta de acción de la comunidad inmediata que conoce la situación y no la denuncia.*
>
> (in Cartagena, ESCNNA is profoundly connected to tourism. A network negotiates sexual services from minors. The price placed on children depends on age and the nationality of tourists. The victims are generally female, aged between 14 and 17. The key factors propelling their participation include poverty and hunger, the neglect or complicity of relatives, and lack of action by the immediate community, which may know of the situation but fail to denounce it.) (Arango-Arias and Hurtado-Díaz 2012, pp. 92–93)

This exploitation of minors is undertaken through networks that are directly and indirectly related to the tourist industry: for example, hotel check-in desks and taxi ranks are switching points between men's arrival and children's exploitation. These locations offer both information about the trade and articulation into it. Such things can also be arranged in advance on line (Arango-Arias and Hurtado-Díaz 2012).

Although the core of the industry is foreign adult men seeking sex with female Colombian children, the demand extends to male minors, some of whom enter prostitution following familial rejection of their sexuality (Castillo and Reyes 2013). As in other countries with similar trends, there is a high incidence of coercion and sexually transmitted disease among the exploited; the Caribbean has the world's highest rates of HIV/AIDS after sub-Saharan Africa (Baral et al. 2012; Djellouli and Quevedo-Gómez 2015).

Two examples from the region reflect the paradoxical, if not contradictory, nature of sexuality in the Colombian Caribbean—and the presence of US citizens. The first occurred during the summit meeting of the Americas in Cartagena in 2012: the case of sex workers servicing numerous Drug Enforcement Agency officials (on repeated visits) and Obama's security-service detail (who declined to pay) (Ryan 2012).[11] The second was the capture of a web of procurers who sold children to US tourists for sexual purposes in the offshore Rosario islands, led by a 22-year-old former beauty queen (Bedoya 2014).[12]

The local press viewed the Obama scandal as an isolated event that did not do justice to the reality of the city and the efforts of local authorities and the national government to promote it. The potential to damage the image of Cartagena and Colombia could be explained away as the result of the character failings of a few secret-service foreigners (Wickcreativo 2012; ¿Cartagena es Pasion? 2012).

Although the event was regarded as "quaint" and even "fun" locally, the mainstream international media described Cartagena as Latin America's Bangkok. For despite diplomatic efforts to diminish the scandal, the episode went viral, and showed the stark reality of the city's true level of sex tourism. It signaled that the image and marketing of Cartagena stereotype Colombian women as products for US custom—export materials—in a shocking link between public diplomacy, country branding, beauty queendom, and social inequality. It is telling that the advisers on the "Colombia is passion" campaign were US experts (Echeverri et al. 2010) put in charge of finding ways to make Colombia and Cartagena attractive places in the eyes of the foreign citizen as a place "that foreigners actually love and enjoy. Of color, festivity, vibrancy and more ... its current realities embodied in the much softer imagery of Colombia is Passion" (Lightle 2017).

The Obama scandal dramatically illustrates the centrality of the USA in Colombian foreign affairs and the image of Cartagena since the 1950s as a destination oriented towards satisfying North American males. The second anecdote—the beauty-queen gang—illustrates that complex organizations of sex work have sprung up, involving various distinct levels and structures of the wider society and tourism in particular to provide foreigners with the trade they are seeking.

Both instances reference the centrality of the female body and the role of beauty queens and other conventionally attractive women working in the culture industries in the construction of gender in Colombia, and its articulation as an international calling card to the world's diplomatic underside and informal economy. Each example signals the casual arrogance and entitlement that peoples around the world experience from US tourists, in contradistinction to the nation's banal, repetitive claims to a high moralism.

CONCLUSION

The international image of Cartagena is not as a site of light-skinned privilege, a fortified city, or an endangered ecology, but a tourist's paradise. It offers spectacular views of the Caribbean from the old town, historic architecture, narrow streets, horse-drawn transportation, luxury hotels, street life, and a cornucopia of music and dance. That panoply hides the realities of massive child sexual exploitation, extreme Afro-Colombian poverty, and leftist intellectuals assassinated by the *paramilitares*.

Successive promotional campaigns designed to entice vast numbers of tourists are clearly not the sole cause of the rise in sex tourism—governmental policies aimed at visitors and the US public and polity cannot be held entirely responsible for what has occurred. But in addition to attracting large numbers of people, these campaigns have focused on gender and sexuality, in keeping with the culturalist focus so beloved of development and diplomacy.

The industry incarnates and indexes a dark underside to Colombia. Local citizenry and overseas visitors alike exploit the vulnerability of the young and the extremely young in an accidental—but entirely unsurprising—impact of the citizen-to-citizen, social-network communication so beloved of the State Department and other advocates. For the reality is that official national branding has become a key instrument of sexual exploitation.

It is clear that state interdiction and public-health campaigns coordinated across the two countries are prerequisites to dealing with the problem. Some strides have been made in that direction, thanks to research and suasion from the third sector and academia. But two governing Pollyannaish fantasies stand in the way of resolving the basic problem. The first is that tourism is regarded as an unproblematic benefit to the Colombian economy that can be promoted with cavalier disregard for gender politics. And it is clearly the case that drawing homologies between young women, male desire, nature, and US visitors over half a century has had malign effects, through the careful curation of female imagery. The second fantasy is that the goodness at the heart of the average American will simply express itself in untrammeled interaction with folks from other, albeit strange, lands, thereby connecting them to the other and finding an unlikely overlap of interests through their common humanity. How twee, when so many businesspeople, militarists, politicians, and officials are reared on doctrines of national, racial, and gender superiority and condescension, and under the specifically arrogant sign of the Monroe Doctrine.

In short, the USA and Colombia must both revise their official views of the region's past and present, and the role of age, masculinity, poverty, and race in person-to-person links between the two nations, which intertwine with economic inequality, both internationally and nationally, and industry policy.

A serious shift in the rhetoric and imagery of development and nation will entail Colombia revisiting its historiography, rewriting its tourism strategy, and rekindling its multicultural vision; and the USA re-educating its people about Colombia and basic sexual justice. Then we might see a reciprocal, realistic, and progressive bilateral relationship that takes responsibility for inequalities and injustices rather than regarding them as aberrant accidents.

NOTES

1. The Ministry of Industry and Tourism has a site dedicated to educational classes and other resources to counter child sexual exploitation: http://escnna.mincit.gov.co/.
2. http://www.state.gov/r/pa/ime/americasmediahub/index.htm.
3. http://www.dane.gov.co/files/censo2005/PERFIL_PDF_CG2005/13001T7T000.PDF.

4. http://whc.unescoorg/en/list/285.
5. http://www.icbf.gov.co/portal/page/portal/PortalICBF/macro-procesos/misionales/restablecimiento/2/LM11.MPM5.P1%20Poblacion%20Especial%20Violencia%20Sexual%20v1.pdf.
6. http://www.cartagenacomovamos.org/cartagena-entre-las-ciu-dades-con-menor-satisfaccion-con-su-calidad-de-vida/.
7. http://www.youtube.com/watch?v=XEuYunbf8Ww.
8. http://www.procolombia.co/noticias/colombia-realismo-magico; http://colombia.travel/realismomagico.
9. A Latin American colloquialism for 'the Giant of the North.'
10. http://www.icbf.gov.co/portal/page/portal/PortalICBF/macro-procesos/misionales/restablecimiento/2/LM11.MPM5.P1%20Poblacion%20Especial%20Violencia%20Sexual%20v1.pdf.
11. http://www.youtube.com/watch?v=EaCaIPKbkf8.
12. http://www.youtube.com/watch?v=fuvMQAYhf48.

REFERENCES

Abello, A. (2016, December). Interview with Anamaria Tamayo Duque and Toby Miller.
Advisory Committee on Cultural Diplomacy. (2005). *Cultural Diplomacy: The Linchpin of Public Diplomacy.* U.S. Department of State. http://www.state.gov/documents/organization/54374.pdf.
Alarma y repudio en Colombia por ataques con ácido. (2014, April 4). *BBC Mundo.* http://www.bbc.com/mundo/noticias/2014/04/140404_colombia_ataques_acido_wbm.
Alsema, A. (2017, May 18). Trump Ignores Colombia's Peace Process, Talks About Venezuela Instead. *Colombia Reports.* https://colombiareports.com/colombia-santos-donald-trump/.
Ang, I., Isar, Y. R., & Mar, P. (2015). Cultural Diplomacy: Beyond the National Interest? *International Journal of Cultural Policy, 21*(4), 365–381.
Arango-Arias, A. L., & Hurtado-Díaz, C. A. (2012). Especificaciones sobre la explotación sexual comercial de niños, niñas y adolescentes (ESCNNA), el turismo sexual y sus relaciones con el discurso capitalista. *Textos y Sentidos, 6,* 79–101.
Baral, S., Beyrer, C., Muessig, K., Potect, T., Wirtz, A. L., Decker, M. R., et al. (2012). Burden of HIV among Female Sex Workers in Low-Income and Middle-Income Countries: A Systematic Review and Meta-analysis. *Lancet Infectious Diseases, 12*(7), 538–549.
Bedoya, N. (2014, October 14). Cartagena Beauty Queen Arrested in Child Sex Tourism Ring Bust. *Colombia Reports.* https://colombiareports.com/beauty-queen-among-five-arrested-cartagena-child-sex-tourism-ring-bust/.
Bello-Urrego, A. del R. (2013). Sexo/género, violencias y derechos humanos: Perspectivas conceptuales para el abordaje de la violencia basada en género

contra las mujeres desde el sector salud. *Revista Colombiana de Psiquiatría, 42*(1), 108–119.

Bernal-Camargo, D. R., Varón-Mejía, A., Becerra-Barbosa, A., Chaib-De Mares, K., Seco-Martín, E., & Archila-Delgado, L. (2013). Explotación sexual de niños, niñas y adolescentes: Modelo de intervención. *Revista Latinoamericana de Ciencias Sociales, Niñez y Juventud, 11*(2), 617–632.

Bolívar, I. J. R. (2007). Reinados de belleza y nacionalización de las sociedades latinoamericanas. *Iconos: Revista de Ciencias Sociales, 28,* 71–80.

Boyer, M. (2002). El turismo en Europa, de la edad moderna al siglo XX (C. L. Rodríguez, Trans.). *Historia Contemporánea, 25,* 13–31.

Brown, J. (2004). Changing Minds, Winning Peace: Reconsidering the Djerejian Report. *American Diplomacy.* http://www.unc.edu/depts/diplomat/archives_roll/2004_07-09/brown_djerejian/brown_djerejian.html.

Browning, C. S., & Ferraz de Oliviera, A. (2017). Introduction: Nation Branding and Competitive Identity in World Politics. *Geopolitics, 22*(3), 481–501.

Büscher, B., & Fletcher, R. (2017). Destructive Creation: Capital Accumulation and the Structural Violence of Tourism. *Journal of Sustainable Tourism, 25*(5), 651–667.

Cabezas Cortés, C. C. (2016). Consideraciones alrededor de regímenes de discriminación género/etnia sobre relaciones laborales en Colombia. In L. A. Montenegro Mora (Ed.), *Retos de las relaciones de trabajo y de la seguridad social en el Siglo XXI* (pp. 71–81). San Juan de Pasto: Editorial UNIMAR.

Caraballo, A. D. (2014). Turismo, modernidad y exclusión social en Cartagena de Indias, 1913–1946. *Alaüla—Revista Estudiantil, 2,* 24–38.

Carbonell, C. (2006). Narrativa etnográfica y análisis sociocultural de las relaciones entre turismo y sexualidad en Cartagena de Indias. *Turismo y Sociedad, 7,* 65–74.

Cartagena Cómo Vamos. (2017). *Cartagena Cómovamos: Informe Calidad de Vida 2016.* http://www.cartagenacomovamos.org/nuevo/wp-content/uploads/2017/07/Presentaci%C3%B3n-para-WEB-ICV-2016.pdf.

¿Cartagena es Pasion? (2012, October 13). *Revista Semana.* http://www.semana.com/nacion/articulo/cartagena-pasion/257186-3.

Castillo, N. C. M., & Reyes, N. E. R. (2013). TICS, comunicación humana y violencia de género contra niños y adolescents víctimas de la explotación sexual comercial: Los casos de Bogotá y Cartagena, Colombia. *Actas—V Congreso Internacional Latina de Comunicación Social—V CILCS.* http://www.revistalatinacs.org/13SLCS/2013_actas/171_Castillo.pdf.

CO. (2017). *Colombia Travel.* http://www.colombia.travel/es/ferias-y-fiestas/independencia-de-cartagena-y-reinado-nacional-de-belleza.

Council on Foreign Relations. (2003). *Finding America's Voice: A Strategy for Reinvigorating U.S. Public Diplomacy.* New York: Council on Foreign Relations.

Criscione, G., & Vignolo, P. (2014). ¿Del Terrorismo al Turismo? Vive Colombia Viaja por ella como dispositivo de movilidad, entre conflicto armado y patrimonio cultural. In M. Chaves, M. Montenegro, & M. Zambrano (Eds.), *El Valor del patrimonio: Mercado, políticas culturales y agenciamientos sociales* (pp. 473–517). Bogotá: Instituto Colombiano de Antropología e Historia.

Cunin, E., & Rinaudo, C. (2008). Consuming the City in Passing: Guided Visits and the Marketing of Difference in Cartagena de Indias (Colombia). *Tourist Studies, 9*(2), 267–286.

De la Hoz Bohórquez, G. A., & Romero Quevedo, J. H. (2016). *Enterremos las armas para que florezca la Vida!!! Comportamiento del homicidio. Colombia, 2015.* Instituto Nacional de Medicina Legal y Ciencias Forenses. http://www.medicinalegal.gov.co/documents/88730/3418907/2.+HOMI-CIDIOS.pdf/70a4c34b-920c-465b-9902-936ffeab4afd.

Departamento Administrativo Nacional de Estadística. (2007). *Colombia una nación multicultural: Su diversidad étnica.* https://www.dane.gov.co/files/censo2005/etnia/sys/colombia_nacion.pdf.

Dinnie, K. (2016). *Nation Branding: Concepts, Issues, Practice* (2nd ed.). London: Routledge.

Djellouli, N., & Quevedo-Gómez, M. C. (2015). Challenges to Successful Implementation of HIV and AIDS-Related Health Policies in Cartagena, Colombia. *Social Science and Medicine, 133*, 36–44.

Echeverri, L. M., Rosker, E., & Restrepo, M. L. (2010). Los orígenes de la marca país Colombia es passion. *Estudios y Perspectivas en Turismo, 19*(3), 409–421.

Echeverri, L. M., ter Horst, E., Molina, G., & Mohamad, Z. (2017). Nation Branding: Unveiling Factors that Affect the Image of Colombia from a Foreign Perspective. *Tourism Planning & Development.* https://doi.org/10.1080/21568316.2017.1362031.

Escovar, A. (2012). Turismo religioso en Colombia. In C. M. Ramos de Balcarce & S. Malnis de Bestiani (Eds.), *Difusión y protección del patrimonio religioso en América Latina* (pp. 343–360). Sáenz Peña: Editorial de la Universidad Nacional de Tres de Febrero.

Fedesarrollo. (1972). Turismo. *Coyuntura Económica.* http://hdl.handle.net/11445/2846.

Gaviria-Castellanos, J. L., Gómez-Ortega, V., & Gutiérrez, P. (2015). Quemaduras químicas por agresión: Caracteristicas e incidencia recogidas en el Hospital Simón Bolívar, Bogotá. Colombia. *Cirugía Plástica Ibero-Latinoamericana, 41*(1), 73–82.

George, B. P., & Panko, T. R. (2011). Child Sex Tourism: Facilitating Conditions, Legal Remedies, and Other Interventions. *Vulnerable Children and Youth Studies, 6*(2), 134–143.

Gilboa, E. (1998). Media Diplomacy: Conceptual Divergence and Applications. *Harvard Journal of Press/Politics, 3*(3), 56–75.

Gómez, C., Alberto, C., Castillo, V. S., & Díaz, K. V. (2015). Analysis of Public Gender Policy in Colombia (1990–2014). *Revista Facultad de Ciencias Contables, Económicas y Administrativas, 5*(2), 175–181.

González, S. M., Gidumal, J. B., & López-Valcárcel, B. G. (2010). La participación de los clientes en sitios web de valoración de servicios turísticos: El caso de Tripadvisor. *Análisis Turístico, 10,* 17–22.

Government Accountability Office. (2007). *U.S. Public Diplomacy: Actions Needed to Improve Strategic Use and Coordination of Research.* http://www.gao.gov/new.items/d07904.pdf.

Granados-Díaz, O. S., & Rodríguez-Cruz, R. (2006). La explotación sexual de los niños en Cartagena de Indias y Bogotá, Colombia. *Revista Infancia Adolescencia y Familia, 1*(2), 247–258.

Guerrero, L. (2013). Burns Due to Acid Assaults in Bogotá, Colombia. *Burns, 39*(5), 1018–1023.

Hernández-Mora, S. (2014, November 6). Colombia: El ridículo histórico del Príncipe Carlos de Inglaterra y del alcalde de Cartagena a cuenta de una placa homenaje al admirante que intentó conquistar la ciudad. *Radio Tierra Viva.* http://radiotierraviva.blogspot.com.co/2014/11/colombia-el-ridiculo-historico-del.html.

Hudson, R. A. (Eds.). (2010). *Colombia: A Country Study* (5th ed.). Library of Congress. https://cdn.loc.gov/master/frd/frdcstdy/co/colombiacountrys00huds/colombiacountrys00huds.pdf.

Instituto Colombiano de Medicina Legal. (2015). *Forensis, datos para la vida.* http://www.medicinalegal.gov.co/documents/88730/1656998/Forensis+Interactivo+2014.24-JULpdf.pdf/9085ad79-d2a9-4c0d-a17b-f845ab96534b.

La Furcia, A. (2016). Los colores de las fantasías. Estudios sobre masculinidades en Colombia: Crítica feminista y geopolítica del conocimiento en la matriz colonial. *Revista Colombiana de Sociología, 39*(1), 47–78.

La nueva Marca País, ¿mejor que las anteriores? (2012, November 9). *Revista Semana.* http://www.semana.com/nacion/articulo/la-nueva-marca-pais-mejor-anteriores/264530-3.

Lamus, D. (2008). Resistencia contra-hegemónica y polisemia: Conformación actual del movimiento de mujeres/feministas en Colombia. *Manzana de la Discordia, 3*(1), 25–37.

Lightle, D. (2017). *David Lightle Nation Branding & Promotion Specialist.* https://davidlightleblog.wordpress.com/my-practice/.

Lindsay-Poland, J., & Tickner, A. B. (2016, May 11). De- or Re-Militarization in Post Peace-Accord Colombia? *NACLA News.* http://nacla.org/news/2016/05/11/de-or-re-militarization-post-peace-accord-colombia.

Londoño, N. H., Valencia, D., García, M., & Restrepo, C. (2014). Factores causales de la explotación sexual infantil en niños, niñas y adolescentes en Colombia. *El Ágora USB Medellín-Colombia, 15*(1), 241–254.

Marcos, A. (2016, October 12). El voto evangélico, clave en la Victoria del 'no' en el plebiscite de Colombia. *El País*. https://elpais.com/internacional/2016/10/12/colombia/1476237985_601462.html.

McNeill, J. R. (2010). *Mosquito Empires: Ecology and War in the Greater Caribbean, 1620–1914*. New York: Cambridge University Press.

Mejia, E. (2007, December 16). *Colombia es Pasión--Creación campaña marca*. https://www.youtube.com/watch?v=hbiYwys-vs4.

Miller, T. (2000). The National Endowment for the Arts in the 1990s: A Black Eye on the Arts? *American Behavioral Scientist, 43*(9), 1429–1445.

Miller, T., & Yúdice, G. (2004). *Política Cultural* (G. Ventureira, Trans.). Barcelona: Gedisa.

Miss Colombia to Sue Letterman. (2001, May 16). *BBC News*. http://news.bbc.co.uk/1/hi/entertainment/1334464.stm.

Mosquera, M. V., & Bozzi, C. O. (2005). El abordaje de la problemática de explotación sexual infantil en Cartagena. *Palabra, 6*, 137–153.

Nasser, M. R. (2012). Feminized Topographies: Women, Nature, and Tourism in *Colombia es Pasión*. *Revista de Estudios Colombianos, 40*, 15–25.

Nasser, M. R. (2013). Bellas por naturaleza: Mapping National Identity on US Colombian Beauty Queens. *Latino Studies, 11*(3), 293–312.

Niesing, E. (2013). *Latin America's Potential in Nation Branding: A Closer Look at Brazil's, Chile's and Colombia's Practices*. New York: Anchor Books.

Nye, J. S. (2002). Limits of American Power. *Political Science Quarterly, 117*(4), 545–559.

Oficina de Estudio Económicos. (2017, Junio). *Boletín Mensual Turismo*. http://www.mincit.gov.co/loader.php?lServicio=Documentos&lFuncion=verPdf&id=81627&name=OEE_LL_Turismo_Junio_18-07-2017.pdf&prefijo=file.

Organización para la Cooperación y el Desarrollo Económico. (2015). *Estudios económicos de la OCDE: COLOMBIA*. http://www.oecd.org/eco/surveys/Overview_Colombia_ESP.pdf.

Pan, B., Xiang, Z., Law, R., & Fesenmaier, D. R. (2011). The Dynamics of Search Engine Marketing for Tourist Destinations. *Journal of Travel Research, 50*(4), 365–377.

PCNT. (1952). *Anales del Primer Congreso Nacional de Turismo: COLOMBIA*. Bogotá: Ministerio de Fomento, Departamento Nacional de Turismo.

Perazzi, J. R., & Merli, G. O. (2016). Análisis de la estructura del mercado laboral en Colombia: Un estudio por género mediante correspondencias multiples. *Cuadernos de Economía*. https://doi.org/10.1016/j.cesjef.2016.02.002.

Procolombia. (2015, July 31). About Cali. http://www.procolombia.co/en/pacific-alliance/about-cali.

Programa de las Naciones Unidas para el Desarrollo. (2015). *Informe sobre desar-rollo humano 2015.* New York: United Nations.

Ryan, E. G. (2012, May 22). Colombian Prostitutes More Addictive Than Colombian Cocaine for U.S. Officials. *Jezebel.* http://jezebel.com/5912278/colombian-prostitutes-more-addictive-than-colombian-co-caine-for-us-officials.

Sancho, V. (2017, August 12). Trump: Posible, opción militar para Venezuela. *El Universal.* http://www.eluniversal.com.mx/articulo/mundo/2017/08/12/trump-posible-opcion-militar-para-venezuela.

Small Arms Survey. (2016, November). *A Gendered Analysis of Violent Deaths.* Research Notes, 63. http://www.smallarmssurvey.org/fileadmin/docs/H-Research_Notes/SAS-Research-Note-63.pdf.

Solano, Y. (2003). Entramado actual del movimiento de mujeres en Colombia. In M. E. Martínez (Ed.), *Cartografía de mujeres, para pensar los derechos* (pp. 98–111). Bogotá: Red Nacional de Mujeres/Corporación Humanizar.

State Department. (2010). *Leading Through Civilian Power: The First Quadrennial Diplomacy and Development Review.* http://www.state.gov/s/dmr/qddr/.

Tokatlian, J. G. (1997). Drogas psicoactivas ilícitas y política mundial: La indud-able e inestable internacionalización de Colombia. In S. Ramírez, & L. A. Restrepo (Eds.), *Colombia entre la inserción y el aislamiento: la política exte-rior colombiana en los años noventa.* Bogotá: Siglo del Hombre Editores/IEPRI, Universidad Nacional.

Toro, G. (2013). La política pública de turismo en Colombia. *Turismo y Sociedad, 2*(2), 9–15.

Torres, J. F. (2011). La Diplomacia Pública en una perspectiva comparada: Una estrategia de la política exterior y su implementación en la política colombi-ana. *Pensamiento Jurídico, 30, 263–293.*

Valle, M. M. (2017). The Discursive Detachment of Race from Gentrification in Cartagena de Indias, Colombia. *Latin American and Caribbean Studies.* https://doi.org/10.1080/01419870.2016.1274419.

Villarreal Méndez, N. (1994). El camino de la utopía feminista en Colombia, 1975–1991. In M. León (Ed.), *Mujer y participación política: Avances y desafíos en América Latina* (pp. 181–204). Bogotá: Tercer Mundo.

Visitcolombia. (2008, March 17). *Colombia, el riesgo es que te quieras quedar* [Colombia, the Only Risk Is Wanting to Stay]. https://www.youtube.com/watch?v=8kUU-DWOqmI.

Wickcreativo. (2012, September 7). *Nuevo logo, nueva imagen, marca país Colombia.* https://www.youtube.com/watch?v=PvVGDHmMbYg.

Wonder Women and Macho Men. (2015, August 22). *Economist.* http://www.economist.com/news/americas/21661800-latin-american-women-are-mak-ing-great-strides-culture-not-keeping-up-wonder-women-and.

World Bank. (1972). *Economic Growth of Colombia: Problems and Prospects: Report of a Mission Sent to Colombia in 1970 by the World Bank.* Chief of Mission and Co-ordinating Author D. Avramovic. Baltimore: The Johns Hopkins University Press.

World Economic Forum. (2015). *Global Gender Gap Report 2015.* https://www. weforum.org/reports/global-gender-gap-report-2015.

Xiang, Z., & Gretzel, U. (2010). Role of Social Media in Online Travel Information Search. *Tourism Management, 31*(2), 179–188.

CHAPTER 6

Entitled to Benevolence? South Korea's Government-Sponsored Volunteers as Public Diplomacy and Development Actors

Kyung Sun (Karen) Lee

From Recipient to Provider of Aid: South Korea in the Changing Terrain of Foreign Aid

Standing in front of a large group of volunteers at the Blue House garden, former President of South Korea (Korea, hereafter), Lee Myung-bak, spoke to a large group of volunteers and government officials, all identically dressed in outdoor vests and brimmed hats printed with the words: "World Friends Korea." Celebrating the third anniversary of the launching of World Friends Korea (WFK), he remarked, "Back then [when Korea received foreign aid], we took what was thrown at us and said 'thank you.' But we need to give with two hands. We need to keep our heads as low as the receiver. That's how Korea's volunteerism is different" (Lee 2012). Lee's brief comment says much about Korea's government-sponsored international development volunteer program. First,

K. S. Lee (✉)
University of Texas, Austin, TX, USA
e-mail: kslee@utexas.edu

© The Author(s) 2018
J. Pamment and K. G. Wilkins (eds.), *Communicating National Image through Development and Diplomacy*, Palgrave Studies in Communication for Social Change, https://doi.org/10.1007/978-3-319-76759-8_6

it is based on a notion that Korea needs to give back having been a recipient. The assertion is designed to project an economically developed, competent image of this country, one that is on a par with the traditional donor countries of the West. At the same time, however, Lee seeks to distinguish Korea from other donors by emphasizing values of humility and respect toward the receiver. In contrast to the deeply ingrained development narrative of moral superiority, Lee emphasizes equality in power relations between the donor and receiver. Finally, by drawing on Korea's culture of bowing one's head in respect toward the other, Lee interprets volunteering as not only an economic or political initiative, but also as a cultural one whose principle is guided by worldviews and values.

Earlier in 2008, Lee proposed an ambitious plan to substantially increase the number of volunteers sent abroad as part of its foreign policy to present itself as an economically competent and culturally attractive nation-state with ethical concerns for global issues. Lee consolidated several government-run volunteer programs under a single program, WFK, thus aligning it more closely with Korea's official development assistance (ODA)[1] administered by the Korea International Cooperation Agency (KOICA). The volunteers were to serve as a platform for the country's public diplomacy (Kondoh et al. 2010). In 2015, 4814 volunteers were sent abroad (KOICA 2016), the second highest in number among government-sending international volunteer programs, behind the US Peace Corps.

Korea's volunteer program represents a steady increase in the number of volunteers coming from countries outside of the West.[2] The increase in non-Western volunteer exchange also aligns with growing interest in public diplomacy among countries outside of the USA and Western Europe. However, scholarship in non-Western voluntary action is "lagging behind" (McBride and Draftary 2005), and scholars are only beginning to look into non-Western volunteer exchanges (Butcher and Einolf 2016; Smith et al., forthcoming). Korea offers an insightful case study in this regard,

---

[1] ODA encompasses resources provided by government members of the Development Assistance Committee (DAC) in the OECD. The resources are given to countries listed in the DAC recipients or multilateral institutions with the objective to promote "the economic development and welfare of developing countries" (OECD 2017).

[2] In 2012, 81% of volunteers in the United Nations Volunteers Program came from the global South, and Chinese volunteering is also growing rapidly in sub-Saharan Africa (Ceccagno and Graziani 2016).

being once a recipient of substantial foreign aid[3] and the first nation-state to be admitted into the Development Assistance Committee (DAC).[4]

This chapter critically engages with Korea's international voluntary action and the changing geopolitics of development. The country actively publicizes its volunteer activities as an embodiment of the ethos of harmony and horizontal relations that volunteerism conveys. However, such an ideal of humanitarianism thinly masks the idea of linear progress and hierarchical world order inherent in Korea's narrative of development, which is worked into the narrative trope of "giving back what it has received." This study looks at the implications of such ingrained principles and ideas upon which development has been historically constructed as asymmetrical hierarchies for relationships between the development actor and the beneficiary. Drawing on critical scholarship of development communication, I highlight how Korean volunteers struggle to navigate the underlying social structures and systems of knowledge that advantage some and disadvantage others as development actors. Embedded in the dominant imaginary of development and Korea's hierarchical worldview, the volunteers are constantly self-aware of their inferior status that is tied to the national, racial, and gendered imaginaries of development. The chapter goes on to discuss implications of such tensions in volunteer–host relations for international development volunteering as grassroots public diplomacy practice.

DEVELOPMENT ASSISTANCE: FROM SOFT POWER TO SOCIAL POWER

The global foreign aid architecture has witnessed shifting terrains, with the rise of new state actors, many of which were once (or still are) recipients of aid and categorized as Third World countries (Mawdsley 2012). In such a context, the act of investing in global public goods to resolve issues such as hunger, health, and gender disparity is increasingly approached as a symbolic tool by which to advance strategically a country's position in the world (Mawdsley 2012; Singh 2017). Historically, volunteering for development programs was established by state agencies

---

[3]From the period 1945 to 1995, Korea received a total amount of US$12 billion in foreign aid (History of Korea's ODA 2012).

[4]In 2010 Korea was admitted to the DAC, becoming the 24th country that is a part of the 30 wealthy bilateral donors.

as part of "grassroots" diplomacy for communicating cultural and diplomatic ideas across territorial boundaries (Hiebert 1996; Hiroshi 1999). International volunteers as public diplomacy actors are valued for their potential to build people-to-people relationships "that later serves as a context for official dialogue and negotiations" (Mueller 2009, p. 102).

Public discourse associates such development intervention programs with the notion of *soft power*. Joseph Nye (2009) who coined the term recognizes development assistance as an "official instrument of soft power" (p. 162), whose investment in global public goods grants the country the ability to influence the recipient of aid through ideas, as opposed to weapons. However, while soft power is said to be an analytical tool (Nye 2017), it presents a simplistic claim that only goes as far as distinguishing the force of attraction and consent as an alternative to or in conjunction with coercive militaristic force. Further, in defining soft power as "the ability to obtain preferred outcomes by attraction and persuasion rather than coercion and payment" (Nye 2014, p. 19), the agent of structural force is dichotomized against the subject of soft power. And despite the different nature of hard and soft power, both work unidirectionally as a top-down imposition of power sources. In such a way, the thesis presents a simplistic structural working of soft power.

The formulation of soft power has been received with much criticism by scholars of communication for essentially embracing cultural imperialism. According to Schiller, soft power "recommends using the instruments of cultural imperialism … for holding onto the global dominator's position" (Schiller 1969/1992, pp. 35–36, cited in Pamment 2015). The point to highlight here is that both soft power and the cultural imperialism thesis see power as being at the disposal of the agent. Just as cultural imperialism received criticism for failing to consider complex relationships (Sparks 2012), soft power fails to take into consideration a multiplicity of actors involved in the unitary conception of agent and subject as well as the social context in which power relations are played out.

In this regard, Peter van Ham's conceptualization of social power, which builds on soft power, focuses not on the specific resources but in the relational process through which one is granted the "capacity to produce, shape and influence the motives, attitudes, roles, and interests of actors" (van Ham 2010, p. 47). In the context of emerging actors in international development and public diplomacy, we need to look at not only what is being done, but also the social mechanisms by which development is practiced. This involves not only intervention strategies (e.g. media campaigns and cultural exchange programs), but how such information, knowledge, and expertise are embedded within the greater structural forces that shape geopolitical relations and which are therefore intersubjective and mutually constituted (Pamment 2015).

With the emergence of previous recipients of aid as donors, scholars have questioned whether and how the new actors may change the current aid landscape (Roussel 2013; Walz and Ramachandran 2011; Woods 2008). A majority of such studies base their claims on policy or resource allocation at the level of intervention programs. From a public diplomacy perspective, given the paradigmatic shift in public diplomacy from persuasion to relationship building (Cowan and Arsenault 2008; Zaharna 2010; Zaharna et al. 2014), it is important to examine how the macro-narrative presented by the donor state takes hold in relational dynamics at a micro-level. Implications for the emergence of "non-Western" donors and the relational power dynamics between the donor and the recipient need to be addressed. This chapter explores how the emerging actors position themselves in relation to hegemonic power structures by considering the connections between development communication and public diplomacy.

Who Can Claim the Power to Problematize? Communicating *About* Voluntary Action

Development communication (Devcom), also known as communication for development (Servaes 1999, 2008) or communication for social change (Grumcio-Dagron and Tufte 2006), refers to "strategic application of communication technologies and processes to promote social change," oftentimes "funded through wealthy agencies and implemented in nation-states with comparably fewer financial resources" (Wilkins 2000, p. 197).

While the origin of the field is traced to post-World War II research on the mass media's effect on experiences of modernity or market-based liberal democracy in Third World countries (McAnany 2012; Shah 2011), over time, critical approaches to development communication have called attention to issues of implicit power relations at play in the development landscape (Wilkins 2000). Specifically, Karin Wilkins calls for the need to consider communication *about* development, or the discursive aspect of power as a "capacity to shape the context in which problems and solutions are determined" (Wilkins 2000, p. 198). How substantive issues become articulated as problems and potential solutions are identified is shaped according to the interests and motivations of those in positions of power.

Critical approaches to development volunteering have illustrated the ways in which the discursive formulations of development take hold in volunteer–host relations. Volunteers instrumentalize the idea of Western superiority in such relationships, for example as American exceptionalism among the US Peace Corps (Hanchey 2015). The host community tends to embrace the notion of the Westerner, which encapsulates assumptions of white masculinity as a marker of authority and competence as a development actor (Georgeou 2012). In such ways, scholars have pointed to the persistence of colonial and imperialistic power dynamics in volunteer–host relations (Grusky 2000; McBride and Daftary 2005) which are shaped by multiple aspects of representation.

METHODS

This study asks *how* people make sense of their experiences and structures, using a qualitative research approach (Creswell 2013). The study is based on in-depth interviews of 15 former volunteers, three former volunteer coordinators, and one KOICA staff member. Volunteer coordinators are contract-based employees of KOICA and are stationed in KOICA's overseas offices. Their responsibility is to monitor volunteers, maintain connection with the headquarters, and to conduct needs research among local host institutions, based on which volunteers with the requested expertise are placed.

The interview participants who were former volunteers and coordinators of the volunteers had served in South/Southeast Asia (Indonesia, Myanmar, Sri Lanka, Thailand, Vietnam), Central/South America (Columbia, Ecuador, Paraguay), and Africa (Egypt, Rwanda, Tanzania, Tunisia). Depending on the particular program, the volunteers stayed abroad for a period of six months to three years, undertaking a wide range of work in the areas of social work, libraries, and the teaching of art, physical education, the Korean language, and taekwondo.

The interviews were semi-structured and lasted between one to two hours each. I found initial interview participants by sending out a request for an interview to returned volunteers listed on WFK-related Facebook pages. Three volunteers responded, and during the interviews I used a snowball sampling method, asking the three interview participants to introduce me to other volunteers they knew (Lindlof and Taylor 2011). Informed consent was sought in regards to the purpose of the research, description of the procedures for the interview questions, and concerns about the risks of participating in the research. Informed consent also ensured confidentiality of records identifying the participant.[5]

The interviews were conducted in Korean and were audio recorded upon permission from the participants. The audio recordings were then transcribed and translated into English by the researcher. The age group of the volunteers, their time spent abroad, and the type of work they were involved in all differ considerably, but, within such variations, the purpose was to try to trace a common thread of themes weaved into their accounts of their experiences in the host institutions.

The in-depth interviews were supplemented by secondary data. These consisted of volunteer training manuals, commissioned reports on volunteer programs run by KOICA, annual reports of WFK, and memoirs of former volunteers. These multiple sources were used to gather contextual information and to triangulate data (Yin 2003). In order to protect the identity of the interview participants, their names have been replaced with pseudonyms. And for the participants who preferred not to have their country of service revealed, I have replaced the name of the country with the broader region.

ENCOUNTERING NATION, RACE, AND GENDER IN POWER DYNAMICS: THE NARRATIVE TROPE OF "GIVING BACK"

South Korea's narrative trope of development, that "we need to give back to the international community what we have received in the past," establishes the legitimacy of intervention by establishing a moral obligation to share Korea's development experience to benefit other nations. The legitimizing discourse remains consistent in the country's international development volunteer program. The institutional discourse often draws on the help Korea received from the US Peace Corps, which served in Korea from 1966 to 1981. The story of the Peace Corps features prominently in an official video publicizing WFK and its volunteer activities. The video begins with images depicting the destruction of the Korean War. Below the black-and-white photos of war-torn cities and hopeless faces of children

---

[5] The study was approved by the Institutional Review Board; Study No. 2015-02-0098.

and women are the words: "The members of the U.S. Peace Corps reached out to heal the pain and devastation in the aftermaths of the Korean War." The video shows American Peace Corps volunteers hard at work among Koreans in rural villages. Then suddenly, the screen abruptly transitions, moving forward to a "modernized" Korea, with fast-moving highways brimming with lights, skyscrapers, and scenes from the World Cup. The text on screen states that Korea is the first country that has received help from the US Peace Corps to develop a global volunteer program, an initiative to share with the world what it has learned from the Peace Corps. The institutional discourse reflects both national pride and moral obligation to pull along those countries that are behind up the linear pathway toward development. Korea's positions itself as a developed, modernized nation by drawing on the U.S. Peace Corps as a symbolic bridge that helped the country to modernize, and in turn, it reinforces its status by emphasizing the commitment to share its development experience with those countries that, in essence, represent Korea's past. It upholds the hierarchical world-view and power relations tied to the dominant discourse of development. In so doing, the institutional discourse engages in the ordering of nation-states, with the USA and Western European countries on the top, followed by Korea in a race to catch up with these developing countries.

The following sections explore how such a hierarchical narrative construction ties and hinders volunteer encounters with their hosts on the ground. I will highlight three themes: (1) volunteers' self-consciousness of their inferior position in comparison to volunteers from Western countries; (2) experience of marginalization as Korean volunteers are not ascribed the credibility and authority of their knowledge and expertise; and (3) how the volunteers navigate the fissures in their relationship with the host. These themes, as will be illustrated in the following sections, cut across aspects of nation, race, and gender.

EMBODYING THE NATION AND CLAIMING LEGITIMACY

In this section, I discuss how the nation figures in the development imaginary as invoked by volunteers in their accounts of their experiences. First, in line with the broader institutional narrative of sharing and respect, volunteers distinguished Korea's program as offering service based on its experience of development and with less imperialistic interest in mind. This was evident, for example, in the following exchange where Kim, a volunteer coordinator from North Africa, explained his work in placing volunteers with host institutions.

There was an agricultural research center that wanted to export their products under their own brand and requested our field office to send an expert in product packaging and branding. I found this to be a just demand, and a meaningful demand, it enables the host to be independent. This is not something that Western donors would do, because they would rather buy the products at a cheaper cost and brand it themselves. We have volunteers in the Senior Advisors Program who are retired from companies like Samsung and CJ with clear capacity to deliver service.

In the above passage, Kim distinguishes Korea's volunteer intervention from the imperialistic interest of Western donors, and at the same time positions Korea as being more economically advanced than the host. However, Kim goes on to express his surprise when many such placements end up with very few positive outcomes. Volunteer coordinators frequently referred to the frustrations expressed by senior experts upon their placement in the host institution. As a retired expert, senior advisors have access to a privileged position in Korean society. They are treated with respect as a professional and as an elder and conferred authority. For Korean senior advisors, rigorous time management, efficiency, and prompt feedback are just a few of the basic tenets of professionalism, a value considered to be central to productivity. However, their expectations were rarely reciprocated by the co-workers of the host institution. Senior experts complained that they were not treated with respect and would oftentimes draw on the stereotypical trope of the laziness of the local co-workers for being economically backward.

What is noteworthy is Kim's explanation of such relational tensions. Kim points to the inferior position of Korea and the lack of political economic influence in comparison to other volunteer-sending states as having a delegitimizing effect on claims to expertise.

To simply think, "I am here to help you, so you follow my lead" is a big mistake. They [senior experts] are not taken seriously by the local people. From the point of view [of the locals], Korea is only a small country with little influence. To them, it is like a joke to see some people from such a small country, not like the US or France, and who know nothing about their [the host country's] culture and pride say, "You follow my lead as I am here to help you." To the locals, [the senior expert] is just someone from some very small country out there.

Kim's comment illustrates the political nature of knowledge, and its validity is constituted in the relational. Kim uses the word "small" to describe the lack of Korea's presence in the host country and the low level of familiarity and interest among the local population. He compares Korea to countries such as Germany, France, and Japan, that have more established, systematized, and sizable development budgets and agendas.

Many volunteers echoed Kim's comments in noticing that, on the ground, they were given different treatment from the volunteers belonging to the US Peace Corps and the Japanese International Cooperation Agency. They attribute the difference in treatment to the lack of cultural and economic clout of Korea. "Even if [the Korean volunteers] speak better English than the Japanese volunteers, they have a much greater advantage because they are Japanese," one volunteer who served in Southeast Asia said. Unlike the Japanese and the US counterparts, the lack of Korea's international presence was commonly seen as the reason for the discriminatory treatment received by the Korean volunteers on ground. The inferior status of the country was perceived to override the individual competency of the volunteers in determining the relational dynamic with the host nationals.

The comments made by the volunteers are indicative of a perceived disjuncture in power relations that arises as the volunteers see their roles as helping to improve the capacity of the host, which may be questioned or dismissed by the host community. The senior experts were separated from their expertise and, instead, embodied by the low level of influence ascribed to the country to which they belong. The embodiment of the nation, in cases of volunteers from Europe or North America, frequently works to ascribe legitimacy of the volunteers. For example, Korean volunteers mention that the German and the Japanese volunteers are respected by the host for their large-scale projects and engineering skills. Within such a discourse, Korean volunteers felt they were not given the legitimacy to claim the role of aid provider, being questioned about their legitimacy based on their (lack of) national image.

PERFORMING TO BE THE "BETTER ASIAN": NAVIGATING THE
RACIALIZED IMAGINARY OF DEVELOPMENT

As the phrase "White man's burden" encapsulates, systemic power issues in development cannot be addressed apart from race. Race constitutes the most visible factor in a volunteer's identity and, as an aspect of representation, works to construct a frame of reference of what a volunteer should look like and, on the other hand, what the recipient of aid should look like. All Korean volunteers who took part in the interview remarked that they were racially ridiculed by the local population in their host countries. Again, the Korean volunteers did not fit the assumption that aid providers are mostly white, undermining their legitimacy as development actors.

The performative aspect of race among Korean volunteers is indicative of their strategic positioning, as perceived by their host counterparts, with respect and credibility. However, rather than attempting to disrupt the racialized identification of the volunteer, most volunteers positioned themselves within such established frames of references. The volunteers' experiences of racial discrimination were much more pronounced in countries outside of Asia. In countries of South and Central America and Africa, the volunteers sought to navigate the racialized hierarchy in power relations by looking "cleaner" and "smart." When the volunteers appeared in public well-dressed and well-groomed, the volunteers noted that they were frequently asked by the host nationals if they were Japanese. Even as the volunteers told the people that they were Korean, they "for some reason," felt better for being addressed as Japanese, as opposed to being labeled as Chinese, which was usually followed by racial ridicule and slurs. In enacting the racialized performance according to the gaze of the host society, however, the volunteers ended up reinforcing the dominant racialized hierarchies.

For the most part, volunteers in Southeast Asia such as Vietnam or Indonesia were less subject to racialized treatment by the host. This is in line with Smith et al.'s (forthcoming) study on South–South volunteering, which points out that similar shades of skin color were associated with "sameness" that fostered identification and friendly relations among volunteers and hosts. In fact, for Korean volunteers in Southeast Asian countries, that their shade of skin tends to be slightly lighter on average than people of Southeast Asia was a source of admiration for the local public. Furthermore, in these countries where the ethnic Chinese comprise a large majority of the upper socio-economic stratum, the volunteers were less subject to racially derogatory comments associated with being Chinese. This demonstrates how racial/ethnic understanding is not homogeneous, but a cultural and political construct that takes on different meanings across parts of the world.

In both situations, the volunteers, rather than challenging established perceptions of legitimacy, sought to navigate within the structure, either by performing so to be perceived as the "better Asian" or enjoying their privileged position.

THE GENDERED IMAGINARY OF DEVELOPMENT IN VOLUNTEER RELATIONS

In many cases, gender worked as an added element of spectacle for the Korean volunteers. Many female volunteers told me that the local children and women would touch their hair and arms. One volunteer jokingly commented, "This is what I imagine it would feel like being a celebrity." In fact, for the female university volunteers that served in Southeast Asian countries where Korean pop music (K-pop) culture had gained widespread popularity, it was common for them to be likened to members of K-pop idol girl bands. K-pop constitutes one of the main components of the so-called Korean Wave (Hallyu), which is used to refer to the country's export of its cultural products globally (Shin 2009). The volunteers' accounts illustrate the ways in which the volunteer–host relationship is mediated by understanding of culture through commercialized celebrities. In fact, K-pop performance is a go-to repertoire in cultural exchange events. In the official WFK blog, one easily comes across photo images of teams of young female volunteers on stage, dressed identically and executing homogenized choreography. K-pop idol girl bands are characterized by their "hypergirlish-femininity that prioritizes submissiveness, pureness, and cuteness over Westernized notions of powerful and independent womanly sexiness" (Oh 2014, p. 56). In reproducing the performative act, the volunteers mediate and are subject to racialized femininity. The accounts of these volunteers illustrate the ways in which K-pop as soft power reinforces the self-stereotyping and transient understanding of the national form as a spectacle, in a way that is self-stereotyping and self-Orientalizing.

Even when they are not performing for the public, Korean female volunteers were frequently seen as novel and subject to the gaze of other foreigners. Cheon, a former volunteer in Ecuador, illustrates being subject to a frame that is defined and captured by white, foreign tourists.

> In the past, I was into taking photos, too. I would always be on the search for great scenes and all. So, I know that being in a touristy city, an Asian girl having a fun time with the locals, it makes a great picture. And I noticed that I was having photos taken of me without knowing.

It was a very unpleasant feeling, to be the one being photographed. A small local girl and an older Asian girl sitting side-by-side having candy, reading a book together in the market square ... these moments were framed by [the foreign tourists] holding up their cameras, and I found it to be really uncomfortable.

The power asymmetry embedded in the act of taking pictures is well documented (Sontag 1977). However, most analyses have examined the divide that separates the passive, silent subject, being framed by the visual composition, from that photographer who has the power to tell the story of the person depicted in the photo. In this case, the volunteer who is an Asian female is also regarded as an added spectacle to the frame. The moment complicates the power asymmetry by adding a layer of racialized and gendered expectations. Although Cheon is there as a facilitator to work on a photovoice project with the girls and women in her village, to an outsider, by being photographed, she is disempowered and silenced, and framed in a simplified way as a racialized and gendered construct.

Professionally, female volunteers oftentimes told me that they were not taken seriously by their male co-workers. Park was a former KOICA volunteer who worked in a local library in Sri Lanka to digitize the library system.

In the beginning, I noticed that the director was treating me not as a colleague but as if I were a child. I felt like an intern in the library. Maybe it was because I'm thin and I look younger than my age?

Then she goes on to explain the culture of gender roles in her village

Where I was, women are mostly confined to the home and did not leave the house often. Even everyday things like grocery shopping was done by men.

Cheon's experience is particularly common for Korean female volunteers, whose smaller physique and youthful appearance is perceived in a childlike way by foreigners. Some volunteers noted that being Asian (as opposed to being a white female volunteer) added to this perception, making it more difficult to maintain an equal stance in positionality with the co-workers in the host institution. In fact, the interview participants' accounts of how they were feminized and infantilized diverge substantially from that of female volunteers of the US Peace Corps, whose positionality as a white American automatically granted them access to masculinity. Therefore, female Peace Corps volunteers were respected "even though" they are women. Hanchey (2015) explains how female volunteers are able to assert masculinity and accepted for their roles, notwithstanding the local culture.

> Rather than having to deal with the gender roles of that particular South American village's culture, she gets to trade her status as a white U.S. American for masculine clout: the positionality of the U.S. American is automatically considered a masculine positionality. (2015, p. 241)

While white female volunteers are given an exceptional status as being apart from the local culture, the Korean volunteers are expected to work through the pervasive stereotype of the Asian woman as being submissive as well as dealing with the gender roles of the host culture.

Hanchey's finding illustrates another layer of gender as being used to construct certain spaces as being associated with masculinity or femininity. My interviews point to such gendered space in the taekwondo academy. Taekwondo is a Korean martial art that emphasizes discipline and spirituality. Han, a university student majoring in international sport management, is a former volunteer who served as a part of the Taekwondo Peace Corps program training students in a Taewondo academy in Tanzania. Upon being asked whether she was discriminated by the male counterparts in the host institution, she stated that she never felt as though she was being treated differently from the other male volunteers. For female volunteers who serve in the Taekwondo Peace Corps, being adept at what is considered to be an elite martial art granted them access to a masculine identity. The Taekwondo Peace Corps presents a masculine identity of the nation through promotion of a martial art that stresses discipline and spiritual training. For this reason, the Taekwondo Peace Corps enjoys a privilege that distinguishes them from most other volunteers. They are frequented by local elites and are granted respect. In this respect, female volunteers, "although they are women," enjoy the same treatment as their male volunteers because they are embedded in a masculine space, just as the female volunteer of the US Peace Corps enjoys a male status due to her country-of-origin that is associated with masculinity.

Conclusion: Reworking the Established Imaginary for Meaningful Relationship-Building

This research has examined South Korea's international development volunteers as an emerging actor in the global aid landscape. Korea legitimizes its government-run volunteer program as a moral obligation to give back the help that was once given to the country. Culturally, it draws on values of respect and identification based on a shared story of economic hardship. But at the same time, the narrative embraces visions of linear economic growth and a hierarchy of the world system. This study highlights the ways in which Korean volunteer and host relations are shaped by the dominant imaginaries of development that is encapsulated in the narrative of Korea.

Korean volunteers' experiences on the ground depict how the idealized actor of development as a white, Euro-American, English-speaking man devalues their work as legitimate development actors. Oftentimes, they are not associated with having expertise, authority, or credibility by the host, a privilege enjoyed by volunteers from traditional donors in the West or Japan. Rather, the capacity of Korean volunteers is equated with the lack of political economic influence of the country and assumptions associated with a hierarchical ordering of race and gender. However, it is noteworthy that the volunteers themselves internalize the hierarchical formulations, and they struggle to conform to such exclusionary practices in navigating the everyday. This oftentimes includes performing the cultural self in a way that subjects the volunteers to be a spectacle which satisfies the gaze of the host.

From a public diplomacy perspective, positioning a volunteer program within the dominant imaginary of development poses challenges for building positive and meaningful relations, and rather may end up furthering cultural misunderstandings based on stereotypes. As stated by van Ham (2010), social power is embedded in relationships, and understanding is intersubjective. It is through subverting such established systems of knowledge that emerging state actors of development may foster friendly ties and mutual understanding with the host. Image projection of cultural attractiveness, such as respect and "shared experiences" of economic hardship, that seeks to distinguish itself from the imperialistic, asymmetrical relations of Western donors only goes as far as thinly masking the hegemonic discourse of development firmly entrenched in Korea's domestic and international development policies. Also, the soft power strategy, which has for the most part constituted a one-way projection of a predefined repertoire of cultural resources spanning traditional and contemporary cultural forms, may only further stereotyping based on the Orientalized gaze rather than being conducive to mutual understanding. The myth of this institutional discourse, carefully selected with elements to uphold the ideological power structure, opens to reveal inherent contradictions. The assumptions of development as linear growth and the idea of a hierarchical world order places Korean volunteers in a subordinate position and the Other as a spectacle based on their country of origin, race, and gender.

According to Nederveen Pieterse, "understanding development as a politics of difference is a step towards making development practice self-conscious with regard to its political and cultural bias, a step towards a practice of reflexive development" (2010, p. 77). Such reflexive exercise involves critical interrogation of power as shaping, negotiating, and subverting relationships. It involves treating culture not as a strategic resource utilized to accrue influence from the target audience, as the soft power thesis posits, but in broadening the understanding of culture as a meaning-making process embedded in relationships, committed to working against and not alongside the established systems of knowledge. Public diplomacy research and practice in conversation with development communication needs to aim at reworking the pervasiveness of Western imaginaries of development by challenging their racialized and gendered nature. Sustained engagement requires more empirical research on emerging actors of international development volunteering, and in practice transcending the narrative of volunteering as helping and sharing and bringing to the fore the established knowledge systems of power in relation to country, race/ethnicity, and gender throughout volunteer training, policy, and evaluation.

REFERENCES

Butcher, J., & Einolf, C. (2016). *Perspectives on Volunteering. Nonprofit and Civil Society Studies.* New York: Springer.

Ceccagno, A., & Graziani, S. (2016). Chinese Volunteering in Africa. *Annali Di Ca' Foscari. Serie Orientale, 52,* 297–333. https://doi.org/10.14277/2385-3042/AnnOr-52-16-11.

Cowan, G., & Arsenault, A. (2008). Moving from Monologue to Dialogue to Collaboration: The Three Layers of Public Diplomacy. *The ANNALS of the American Academy of Political and Social Science, 616*(1), 10–30.

Creswell, J. W. (2013). *Research Design: Qualitative, Quantitative, and Mixed Methods Approaches.* Thousand Oaks, CA: Sage.

Georgeou, N. (2012). *Neoliberalism, Development, and Aid Volunteering.* New York: Routledge.

Grumcio-Dagron, A., & Tufte, T. (2006). *Communication for Social Change Anthology: Historical and Contemporary Readings.* CFSC Consortium, Inc.

Grusky, S. (2000). International Service Learning: A Critical Guide from an Impassioned Advocate. *American Behavioral Scientist, 43*(5), 858–867. https://doi.org/10.1177/00027640021955513.

Hanchey, J. (2015). Constructing American Exceptionalism: Peace Corps Volunteer Discourses of Race, Gender, and Empowerment. In M. W. Kramer, L. K. Lewis, & L. M. Gossett (Eds.), *Volunteering and Communication* (Vol. 2, pp. 233–250). New York: Peter Lang.

Hiebert, M. (1996). Money Isn't Everything. *Far Eastern Economic Review, 159*, 62.

Hiroshi, A. (1999, October–December). Japan's Overseas Volunteers Make a Difference at Home, Too. *Japan Quarterly, 46*(4), 77–85.

History of Korea's ODA. (2012). Retrieved September 28, 2017, from https://www.odakorea.go.kr/eng.overview.History.do.

KOICA. (2016). *World Friends Korea: Statistical Report, 2015*. Seongnam, South Korea: KOICA.

Kondoh, H., Kobayashi, T., Shiga, H., & Sato, J. (2010). Diversity and Transformation of Aid Patterns in Asia's "Emerging Donors" (Working Paper No. 21). JICA Research Institute. Retrieved from http://hdl.handle.net/10685/76.

Lee, S. W. (2012, June 1). President Lee, "Volunteering is about Learning, Not Giving." *Yonhap News*. Retrieved from http://news.naver.com/main/read.nhn?mode=LSD&mid=sec&sid1=100&oid=001&aid=0005634423.

Lindlof, T. R., & Taylor, B. C. (2011). *Qualitative Communication Research Methods*. Los Angeles, CA: Sage.

Mawdsley, E. (2012). *From Recipients to Donors: Emerging Powers and the Changing Development Landscape*. London, UK: Zed Books.

McAnany, E. G. (2012). *Saving the World: A Brief History of Communication for Development and Social Change*. Urbana: University of Illinois Press.

McBride, A. M., & Draftary, D. (2005). *International Service: History and Forms, Pitfalls and Potential* (CSD Working Paper No. 05-10). Retrieved from https://csd.wustl.edu/Publications/Documents/WP05-10.pdf.

Mueller, S. (2009). The Nexus of US Public Diplomacy and Citizen Diplomacy. In N. Snow & P. M. Taylor (Eds.), *Routledge Handbook of Public Diplomacy* (pp. 101–107). New York: Routledge.

Nye, J. S. (2009). Get Smart: Combining Hard and Soft Power. *Foreign Affairs, 88*(4), 160–163.

Nye, J. S. (2014). The Information Revolution and Soft Power. *Current History, 113*(759), 19–22.

Nye, J. S. (2017, February). Soft Power: The Origins and Political Progress of a Concept. *Palgrave Communications, 3*. Available at SSRN: https://ssrn.com/abstract=2942713 or http://dx.doi.org/10.1057/palcomms.2017.8.

OECD. (2017). *Official Development Assistance—Definition and Coverage*. Retrieved September 30, 2017, from http://www.oecd.org/dac/stats/officialdevelopmentassistancedefinitionandcoverage.htm.

Oh, C. (2014). The Politics of the Dancing Body: Racialized and Gendered Femininity in Korean Pop. In Y. Kuwahara (Ed.), *The Korean Wave: Korean Popular Culture in Global Context.* New York: Palgrave Macmillan.

Pamment, J. (2015). Media Influence, Ontological Transformation, and Social Change: Conceptual Overlaps Between Development Communication and Public Diplomacy. *Communication Theory, 25*(2), 188–207.

Pieterse, J. N. (2010). *Development Theory.* Sage.

Roussel, L. W. (2013). The Changing Donor Landscape in Nicaragua: Rising Competition Enhances Ownership and Fosters Cooperation. *Journal of International Development, 25*(6), 802–818. https://doi.org/10.1002/jid.2932.

Schiller, H. I. (1969). *Mass Communications and American Empire* (2nd ed.). Boulder: Westview.

Servaes, J. (1999). *Communication for Development: One World, Multiple Cultures.* Cresskill, NJ: Hampton Press. Retrieved from http://library.wur.nl/WebQuery/clc/1670588.

Servaes, J. (2008). *Communication for Development and Social Change.* New Delhi, India: Sage.

Shah, H. (2011). *The Production of Modernization: Daniel Lerner, Mass Media, and the Passing of Traditional Society.* Philadelphia: Temple University Press.

Shin, H. (2009). Have You Ever Seen the Rain? And Who'll Stop the Rain?: The Globalizing Project of Korean Pop (K-pop). *Inter-Asia Cultural Studies, 10*(4), 507–523. https://doi.org/10.1080/14649370903166150.

Singh, J. P. (2017). Beyond Neoliberalism: Contested Narratives of International Development. In A. Miskimmon, B. O'Loughlin, & L. Roselle (Eds.), *Forging the World: Strategic Narratives and International Relations* (pp. 134–163). Ann Arbor: University of Michigan Press.

Smith, M. B., Laurie, N., & Griffiths, M. (forthcoming). South-South Volunteering and Development. *The Geographical Journal.* https://doi.org/10.111/geoj.12243.

Sontag, S. (1977). *On Photography.* London: Penguin Books.

Sparks, C. (2012). Media and Cultural Imperialism Reconsidered. *Chinese Journal of Communication, 5*(3), 281–299. https://doi.org/10.1080/17544750.2012.701417.

van Ham, P. (2010). *Social Power in International Politics.* Oxon, England: Routledge.

Walz, J., & Ramachandran, V. (2011). *Brave New World: A Literature Review of Emerging Donors and the Changing Nature of Foreign Assistance* (Center for Global Development Working Paper 273). Retrieved from http://www.cgdev.org/content/publications/detail/1425691.

Wilkins, K. G. (2000). Accounting for Power in Development Communication. In K. G. Wilkins (Ed.), *Redeveloping Communication for Social Change: Theory, Practice, and Power* (pp. 197–210). Boulder, CO: Rowman & Littlefield.

Woods, N. (2008). Whose Aid? Whose Influence? China, Emerging Donors and the Silent Revolution in Development Assistance. *International Affairs, 84*(6), 1205–1221. https://doi.org/10.1111/j.1468-2346.2008.00765.x.

Yin, R. K. (2003). *Case Study Research: Design and Methods* (3rd ed.). Thousand Oaks, CA: Sage.

Zaharna, R. S. (2010). *Battles to Bridges: U.S. Strategic Communication and Public Diplomacy after 9/11*. New York, NY: Palgrave Macmillan.

Zaharna, R. S., Arsenault, A., & Fisher, A. (2014). *Relational, Networked and Collaborative Approaches to Public Diplomacy: The Connective Mindshift*. London: Routledge.

CHAPTER 7

The Slow Reunification of Development Assistance and Public Diplomacy: Exchange and Collaboration Activities Through the Swedish Institute 1973–2012

Andreas Åkerlund

INTRODUCTION

They are estranged siblings, public diplomacy (PD) and development communication (Devcom), according to James Pamment. They share the origin in the same communication theories and the political context of the Cold War. They are both aiming at social change across national borders, and struggling with similar problems of "asymmetrical power relations and the ambiguous objective of influence over others" (Pamment 2015, p. 2). A common problem both fields had to manage historically was the impact of decolonization and the related need for stable institutions and social and economic development. One can surely conclude that both PD and Devcom during the Cold War were instigators of modernization and that social change was to be brought about through

A. Åkerlund (✉)
Södertörn University, Stockholm, Sweden
e-mail: andreas.akerlund@sh.se

© The Author(s) 2018   143
J. Pamment and K. G. Wilkins (eds.), *Communicating National Image through Development and Diplomacy*, Palgrave Studies in Communication for Social Change, https://doi.org/10.1007/978-3-319-76759-8_7

information and through influencing attitudes. In the words of Pamment they "seem to share the goal of prompting personal transformation by mediating modernity" (Pamment 2015, p. 8). In short: the right information and experiences would alter the ways foreign citizens experience the world which in turn would bring about social change and political stability.

In line with the work of Pamment, this chapter also highlights the relationship between official development assistance (ODA) and public diplomacy. It is one thing to conclude that both fields share communicative goals or intellectual origins; another is to show similarities in practices and organizational and financial overlaps. It is possible to conclude that ODA and PD are estranged siblings within the field of communication theory, but this notion also raises the question of their relationship on the practical, organizational level.

A suitable concept through which this relationship can be investigated is the idea of education. Pamment quotes Wilbur Schramm on the importance of information for awakening the political consciousness of foreign target groups: "the more information they get, the more they are interested in political developments. The more education they have, the more they seek information" (Schramm 1963, p. 36). Following this line of argument, educating the foreigners who are to be influenced is of crucial importance, as education would not only enable them to seek information, but also sets the frames for the interpretation of that very information. It is worth noting that only one year after this article by Schramm, Philip H. Coombs recommended that a larger proportion of US Agency for International Development (USAID) funds should be directed towards developing education, human resources, and cultural institutions. This aid should be combined with an elite approach, focusing the "movers and shapers" of the target countries (Coombs 1964, pp. 128–132). Coombs's book described education and culture as the "fourth dimension of foreign policy," thus placing both education and development assistance under the larger umbrella of public diplomacy.

Within public diplomacy theory exchange of persons is considered one core activity as formulated by Nicholas J. Cull, the others being listening, advocacy, cultural diplomacy, and news broadcasting (Cull 2008). Exchange for educational and/or research purposes is a large portion of the personal exchanges conducted by public diplomacy actors. One function of exchange from a PD perspective is relation-building based on an idea of reciprocity or mutuality. This does not equal a just quantitative balance of traveling persons. Instead exchange should be beneficiary for the sending as well as the receiving country. PD exchange is deliberate as it is normally part of a treaty or partnership and thus an "activity pursued in order to serve distinct purposes" (Lima 2007, p. 238). Exchanges are interactive as they are thought to transfer knowledge about other countries and cultures through interaction between program participants and the host society. Therefore exchange programs are regarded as an excellent way to create trust and to promote mutual understanding (Lima 2007, p. 239; Mulcahy 1999, pp. 25–27). Consequently they are not ideal vehicles for transmitting an official or controlled image of the country or for direct advocacy or propaganda activities. "Building relationships are very different from selling messages because it involves a genuine exchange and means that people are given a 'warts and all' picture of the country" (Leonard et al. 2002, p. 18).

Another function of exchange programs is the intended transfer of knowledge and values. Christopher Medalis points to the importance of the Fulbright Program during the 1989–1991 transition in Hungary. US scholarships strengthened the English language, promoted knowledge transfer in other academic fields such as law, and helped reform academic institutions in Hungary. Medalis thus concludes that PD exchange is important for knowledge transfer, especially in transition periods (Medalis 2012). A similar function for de-Stalinizing Polish social sciences had the short-lived Ford Foundation program with Poland 1957–1961 (Czernecki 2013). Another similar example is of course the role played by exchange programs in the re-education of occupied Germany, Austria, and Japan after World War II (Coombs 1964, pp. 98–102; Mulcahy 1999, p. 15).

Education has been a central part of modern development assistance ever since 1945 if not earlier. During the 1960s theories on educational expansion and economic development developed within UNESCO and other international actors (Mundy 1998, p. 458). Development assistance can thus be understood as one of the driving rationales behind the post-1945 internationalization of higher education (de Wit 2002, p. 87). The idea of a knowledge driven economic development leads to the education and training of highly qualified individuals from ODA-receiving countries. This education is however mainly available abroad, making academic mobility necessary (Fellesson and Mählck 2013, pp. 11–13). Academic mobility is also considered one possible way of technology transfer to developing countries (Hoekman et al. 2005,

p. 1590). The idea of assistance and development through higher education has in turn been criticized for being imperialistic and leading to a Western dominance in knowledge creation (Selvaratnam 1988) and for causing brain drain through facilitating South–North academic migration (Tsang 2000, p. 149). Exchange programs aimed at education and research must however be considered key features of development assistance directed at capacity building, knowledge development, and technology transfer.

THE SWEDISH INSTITUTE, EXCHANGE PROGRAMS, AND THE DETACHMENT OF DEVELOPMENT ASSISTANCE

Educational exchange is thus a central activity within both PD and ODA, and therefore also a suitable case study. The organizational setting in which the internal relationship between these two fields will be investigated in this chapter is the Swedish PD organization, the Swedish Institute (SI). This institute was established in 1945 as a joint venture between the state, commercial interests, and civil society. In 1970 it was reorganized into a state foundation and in 1998 it was once again transformed, this time into a state agency. The Institute has thus over time been successively moved from being a semi-independent organization at arm's length from the state to an agency under direct state control.

Exchange of persons has been a core task of the Institute since its founding in 1945. Noteworthy is that the Swedish government's funds for exchange activities have grown over time. This is illustrated by the fact that the share of costs for long or short-term mobility scholarships within the total SI budget has risen over time from around 7–8% in the 1950s to over 30% in the mid-1990s (Åkerlund 2015, p. 121). This rise in costs for educational exchange goes hand in hand with a development towards integrating more and more geographical areas in SI exchange during the entire Cold War. It is possible to see this as a three-step process. Exchange activities in the 1950s were primarily directed towards Western Europe; Warsaw Pact countries were included in the 1960s through the signing of bilateral cultural programs, and during the 1970s scholars from countries in the so-called developing world started to be offered Swedish scholarships (Åkerlund 2014).

In the Swedish case, PD and ODA are really born out of the same organizational setting, since Swedish foreign aid actually has its institutional origins in the SI and the aid given to war ridden Europe, and especially to Germany after World War II (Lindner 1988). The Institute administered a visitors program for mainly German academics with the dual purpose to re-establish the international contacts of German science and to help re-establish democratic ideals and institutions in the country. Around 600 persons came to Sweden on short-term scholarships through this program between 1946 and 1952 (Fischer 2013). The Institute was also involved in other educational measures primarily in collaboration with the Swedish Committee for International Aid (Svenska komittén för internationell hjälpverksamhet) and the Joint Committee for Democratic Reconstruction (Svenska komittén för demokratiskt uppbyggnadsarbete) (Mays 2011; Müssener 1974, pp. 262–270). Starting in 1951, the Institute also started offering bilateral long-term scholarships for West German academics, initially financed by the Committee for International Aid (Svenska Institutet 1952, p. 31). This is the first, but by no means the last, example of academic exchange considered as part of foreign aid activities.

As the Central Committee for Swedish Technical Assistance to Less Developed Areas was established in 1952, the Swedish Institute unit for technical assistance was made the administrative secretariat of the committee (Nilsson 2004, pp. 5–6). The Committee members were civil society organizations alongside commercial enterprises. There were strong political and economic reasons for Sweden to engage in development assistance. Helping the so-called Third World was a matter of credibility for the Swedish neutrality policy and the idea of Sweden as a representative of an ideological Third Way, between capitalism and communism (Bjereld et al. 2008, pp. 210–215). There was also an economic argument used by the committee towards the representatives from trade and industry, namely that technical assistance might contribute to Swedish exports by creating goodwill in potential markets (Glover 2011, pp. 80–82). The Central Committee was dissolved in 1961 and replaced in 1962 by the Board for International Assistance, which later was to become the Swedish International Development Cooperation Agency (SIDA). This meant that questions related to development assistance were removed from the SI and were situated in this new state agency. According to Nikolas Glover this change should be understood as part of a general trend toward specialization of the Swedish contacts with the international community (Glover 2011, p. 119). Technical assistance and cultural contacts were from 1962 handled by separate organizations. One practical result of this division was that the UNESCO scholarships intended for recipients from developing countries and handled by the SI were transferred to the new agency.

1973–1990: RE-ENTER ODA

This division of labor lasted for roughly 10 years. Starting in the early 1970s there was a step-by-step process where ODA funding of SI exchange activities became increasingly common. Looking closer at this process one can identify two rationales behind it: one related to the organizational/administrative capacity of the Institute and one related to the funding sources of scholarships.

The changes described below need to be related to the Swedish foreign policy of that time. Ever since the early 1960s Sweden had actively taken a neutral position between the two power blocs. With this policy of the third way followed internationalism as an important pillar of what is normally referred to as the Nordic or Swedish model of security policy (Goldmann 1991). These internationalist values included global redistributive justice, solidarity with the so-called Third World, and a strong support for the United Nations and other international organizations (Bergman 2006, p. 73). Development assistance and a policy aiming to put the problems of the developing countries on the agenda of world politics played an important role in this activist foreign policy (Bjereld et al. 2008, pp. 241–251).

EXTERNALLY FUNDED PROGRAMS

In 1973 the UNESCO scholarships were retransferred to the SI from SIDA. From this year on the Institute was responsible for administrating the Swedish participation in various UN financed scholarship schemes for recipients from Eastern Europe or so-called developing countries. This was a return to the situation before 1962, which in practice meant that the SI coordinated the Swedish part of multilateral educational programs aiming at knowledge transfer from the developed to the underdeveloped world.

Apart from coordinating the multilateral schemes, the SI was also given more responsibility within the national context. The first example for this was triggered by political turmoil in South America. As a result of the *coup d'état* in Chile on September 11, 1973, the Swedish economic support to the Allende government's plan for economic development was taken back. The money, originating in the SIDA budget for 1974, was instead used for relief activities for Chilean refugees. One of these activities was creating a special scholarship program for Chilean academics to come and do research at Swedish facilities: 32 exiled researchers entered the program which ran continuously until 1979 (Åkerlund 2016a, pp. 88–92). The program was financed by SIDA but carried out by the SI. This program as such is an interesting case study in how scholarships for academics can be used to support political refugees, but in the context of this chapter it stands as an example of a phenomenon that was growing more and more common during the 1970s. It was not only the scholarships financed by international organizations that were transferred to the institute in the mid-1970s, for this was also the decade in which Swedish ODA agencies started to assign the task of carrying out their exchange programs to the SI.

There are numerous examples for this as visible in the presentation of the Institute's external assignments in the yearly reports. Beside the Chile program described above (1974–1979, financed by SIDA), there was also a scholarship program for Portuguese experts (1975–1982, SIDA), for recipients for a number of undefined "developing countries" (1977–1979, SIDA), for Vietnamese researchers (1978–1981, SAREC[1]), for Swedish students of Vietnamese (1980, SIDA), and funds for curative work for Chinese students (1980–1982, BITS[2]).[3] It is obvious that the expertise built up within the SI within the fields of international exchange and international education was attractive for the ODA agencies. Instead of administrating time-limited scholarship schemes themselves they preferred to assign them to a more experienced actor.

In the context of Swedish ODA at this time, these exchanges were however relatively small and the majority of educational aid was distributed directly by the ODA agencies. In 1977 education and research was the largest sector of aid passing through SIDA, making up 15% of the grand total (SOU 1977:13, p. 214). Scholarship and exchange of students and researchers are not treated separately in the 1977 inquiry

---

[1] SAREC: Swedish Agency for Research Cooperation with Developing Countries (Styrelsen för U-landsforskning).

[2] BITS: Swedish Agency for International Technical and Economic Cooperation (Beredningen för internationellt tekniskt-ekonomiskt samarbete).

[3] As seen in Svenska Institutet (1975, p. 10; 1976, p. 55; 1977, p. 56; 1978, p. 25; 1979, p. 25; 1980, p. 36; 1981, p. 37; 1982a, p. 48).

into development assistance. The part on technology transfer mainly discusses the strengthening of infrastructure for research and technology application in the developing world (SOU 1977:13, pp. 191–192). In 1988 the various research training exchanges of SAREC comprised of over 500 scientists visiting Swedish facilities (Brodén Gyberg 2013, pp. 154–155). Although assigned the responsibility for some exchange programs, the major division of labor between the SI and the ODA agencies was still upheld. During this period aid was above all concerned with technological development, whereas Swedish public diplomacy was still primarily directed towards either developed Western countries or the communist bloc. The SI was therefore a PD organization carrying out minor exchange programs on behalf of ODA agencies, but cannot be labeled a development assistance actor in its own right.

Combining PD and ODA

In 1975 the Ministry for Foreign Affairs started to investigate what was called "cultural cooperation with developing countries." Information about Sweden had, according to an internal memo, mainly been directed towards Western Europe and the USA, which the ministry considered a problem. There were strong arguments in favor of a widened cultural exchange, both from an ODA and a PD perspective. The interest in information about Sweden in developing countries would be bigger if the countries had the same possibilities to present themselves in Sweden. This would in turn benefit the internal Swedish communication about developing country issues. In the end, culture was deemed important for Swedish ODA in general, but also for trade and foreign policy: "collaboration within the area of culture could also be a complement to and a gateway to an intensified collaboration in economic and political questions and therefore an important component in a coordinated ODA-policy" (Andersson 1975, p. 5).

The question of cultural collaboration with developing countries was discussed in the state inquiry on ODA policy (SOU 1977, pp. 119–120) and in the inquiry on international exchange of culture and information, which also recommended a trial project for intensified cultural exchange between Sweden and ODA recipients (SOU 1978, p. 25). In the project, designed by SIDA, the SI, and the Culture Council, the contribution of the SI was to run a short-term scholarship program for experience exchange, open to applicants from all developing countries (SIDA et al. 1980). The project ran over four years and was financed directly over the state ODA budget.

One interesting aspect of this idea of ODA-financed cultural exchange is the argumentation that PD and ODA could be mutually supportive. Knowledge about other cultures would benefit the Swedish internal discussion about development aid, and knowledge about Sweden in the recipient countries would be of benefit for Swedish projects in these countries. It can be noted that this argumentation is very similar to the function of international exchange within public diplomacy as conceptualized by Cull (2008), de Lima (2007), or Leonard et al. (2002). The aim of cultural cooperation was mutual understanding and something that would benefit both participants.

The next step in this process of merging Swedish PD with ODA was the establishment of a special scholarship program for recipients from ODA countries. The reason behind this was originally financial problems within the unilateral guest scholarship program managed by the SI. This program was established in 1972/1973 as a result of changed rules for Swedish study assistance which excluded foreign students from this financing source. The guest scholarships were open to applicants from the whole world, which made them different from bilateral exchange with a fixed number of scholarships for specific countries. The majority of scholars from the world's poorer countries entering Swedish higher education through the SI arrived through this program as poorer countries normally could not offer the reciprocity needed for bilateral exchange.

By 1980 the guest scholarship program had serious financial problems due to underfunding. The SI therefore had to reduce the number of scholarships below the 100 annual scholarships decided on by parliament to 94 for the year 1980/1981, to 87 for 1981/1982, and to only 82 for 1982/1983, which was the lowest number ever (Rylander 2010, p. 8; Svenska Institutet 1982a, p. 40). In an attempt to solve this the SI proposed that some long-term scholarships could be financed within the ODA line for cooperation with developing countries. The proposed program, called the U-scholarships, was in practice a smaller copy of the guest scholarship program, applying the same rules, but open only to applicants from countries receiving Swedish ODA (Svenska Institutet 1982b). The plan was approved by the ODA-agency BITS and a three-year trial was initiated. Eligible for nomination were a selected number of ODA-receiving countries (Rylander 1985, pp. 3, 6).[4]

Parallel to the U-scholarships, the Swedish government started to strengthen guest scholarships by adding funds from the ODA budget. In the annual report from 1985/1986 it is stated that the number of guest scholarships could once again be held at 100. This was made possible by an addition from funds for development aid (Svenska Institutet 1986, p. 26). At first only considered a temporary solution, the financing of the guest scholarship program partly through the ODA budget was made permanent. The U-scholarship program was continued until the academic year 1987/1988 and after that the resources were added to the guest scholarships (Svenska Institutet 1988, p. 22). From 1985/1986 academics from developing countries, according to the OECD definition, were guaranteed half of the available scholarship months within the guest scholarship program (Rylander 2010, p. 8).

OVERALL CHANGES

During the 1970s and 1980s ODA-financed academic exchange slowly entered the SI. Between 1973 and 1990 the ratio of ODA funds related to the basic allocation the SI received from the Ministry for Foreign Affairs and the second largest financier, the Ministry for Education, never exceeded 20% of the grand total, as seen in Fig. 7.1. Here the 19.9% ODA funds in the budgetary year 1987/1988 is explained through this being the last year of the U-scholarships alongside a 50% funding of the regular guest scholarships through ODA. The trend towards a larger part of money for development aid in the total budget of the SI during this period is however easy to recognize.

Although ODA entered the institute during this period it was still a minor financing source. As visible in the nomination process for the U-scholarships as well as in the external assignments, the recipients of ODA scholarships came primarily from nonindustrialized countries in Asia, Africa, or Latin America. There was little directly formulated thought on the relationship between aid and public diplomacy, although

[4]For the academic year 1983/1984, ten countries were invited to nominate: Algeria, Cuba, Dominican Republic, Iraq, Mexico, Nigeria, Pakistan, Peru, Sudan, and Zimbabwe. For the academic year 1984/1985, five countries were added: India, Jordan, Malaysia, Tunisia, and Vietnam.

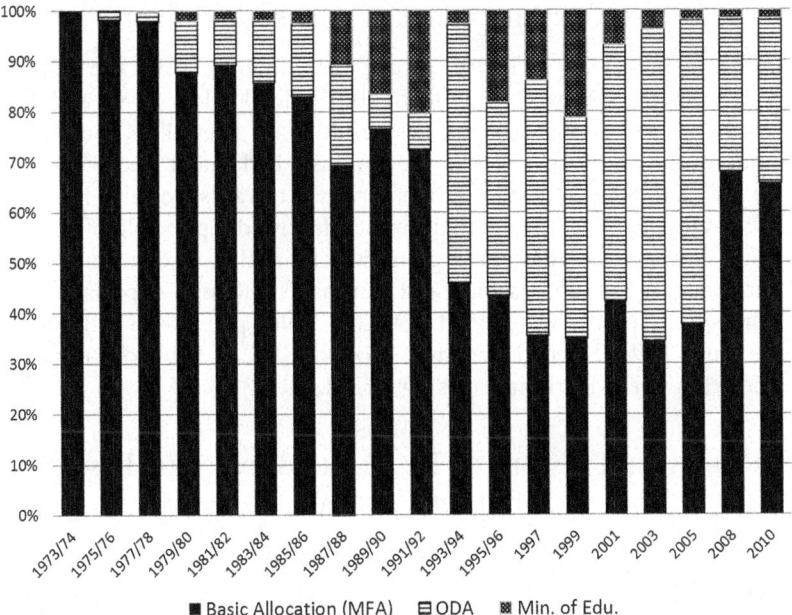

Fig. 7.1 Relationship between the three major funding sources of the SI Basic Allocation (*Note* Funding from the Ministry for Foreign Affairs, ODA, and allocations from the Ministry for Education 1973–2010, showing every second budgetary year, except between 2005 and 2008 where the span is three years. *Source* Prop. 1976/77:100; Prop. 1978/79:100; Prop. 1980/81:100; Prop. 1982/83:100; Prop. 1984/85:100; Prop. 1986/87:100; Prop. 1988/89:100; Prop. 1990/91:100; Prop. 1992/93:100; Prop. 1996/97:1; Svenska Institutet 1974, 1976, 1994, 1997, 1999, 2001, 2003, 2005, 2008, 2010)

the idea that wider cultural cooperation could be of benefit both to Sweden and to the aid receiving country indicates that the idea of two mutually benefitting practices started to gain ground in the mid-1970s after the institutional separation in 1962. The mutual benefit between PD and ODA was thus primarily situated on the practical and organizational level. Letting the SI manage a larger and larger part of exchange activities was practical for the ODA agencies, whereas using development aid for scholarships was a way to maintain the desired level of academic exchange through the SI.

1990–2010: Aid, Trade, and Eastern Europe[5]

For the SI the 1990s were to become very different from the 1980s. The reasons for this were the fall of the Berlin Wall in 1989 and the political turmoil and social changes resulting in the fall of European Communism. As early as 1990 the Swedish Parliament decided on a large aid and cooperation program directed towards Eastern Europe. A 1996 OECD survey shows that Sweden followed a principle of directing aid towards an adjacent region, which in this case meant three Baltic States—Estonia, Latvia, and Lithuania—Russia—especially the north-western part—and Poland (OECD 1996, pp. 51–53). Between 1990 and 1994 Sweden directed around SEK 4.3 billion towards cooperation in the Baltic area (Ds 1994:134, p. 19).

From Value Transfer to Economic Boost: The Eastern Europe Programs

Four interrelated aims guided the Swedish engagement in Eastern Europe during the 1990s:

• to promote common security;
• to deepen the culture of democracy;
• to support a socially sustainable economic transition;
• to support an environmentally sustainable development. (Hedborg 1998, p. 16)

The SI was heavily involved in the assistance directed towards Eastern Europe. It was given responsibility for ODA-financed exchange and collaboration programs, primarily directed at the Baltic States, Russia, and Poland, but later on also involving other previously communist states. This meant that this region rapidly became the most important target for the Institute. For 1993/1994, 38.8% of the Institute's operative budget was directed towards Central and Eastern Europe (Svenska Institutet 1994, p. 14). By 1998 this percentage had risen to 58 (Eduards and Sylwan 2000, p. 1). Isolating only the area of programs for persons exchange within studies and research for 1993/1994 shows that 45% of

---

[5] For a more detailed account of the Swedish PD towards Eastern Europe after 1989, see Åkerlund (2016b).

the money spent went to exchanges with Eastern Europe alone (Svenska Institutet 1994, p. 39).

In comparison to the situation before 1989, the scholarship and collaboration programs managed by the SI and directed towards Eastern Europe were clearly tied to the overall aims of assistance. Prioritized areas were studies and research related to "democracy," "market economy," and "ecological improvement" (Svenska Institutet 1994, pp. 14–15). The Institute's assignments in 1993/1994 included: individual short-term and long-term scholarships for students and researchers funded by the Swedish state and the Nordic Council of Ministers, funds for various forms of research collaboration on an institutional level between Swedish and Eastern European universities, and research facilities as well as a program for the exchange of experts (Svenska Institutet 1994, pp. 29, 35–36).

But why was the SI assigned these large programs? The main motive was the directed transfer of two almost inseparable things, namely *values* and *knowledge*, to Eastern Europe. In government publications these exchange programs are normally pictured as supporting the development of democracy (Ds 1994:134, p. 44; Eduards 2000, p. 55; Metell and Ganuza 1994, p. 6). Although seldom exactly defined how exchanges would support democratic development, it is possible to understand this thought through the idea of exchange as formulated by Leonard et al. (2002). Knowing a democratic society "warts and all" would be beneficial for the internalization and diffusion of democratic values. A 1994 government evaluation clearly defined the function of the SI programs as "general knowledge transfer and education in the environmental area" (Ds 1994:134, pp. 54–55). A more specific special evaluation of the SI research collaboration programs showed that a majority of available funds (33.6% or over SEK 14 million) had gone to collaboration projects aiming at knowledge transfer within economics (Metell and Ganuza 1994, Table 10).

Looking at the programs directed at Eastern Europe during the period between 1990 and 1997 it is not only clear that their main aim was a transfer of knowledge and values; it was also a transfer going in one direction. Any Swedish benefits from the assistance, apart from political stability in the neighboring region, were rarely if ever brought up. In retrospect the aims chosen for Swedish assistance are interesting as examples of the view of Western democracies on the former communist dictatorships. Particularly in the field of economics, the aim was to guide the economic transition from a planned to a liberal market economy. As Philipp Ther has shown in his book on neoliberal Europe after 1990, there were for a majority of reformers no alternatives to a neoliberal shock therapy for the Eastern economies (Ther 2014, p. 32 and *passim*). The question is really if there was any space for mutual learning from this position.

The aid programs towards Eastern Europe were during this early phase primarily directed at assisting change in the target countries. The question of eventual benefits for Sweden was secondary. This changed in June 1996 as the Swedish Parliament decided on a multi-billion SEK program to cut unemployment and to support economic growth, the so-called occupational bill. This bill combined ODA, foreign policy, and labor market politics. It stated that the emerging markets around the Baltic Sea were central for future Swedish economic development at the same time as a stable political and economic situation in these countries was a foreign policy interest (Prop. 1995/96:222).

One result of this bill was the "Baltic Billion," a one billion SEK program for cooperation over the Baltic Sea with the aim to "stimulate economic exchange, growth and employment in Sweden and the Baltic Region, and to strengthen the position of Swedish companies in the region" (Government Offices of Sweden 2004). Responsible for this program was the Ministry of Enterprise and Trade (Eduards 2000, p. 147).

In 1997 the SI established the Visby program, fully funded from the Baltic Billion. This collaboration program included both funds for research collaboration as well as individual scholarships for researchers in the Baltic Area. The focus was similar to the existing programs, as the focus should be on natural sciences, economy, law, and social sciences—areas corresponding to the four aims of assistance to the region. In 1998 this was further accentuated as the government permitted funds to be used for other parts of Russia than the north-west if it could be assumed that this would "promote the reform process" (Eduards and Sylwan 2000, p. 20).

The Visby program is an excellent example of how development assistance, public diplomacy, and trade politics were merged. In the Baltic Billion the evaluators concluded that the double aim had created results in three distinct areas:

- Benefits for Swedish trade and occupation;
- Development assistance beneficial for Sweden;
- Development assistance beneficial for the Baltic Region.

Although the evaluation found few direct benefits for trade and labor markets it concluded the Billion was a success. It had created a positive image of Sweden in the area as well as stable networks between persons, state agencies, and companies, which could be beneficial in the long run. Knowledge exchange was also put forth as a clear result beneficial for the target countries around the Baltic Sea (Boston Consulting Group 2004a, pp. 4–5). The Visby program was described as a success as well, although it had not promoted growth or employment in the region, nor contributed to ecological sustainability in any noticeable way. It had however strengthened the image of Sweden in the Baltics, it had promoted democracy and political stability, knowledge exchange as well as cultural understanding (Boston Consulting Group 2004b, pp. 111–115).

Compared to the period before 1990 it is obvious that PD and ODA had moved closer together during the assistance and collaboration programs for Eastern Europe, and especially with the Visby program. This was no longer only organizational collaboration at a practical level. Instead there was an idea that the purposes of both PD and ODA could be served within the same program. This was only the beginning of a merging of PD and ODA, which was continued in the following decades.

1998 AND BEYOND: A STATE PD AGENCY WORKING FOR AID AND TRADE

In 1998 the Swedish Institute was reorganized and turned into a government agency (Svenska Institutet 1998, p. 1). This meant that the Institute was tied closer to the Ministry for Foreign Affairs. The reorganization alongside the trade and occupation focus of the Visby program slowly transformed Swedish public diplomacy. According to James Pamment there has been a shift towards separated public diplomacy as a "short-term, pragmatic, reactive task" from more long-term cultural diplomacy. Public diplomacy is now seen as a promotional tool to sell "Brand Sweden" (Pamment 2013, pp. 101–102):

"Rather than identifying itself simply as a cultural or exchange diplomacy organization, the SI now considers itself a public diplomacy actor with the remit of using culture, values and information to promote Sweden as a competitive trading country" (Pamment 2013, p. 102).

A restructuring of Swedish public diplomacy underlining this change is the responsibility of the SI being moved from the Ministry for Foreign Affairs' press office to the ministry's office for EU internal markets and the promotion of Swedish trade. The Institute's development after 1998 can therefore best be understood in terms of Symogy Varga, who sees a merging of foreign policy and trade policy under the headline "commercial diplomacy" as a central feature of the post-1990 development (Varga 2013). The Visby program is probably one of the best examples of this development.

There is however a third component to this equation, neglected by Varga, and that is the adding of development assistance, or more correctly, the educational aspect of development assistance, as a supportive moment in modern trade-oriented public diplomacy. The reason for this is of course the idea of a knowledge-oriented economic development, where higher education and research play an important role for economic growth and employment. This notion is visible in state inquiries from the early 2000s on the collaboration with Eastern Europe. According to the findings of many such studies, economic development, both in Sweden and the receiver countries, should not be considered separate from education and research (Ds 2002:46, p. 151, SOU 2000:122; Eduards 2000, p. 152; Högskoleverket 2003, pp. 16–18). Educational assistance and scientific exchange could thus be motivated in three ways: as development assistance, helping other countries to build capacities; as public diplomacy, influencing foreign publics, shaping Sweden's image abroad, and creating contacts and networks; and as a key factor for Swedish economic growth, as these two things together facilitated export as well as the recruitment of trained personnel for Swedish companies.

The Visby program contributed to all three of these areas, as described above. The funding of the program also neatly illustrates how ODA, trade, and PD coincide. As the funding from the Baltic Billion ended in 2002, the program was financed out of the general Swedish ODA budget until 2006. After 2006 the program then moved to be included in the Ministry for Foreign Affairs budget line for "general international cooperation" (Åkerlund 2015, p. 134; Eduards 2006). Thus over the period of 13 years the Visby program belonged to all three areas. The content of the program however did not change more than marginally. The high amount of ODA in the SI budget is shown in Fig. 7.1. The large difference in allocation happening between 2005 and 2008, visible as a decline in ODA funding, depends completely on this budgetary change, which also indicates the size of the Visby program within the Institute.

The Visby program still exists, but has changed geographical focus over the years due to EU enlargement. As Poland and the three Baltic states entered the EU in 2004 they were no longer part of the program. From 2005 the only countries eligible for this program were Russia, Belarus, and Ukraine (Svenska Institutet 2005, pp. 41–42). Eastern Europe is still an important region for the SI; it is just not the same Eastern Europe as in the 1990s. Programs directly initiated by the reorganized ODA-agency SIDA (established in 1995 through the merging of various ODA agencies) included scholarships for Caucasus and Moldova (1997–2005) and the Master in Sweden for Eastern Europe (MSEE) program (2006–2010) (Svenska Institutet 1998, p. 25, 2005, p. 31, 2010, p. 55).

Besides the Visby program there were other scholarship programs directed at the former communist countries. Between 1997 and 2000 the Ministries for Employment, Education and Foreign Affairs cofinanced a program called the Baltic Scholarships, available for applicants from the same area. The Baltic scholarships merged with the Visby program in 2000 (Svenska Institutet 2000, p. 29). The so-called Eastern Europe scholarships (*Östeuropastipendier*) were directed towards countries outside the Baltic area, with most applicants coming from Bulgaria, Romania, and the parts of Russia not eligible for the Visby program. This program was initiated in 1998 and abandoned in 2006 (Svenska Institutet 2006, p. 42), probably as a result of Bulgaria and Romania entering the EU in 2007. The SI was also responsible for scholarship programs directed towards Eastern Europe initiated by the ODA agency SIDA. Examples include the program directed towards Caucasus and Moldova and the MSEE which included Belarus and Ukraine, Moldova and the Balkans, Armenia, Azerbaijan, and Georgia as well as Kyrgyzstan and Tajikistan. Even the Swedish–Turkish scholarship program (2008–2011) is in the yearly reports defined as a part of SI's support to Eastern Europe (Svenska Institutet 2005, p. 31, 2010, p. 56).

This geographical focus on Eastern Europe partly hides the fact that ODA-financed exchange with other parts of the globe also increased after 1998; 2001 was the first year when international development cooperation was given its own heading in the SI annual report and here it may be seen that the Institute managed short term expert exchanges with large parts of the world, handed out 66 guest scholarships to applicants from countries on the OECD/DAC list of ODA recipients, and also ran an independent program for South African students (Svenska Institutet 2001, pp. 25–29). Exchanges of experts and guest scholarships were also a part of the development assistance in 2005 as well as the Caucasus/Moldova program mentioned above. The SI also handled scholarships for Chinese students, for doctoral candidates from ODA countries (SIDA), for "key personnel in developing countries" for master's studies in Sweden (SIDA) and a Swedish–Turkish master's program on behalf of the general consulate in Turkey (Svenska Institutet 2005, pp. 29–31). By 2010 ODA-financed management related programs had entered the SI. The Institute ran a program on Corporate Social Responsibility for young managers from India and China, a Young Leaders Visitors Program for opinion makers from Sweden and the MENA area, as well as a leadership program for young female social entrepreneurs from Egypt, Syria, Jordan, Morocco, and the West Bank/Gaza (Svenska Institutet 2010, p. 44).

The last larger change in SI scholarship granting is directly related to the commercialization and commodification of Swedish higher education. In 2011 the country introduced tuition fees for non-EU students as a result of the government proposition "Compete with Quality" (Prop. 2009/10:65). At the same time ODA funding was set aside for the creation of the "Swedish Institute Study Scholarships" for students from OECD/DAC countries. According to the SI the overall aim of this program is to "contribute to the qualified competence supply in the developing countries" (Svenska Institutet 2012, pp. 38–39). Parallel to this, a 2011 inquiry into higher education in development cooperation suggested the creation of a framework for capacity building and competence supply in developing countries and for the internationalization of Swedish higher education. The program would develop master's programs in developing countries in collaboration with Swedish universities and be developed and coordinated by the SI, based on the Institute's experiences with international cooperation and scholarship handling (Ds 2011:3, pp. 98–100). This last proposal underlines the presently strong position of the SI within the fields of both international higher education as well as development assistance.

OVERALL CHANGES

The fall of communism accelerated a process already in movement, namely the slow merging of Swedish public diplomacy activities with development assistance. After 1990 the SI administered large exchange programs, which differed from the other programs of the Institute as they were to contribute to the direct transfer of values and knowledge, not primarily for the benefit of Sweden or Swedish interests. The centrality of ODA after 1990 is indicated in Fig. 7.1. The sums assigned to the SI for the assistance and collaboration programs for Eastern Europe were huge and had an important impact on the SI as an institution (Eduards and Sylwan 2000, p. 7). The conclusion is that the post-1990s activities moved ODA from the periphery to the center of the Institute's work. The Visby program and the Baltic Scholarship scheme added yet another aspect as they had an outspoken aim to enhance exports and generate revenue through contact building and culture promotion alongside development assistance. The centrality of academic exchange within the Baltic Billion cannot be underestimated as 21% or SEK 210 million went into the Visby program (Boston Consulting Group 2004b, pp. 107, 444).

The assignment of Eastern European collaboration programs to the SI transformed the Institute. Exchange and collaboration within the field of ODA, which up until then had been a secondary task, now became its primary assignment. The entry of a number of former communist countries into the EU in the 2000s did not slow this development. Instead the idea of academic exchange as beneficial for the transfer of values and knowledge has been maintained, but directed towards other parts of the globe as illustrated by various exchange programs for ODA-recipient countries.

CONCLUSIONS

This chapter has applied a long historical perspective on the relationship between Swedish PD and ODA. Focusing on the field of exchange of persons, and more specifically scholarly exchange, it has brought up their common organizational roots within the SI, the organizational separation in 1962, and finally a slow merging of the two, starting around the mid-1970s. From around 1990 this merging process accelerated as a result of the fall of Eastern European communism as well as an increasing importance of higher education within Swedish ODA. On the organizational level and in this very special case, it is actually not wrong to ask how estranged PD and ODA are. Historically their total separation was not longer than roughly 10 years between 1962 and 1973.

The case treated in this chapter shows the complexity of the internal relation between ODA and PD. It is actually possible to see them both as subordinated to the other at the same time. It is on the one hand obvious that the amount of ODA financed exchange activities within the SI has risen over time. This curtailed the relative autonomy of the SI as target groups or target countries were increasingly determined by assistance policy. The mission to work for democracy and social change abroad is also very different from the assignment to work for Swedish interests on a global level as pointed out in the evaluation of the SI's work towards Eastern Europe (Eduards and Sylwan 2000, p. 7). In this formulation we find one of the main reasons for the rising ODA activity of the SI. Although democracy was proposed to be an overall aim of Swedish ODA already in 1977 (SOU 1977:13, pp. 38–40), it was during the political transformation in Eastern Europe that this aim was given the same dignity as technical assistance as seen in the four interrelated aims presented above. As assistance was redirected from mainly technical assistance, where technology transfer was the main purpose of academic exchange, to democracy and social change, it also opened up for the SI, as a PD institute, the ability to play a more central role within ODA.

At the same time it is possible to conclude that ODA funds have increasingly been used to finance activities of a PD character. The 1980s decisions to open up for a wider cultural cooperation with developing countries or to fund 50% of the guest scholarships through the ODA budget are two early examples of this. Making the Visby program, originally aiming at promoting exports and commercial networking in the Baltic region, a part of the development assistance to post-communist Eastern Europe is a more recent example. The last example, however, was the establishment of the 2011 Study Scholarships: a way to compensate for the loss of affordable study possibilities in Sweden, the practical result of the tuition fees for many persons, through an ODA-financed scholarship program.

The last two examples touch on the crucial changes within global higher education during the last 25 years, which have had an important impact on both PD and ODA. The commodification of education and the ideas of a global educational market (Altbach 2002), in combination with the ideas of a knowledge driven economic development, have made higher education and research a central aspect of both public diplomacy and development assistance. Against this view on education as a creator of revenue it is easy to understand the more commercial focus of contemporary public diplomacy as presented by Varga or Pamment (Pamment 2013; Varga 2013). As visible in the Visby program, the idea of enhancing academic exchange for commercial and labor market purposes was easily combined with the notion of international collaboration for democracy and social change. Here it is impossible to distinguish aid from trade from public diplomacy as the idea of exchanging persons is thought to benefit all three areas.

But the history doesn't stop with the Eastern European transformation. According to Sajita Bashir, global ODA commitments for higher education increased 2.4 times between 1999 and 2004, with three countries, France, Germany, and Japan, contributing around 80% of the 2004 total of USD 3.292 million (Bashir 2007, p. 21). In an attempt to explain this rise Bahir points to foreign policy interests such as promoting skilled migration, creating conditions for investments, penetrating foreign markets, or geopolitical interests. Unlike the way ODA in this sector used to work, she writes, the current aid is not used to strengthen domestic higher education, but is mainly used for mobility (Bashir 2007, p. 25). It is obvious that strong countries with education in research, which however lack the linguistic capital of English, are presently using their ODA to create global flows of students in order to strengthen their domestic educational sector. Sweden cannot compete with Germany, France, or Japan when it comes to the sums invested, but these recent developments show that the strategy is similar. In this process it is, once again, impossible to keep PD and ODA apart, especially when they are both present in the same organization, as is the case with the SI.

References

Åkerlund, A. (2014). The Impact of Foreign Policy on Educational Exchange: The Swedish State Scholarship Program 1938–1990. *Paedagogica Historica, 50*(3), 390–409.

Åkerlund, A. (2015). For Goodwill, Aid and Economic Growth: The Funding of Academic Exchange Through the Swedish Institute 1945–2010. *Nordic Journal of Educational History, 2*(1), 119–140.

Åkerlund, A. (2016a). *Public Diplomacy and Academic Mobility in Sweden: The Swedish Institute and Scholarship Programs for Foreign Academics, 1938–2010.* Lund: Nordic Academic Press.

Åkerlund, A. (2016b). Transition Aid and Creating Economic Growth: Academic Exchange Between Sweden and Eastern Europe Through the Swedish Institute 1990–2010. *Place Branding and Public Diplomacy, 12*(2), 124–138.

Altbach, P. G. (2002). Knowledge and Education as International Commodities: The Collapse of the Common Good. *International Higher Education, 28,* 2–5.

Andersson, G. (1975, October 29). *Kulturellt samarbete med U-länder.* (Memo). Vol. 1, IN11, 1920-års dossiersystem [Dossier System of 1920], 2219-03-3, UD [Ministry for Foreign Affairs], Riksarkivet [Swedish National Archives].

Bashir, S. (2007). *Trends in International Trade in Higher Education: Implications and Options for Developing Countries.* Washington, DC: The World Bank.

Bergman, A. (2006). Adjacent Internationalism: The Concept of Solidarity and Post-Cold War Nordic-Baltic Relations. *Cooperation and Conflict, 41*(1), 73–97.

Bjereld, U., Johansson, A. W., & Molin, K. (2008). *Sveriges säkerhet och världens fred: svensk utrikespolitik under kalla kriget.* Stockholm: Santérus.

Boston Consulting Group. (2004a). *Utvärdering av den första Östersjömiljarden: Del I.*

Boston Consulting Group. (2004b). *Utvärdering av den första Östersjömiljarden: Del II (Appendix 2: utvärderingar).*

Brodén Gyberg, V. (2013). *Aiding Science: Swedish Research Aid Policy 1973–2008.* Linköping: Linköping University Press.

Coombs, P. H. (1964). *The Fourth Dimension of Foreign Policy: Educational and Cultural Affairs.* New York: Harper & Row.

Cull, N. J. (2008). Public Diplomacy: Taxonomies and Histories. *The Annals of the American Academy of Political and Social Science, 616*(1), 31–54.

Czernecki, I. (2013). An Intellectual Offensive: The Ford Foundation and the Destalinization of the Polish Social Sciences. *Cold War History, 13*(3), 289–310.

de Lima, A. F. (2007). The Role of International Educational Exchanges in Public Diplomacy. *Place Branding and Public Diplomacy, 3*(3), 234–251.

De Wit, H. (2002). *Internationalization of Higher Education in the United States of America and Europe: A Historical, Comparative and Conceptual Analysis.* Westport: Greenwood Press.

Ds 1994:134: Sveriges samarbete med Central- och Östeuropa. (1994). Stockholm: Fritzes.

Ds 2002:46: Östersjöprogram för framtiden: Studie gällande behovet av fortsatta särskilda statliga insatser för att främja näringslivsutveckling i Östersjöregionen efter år 2003. (2002). Stockholm: Fritzes.

Ds 2011:3: Högre utbildning i utvecklingssamarbetet: En analys av högre utbildning inom ramen för svenskt utvecklingssamarbete och politiken för global utveckling. (2011). Stockholm: Fritzes.

Eduards, K. (2000). *SOU 2000:122 (Bilaga): Att utveckla samarbetet med Central-och Östeuropa: Utvärdering av utvecklingssamarbetet.* Stockholm: Fritzes.

Eduards, K. (2006). Visbyprogrammet: Ny uppdragsformulering (Internal Report for the Ministry for Foreign Affairs).

Eduards, K., & Sylwan, M. (2000). *Svenska Institutets Östeuropaverksamhet: Utvärdering* (Internal evaluation).

Fellesson, M., & Mählck, P. (2013). *Academics on the Move: Mobility and Institutional Change in the Swedish Development Support to Research Capacity Building in Mozambique.* Uppsala: Nordiska Afrikainstitutet.

Fischer, J. (2013). *Studiebesök i Sverige - mer än bara vetenskap? Om Svenska Institutets inbjudan av akademiker från krigshärjade länder i efterkrigstidens Europa 1947–1952.* B-Thesis in History, Uppsala University.

Glover, N. (2011). *National Relations: Public Diplomacy, National Identity and the Swedish Institute 1945–1970.* Lund: Nordic Academic Press.

Goldmann, K. (1991). The Swedish Model of Security Policy. *West European Politics, 14*(3), 122–143.

Government offices of Sweden. (2004, April 21). The Baltic Billion Funds—Promotion of Trade and Industry in the Baltic Region. Retrieved from http://www.government.se/sb/d/3095.

Hedborg, E. (1998). *A Good Neighbourhood: Sweden's Cooperation with Central and Eastern Europe.* Stockholm: Ministry for Foreign Affairs.

Hoekman, B. M., Maskus, K. E., & Saggi, K. (2005). Transfer of Technology to Developing Countries: Unilateral and Multilateral Policy Options. *World Development, 33*(10), 1587–1602.

Högskoleverket. (2003). *Över Östersjön: Om högskola och högskolesamarbete i Sveriges östra närområde* (Vol. 2003:8 R). Högskoleverket.

Leonard, M., Stead, C., & Smewing, C. (2002). *Public Diplomacy.* London: Foreign Policy Centre.

Lindner, J. (1988). *Den svenska Tysklands-hjälpen 1945–1954.* Umeå: Umeå University.

Mays, C. (2011). *For the Sake of Democracy: Samarbetskommittén för demokratiskt uppbyggnadsarbete and the Cultural Reconstruction of Post-World War II Europe.* Masters Thesis in History, Uppsala University.

Medalis, C. (2012). The Strength of Soft Power: American Cultural Diplomacy and the Fulbright Program during the 1989–1991 Transition Period in Hungary. *AUDEM: The International Journal of Higher Education and Democracy, 3*(1), 144–163.

Metell, K., & Ganuza, E. (1994). *En översyn av Svenska institutets program för högskolesamarbete med Öst- och Centraleuropa.* Stockholm: SASDA.

Mulcahy, K. V. (1999). Cultural Diplomacy and the Exchange Programs: 1938–1978. *The Journal of Arts Management, Law, and Society, 29*(1), 7–28.

166 A. ÅKERLUND

Mundy, K. (1998). Educational Multilateralism and World (Dis)Order. *Comparative Education Review, 42*(4), 448–478.

Müssener, H. (1974). *Exil in Schweden: politische und kulturelle Emigration nach 1933.* München: Hanser.

Nilsson, P. Å. (2004). *Svenskt bistånd till den tredje världen: dess uppkomst under 1950-talet: en studie av SIDA:s och NIB:s föregångare: Centralkommittén för svenskt tekniskt bistånd till mindre utvecklade områden.* Hammerdal: Hammerdal förl. och reportage.

OECD. (1996). *Assistance Programmes for Central and Eastern Europe and the Former Soviet Union.* Paris: OECD.

Pamment, J. (2013). *New Public Diplomacy in the 21st Century: A Comparative Study of Policy and Practice.* London: Routledge.

Pamment, J. (2015). Media Influence, Ontological Transformation, and Social Change: Conceptual Overlaps between Development Communication and Public Diplomacy. *Communication Theory, 25*(2), 188–207.

Prop. 1976/77:100 (Med förslag till statsbudget för budgetåret 1977/78).

Prop. 1978/79:100 (Med förslag till statsbudget för budgetåret 1979/80).

Prop. 1980/81:100 (Med förslag till statsbudget för budgetåret 1981/82).

Prop. 1982/83:100 (Med förslag till statsbudget för budgetåret 1983/84).

Prop. 1984/85:100 (Med förslag till statsbudget för budgetåret 1985/86).

Prop. 1986/87:100 (Med förslag till statsbudget för budgetåret 1987/88).

Prop. 1988/89:100 (Förslag till statsbudget för budgetåret 1989/90).

Prop. 1990/91:100 (Förslag till statsbudget för budgetåret 1991/92).

Prop. 1992/93:100 (Förslag till statsbudget för budgetåret 1993/94).

Prop. 1995/96:222 (Vissa åtgärder för att halvera arbetslösheten till år 2000, ändrade anslag för budgetåret 1995/96, finansiering m.m.).

Prop. 1996/97:1 (Förslag till statsbudget för budgetåret 1997).

Prop. 2009/10:65 (Konkurrera med kvalitet – studieavgifter för utländska studenter).

Rylander, U. (1985). *Redogörelse för försöksverksamhet med stipendier för sökande från vissa u-länder.* Vol. 12, IN11, 1920-års dossiersystem [Dossier System of 1920], 2219-03-3, UD [Ministry for Foreign Affairs], Riksarkivet [Swedish National Archives].

Rylander, U. (2010). *Stipendier skapar relationer: En uppföljning av Svenska institutets gäststipendiater 1973–1997.* Stockholm: The Swedish Institute.

Schramm, W. (1963). Communication Development and the Development Process. In L. W. Pye (Ed.), *Communications and Political Development* (pp. 30–57). Princeton: Princeton University Press.

Selvaratnam, V. (1988). Higher Education Co-operation and Western Dominance of Knowledge Creation and Flows in Third World Countries. *Higher Education, 17*(1), 41–68.

SIDA et al. (1980, December 16). *Promemoria angående former för och finansiering av kulturutbytet med u-länderna utarbetad i samråd mellan SIDA,*

Statens kulturråd och Svenska institutet. (Memo). Vol. 1, IN11, 1920-års dossiersystem [Dossier System of 1920], 2219-03-3, UD [Ministry for Foreign Affairs], Riksarkivet [Swedish National Archives].
SOU 1977:13: Sveriges samarbete med U-länderna: huvudbetänkande. (1977). Stockholm: Liber.
SOU 1978:56: Kultur och information över gränserna. (1978). Stockholm: Liber.
SOU 2000:122: Att utveckla samarbetet med Central- och Östeuropa: betänkande. (2000). Stockholm: Fritzes.
Svenska Institutet. (1952). *Verksamheten 1951–52.*
Svenska Institutet. (1974). *Verksamhetsberättelse budgetåret 1973/74.*
Svenska Institutet. (1975). *Verksamhetsberättelse budgetåret 1974/75.*
Svenska Institutet. (1976). *Verksamhetsberättelse budgetåret 1975/76.*
Svenska Institutet. (1977). *Verksamhetsberättelse budgetåret 1976/77.*
Svenska Institutet. (1978). *Verksamhetsberättelse budgetåret 1977/78: Del 1 text.*
Svenska Institutet. (1979). *Verksamhetsberättelse budgetåret 1978/79: Del 1 text.*
Svenska Institutet. (1980). *Verksamhetsberättelse budgetåret 1979/80: Del 1 text.*
Svenska Institutet. (1981). *Verksamhetsberättelse budgetåret 1980/81: Del 1 text.*
Svenska Institutet. (1982a). *Verksamhetsberättelse budgetåret 1981/82: Del 1 text.*
Svenska Institutet. (1982b, August 26). *Förslag till finansiering av vissa stipendier över anslaget III ht C2 Bilateralt utvecklingssamarbete.* Memo.
Svenska Institutet. (1986). *Verksamhetsberättelse 1985/86.*
Svenska Institutet. (1988). *Verksamhetsberättelse 1987/88.*
Svenska Institutet. (1994). *Verksamhetsberättelse 1993/94.*
Svenska Institutet. (1997). *Årsredovisning 1997.*
Svenska Institutet. (1998). *Årsredovisning. Verksamhetsåret 1998.*
Svenska Institutet. (1999). *Årsredovisning 1999.*
Svenska Institutet. (2000). *Årsredovisning 2000.*
Svenska Institutet. (2001). *Årsredovisning 2001.*
Svenska Institutet. (2003). *Årsredovisning 2003.*
Svenska Institutet. (2005). *Årsredovisning 2005.*
Svenska Institutet. (2006). *Årsredovisning 2006.*
Svenska Institutet. (2008). *Årsredovisning 2008.*
Svenska Institutet. (2010). *För Sverige i världen. Svenska institutets årsredovisning 2010.*
Svenska Institutet. (2012). *För Sverige i världen. Svenska institutets årsredovisning 2012.*
Ther, P. (2014). *Die neue Ordnung auf dem alten Kontinent: Eine Geschichte des neoliberalen Europa.* Berlin: Suhrkamp.
Tsang, M. C. (2000). The Economics and Resourcing of Education. In B. Moon, M. Ben-Peretz, & S. A. Brown (Eds.), *Routledge International Companion to Education* (pp. 128–152). London and New York: Routledge.
Varga, S. (2013). The Marketization of Foreign Cultural Policy: The Cultural Nationalism of the Competition State. *Constellations, 20*(3), 442–458.

CHAPTER 8

State–Civil Society Partnerships in International Aid and Public Diplomacy: The Case of Turkey and Somalia

Senem B. Çevik, Efe Sevin and Banu Baybars-Hawks

International development and public diplomacy have a complex and interconnected relationship. Public diplomacy is a political tool. Countries engage in public diplomacy activities with the expectation of managing the international environment (Cull 2009). In other words, there is an inherent objective of contributing to the achievement of foreign policy goals (Glassman 2008). International development, on the other hand, is geared towards providing countries with the know-how and resources to help developing countries to reduce poverty, increase their capacity to provide fundamental services to their citizens, and

S. B. Çevik (✉)
University of California, Irvine, CA, USA
e-mail: scevik@uci.edu

E. Sevin
Reinhardt University, Waleska, GA, USA

B. Baybars-Hawks
Kadir Has University, Istanbul, Turkey

© The Author(s) 2018   169
J. Pamment and K. G. Wilkins (eds.), *Communicating National Image through Development and Diplomacy*, Palgrave Studies in Communication for Social Change, https://doi.org/10.1007/978-3-319-76759-8_8

eventually to prevent conflicts (Fukuda-Parr 2007). These objectives prioritize the needs of the aid recipient country over the practitioner country, to such an extent that development practitioners argue that development aid should try to stay anonymous (Stewart 2012). The main objective of international development is to ensure that developing countries establish the necessary infrastructure to fulfill the needs of their societies. A successful international development campaign helps countries develop their own capacities to satisfy the needs of their people. Once we see international development as a public diplomacy tool and start "branding" the development projects with logos and slogans, the development objective loses its priority (Stewart 2012). It becomes more important to promote the source of the aid, rather than to develop the internal capacities of countries. Yet, despite this inherent dilemma, public diplomacy and international aid still go hand-in-hand. Countries see international development as a feasible platform to engage with foreign publics.

In this chapter, we conceptualize development as a two-level public diplomacy opportunity. At the first—state—level, countries use their financial and operational resources to increase the capabilities of other countries. Known generally as official development assistance (ODA), state-level aid enables practitioner countries to engage with foreign publics as well as foreign governments. The second—civil society—level includes non-governmental organizations, such as charitable foundations, engaging in development activities. These aid campaigns have an indirect impact on public diplomacy efforts of countries. In certain instances, states can coordinate their activities with non-state actors. Even in the cases where countries do not necessarily sanction their civil society groups, domestic activities influence the way countries are perceived internationally. The "state–civil society partnership" concept in the chapter title does not necessarily refer to the coordination of these activities, but rather to an implicit cooperation. Indeed, both civil society and state actors execute international development campaigns that are likely to yield relevant public diplomacy outcomes. Yet, with the lack of an overall strategic objective and/or planning, the question of "how" needs to be discussed. How do these implicit partnerships work? How can we observe their impact on bilateral relations? How do they manifest their influence on countries' public diplomacy campaigns?

This chapter introduces Turkey as a crucial case in our understanding of the relationship between ODA and public diplomacy (Gerring 2009).

Turkey situates development aid as a fundamental public diplomacy and promotion tool. Despite being relatively new[1] to the fields of public diplomacy and international development, the country has taken steps to establish itself as an active public diplomacy actor and a generous donor to development and humanitarian projects. Turkey takes pride in and promotes itself through being a donor country and drastically increasing both its official humanitarian and development assistance contributions.[2] The Turkish case expands our theoretical understanding by integrating an influential case (Seawright and Gerring 2008). This chapter specifically focuses on Turkey's development efforts in Somalia due to the extensive Turkish state and non-state presence in the country (Achilles et al. 2015). Therefore, this particular single-case provides the opportunity for an important number of observations.

The rest of the chapter is composed of four sections. First, we provide a working definition of public diplomacy and an analytical framework that we will use in the case study. Second, we introduce the overall structure of Turkish public diplomacy and international aid by providing an analysis at the discursive and institutional levels. Third, we present the case of Turkish involvement in Somalia. We conclude the chapter by explaining how Turkey uses state and NGO-led development projects together to reach its foreign policy objectives, and we assess the communication between these two levels.

PUBLIC DIPLOMACY AND INTERNATIONAL AID

Public diplomacy is becoming an established field of study and practice. In academia, there are journals and special issues devoted to the subject, as well as graduate programs training the next generation of scholars. In the policy-making world, an increasing number of countries explicitly embrace the concept and start up institutions bearing the name of public diplomacy. Yet, perhaps not unexpectedly, this high level of interest does not necessarily yield to a universally accepted definition of the term

[1] The concept of public diplomacy was not mentioned in political discourse until 2004. The first institution bearing the name "public diplomacy" was established in 2010.

[2] Turkey was one of the five biggest government donors of humanitarian assistance according to the Global Human Assistance 2013 report. This fact is repeatedly used in the official promotion documents. The report can be accessed at: http://www.globalhumanitarianassistance.org/wp-content/uploads/2013/07/GHA-Report-2013.pdf.

or standards of operations (Gregory 2008). Rather, various disciplines and countries tend to bring in their own priorities and enrich discussions in the field. For the purposes of this research, we follow a state-centric view of public diplomacy. Thus, public diplomacy is used to refer "to the communication-based activities of states and state-sanctioned actors aimed at non-state groups in other countries with the expectation of helping to achieve foreign policy goals and objectives" (Sevin 2014, pp. 36–37). The definition intentionally ignores grassroots, or people-to-people (Payne 2009), diplomacy activities. As we argued above, these activities only have an indirect influence on public diplomacy as grassroots diplomacy does not necessarily follow government objectives or policies. Civil society initiatives are included in the research to the extent that they are implicitly or explicitly coordinated with governmental objectives.

ODA includes all development-related expenditures carried out by official agencies—state and local governments, as well as their executive agencies—to support development related campaigns (OECD n.d.). Within this perspective, ODA is parallel to the state-centric view of public diplomacy. One of the criteria for ODA is the inclusion of state actors. However, ODA is not the only method for engaging in development activities. In fact, in 2012, non-state actors globally spent over USD 4 billion in development projects which constitutes one-fourth of all humanitarian assistance spending (Stirk 2014).

As James Pamment (2015, 2016) argues, there is an important link between public diplomacy and international development. Building on the existing models of communication and development, he suggests a communication *of* development understanding. Before this addition, communication was seen either as a tool to contribute to development (communication *for* development as in the case of ICT4D) or a way to discuss development projects (communication *about* development). Communication of development highlights the aspect that has not been embraced by communication or development scholars—the marketing and stakeholder communication.

Turkey's public diplomacy activities reflect a *communication of development* understanding to mobilize grassroots engagement and *communication about* development in the field where aid initiatives take place. Therefore, there is simultaneously a narrative and network level approach in the way Turkey utilizes public diplomacy. Promoting the aid initiatives at home and abroad has become part and parcel of Turkey's nation branding, which positions the country as a "donor state" and generous country. This brand narrative is interrelated with Turkey's foreign policy objectives of becoming more prominent in global affairs and where it perceives itself in world affairs (Davutoğlu 2012; MFA 2016). In turn, this narrative facilitates and encourages grassroots engagement in the field. Turkish public diplomacy sees ODA as a point of pride—not only to promote itself as a "generous" country in the international arena but also as a tool to engage with foreign publics while simultaneously consolidating support for Adalet ve Kalkınma Partisi/Justice and Development Party (AKP) foreign policies (Çevik 2015). Cemalettin Haşimi, former coordinator of the Office of Public Diplomacy (KDK),[3] posits that there is a "Turkish model"[4] of public diplomacy that is flexible and receptive. In this model, Turkey does not follow long-term development strategies that are formulated *in* Ankara and *by* Ankara. Rather, the country monitors the needs and demands of developing societies and adjusts its development budget/aid programs according to needs. Hasimi uses the example of Somalia to illustrate this model. Following the 2011 East Africa drought, Turkey responded to the Somalia plight and was able to reshuffle its resources to provide assistance. Moreover, the intervention in Somalia was not limited to ODA. Several "political and socio-economic groups, trade organizations, NGOs, and others" were included (Wasuge 2016, p. 12). Therefore, the country was able to engage with the Somali public in a variety of ways.

Turkey's development aid utilizes grassroots engagement amongst the donor and recipient, as well as communication amongst stakeholders. This engagement understanding is in line with R. S. Zaharna's arguments on soft power differential (2007) and networked public diplomacy (2014). Conceptualizing soft power, Zaharna differentiates between two different types of public diplomacy based on their communication approaches. The initiatives that rely on mass communication wield soft power and focus on message dissemination, whereas network communication approaches value message exchange, relationship building, and network creation, thereby creating soft power (Zaharna 2007, p. 221). In networked public diplomacy, Zaharna details how to analyze

---

[3] Personal interview with one of the authors (Sevin), March 15, 2013.

[4] "Turkish model" is an argument put forth by the Turkish state and government that suggests the existence of a unique Turkish foreign and humanitarian aid model. This narrative is aimed at differentiating Turkey from other donor countries and is also used as an apparatus to gain domestic support in foreign policy regarding aid.

Table 8.1   Elements of networks (*Source* Zaharna 2014)

Network overview	What does the network look like?
Network structure	How strong are the relations?
Network synergy	How does the network build internal and external connections?
Network strategy	What purposes does the network serve?

network communication-based public diplomacy and identifies four layers. Accordingly, an analysis should include a network overview (overall communication understanding), network structure (the relations within a network), network synergy (relationship building strategies), and network strategy (messaging strategy in a network) (Zaharna 2014).

Thus, an analysis of Turkish engagement in Somalia should provide explanations for the four items and relevant questions summarized in Table 8.1. In order to provide a more inclusive analysis, the next section presents a short institutional overview of Turkish public diplomacy and international development at the state and non-state levels. It should be noted that the next section does not necessarily include all the actors in the Turkish public diplomacy scene, but is rather structured as a backdrop for understanding the case of this nation's involvement in Somalia.

TURKISH PUBLIC DIPLOMACY AND INTERNATIONAL DEVELOPMENT

Turkey is a latecomer to the public diplomacy scene. Up until 2004, the country did not use the term in official documents—despite engaging in strategic communication practices that resemble public diplomacy. The first institution bearing the name public diplomacy—the Office of Public Diplomacy—was established in 2010 (Başbakanlık 2010). In terms of a public diplomacy narrative Turkey labels itself as the most generous country given the fact that the country uses 0.21% of its GDP for development projects with USD 3.3 billion (KDK 2014). In 2014, this figure increased to USD 6.4 billion, with over USD 2 billion spent on development and humanitarian assistance projects regarding the crisis in Syria (KDK 2015b). Moreover, the Office of Public Diplomacy (KDK) also includes information about the activities of Turkish civil society organizations. The Turkish state provides USD 40 million in funding to Turkish organizations, which in return have spent over USD 350 million in development projects (KDK 2015b). In this section, we introduce Turkish public diplomacy under two headings with the intention of highlighting the network structure, how these networks operate internally as well as externally, and the purposes these networks serve. First, we discuss how Turkish political leadership justifies its investment in public diplomacy and development projects. Second, we focus on the state and non-state institutions.

POLITICAL DISCOURSE BEHIND TURKISH PUBLIC DIPLOMACY: AID AS "MANIFEST DESTINY"

It is imperative to investigate the rationale and discourse behind Turkey's public diplomacy in order to understand the purpose of development aid networks, their operations, and the connectedness of the institutional landscape. Turkey's development aid is grounded on a values-based foreign policy rhetoric that has been a central theme proposed by Ahmet Davutoğlu[5] (2013b). This discourse positions Turkey as a humanitarian, morally driven state formulating its foreign policy on global values such as equal representation, global governance, and eradicating inequalities. Some of the key components manifested in political rhetoric (such as aid as a moral duty, Muslim brothers, brethren, defending the interests of all aggrieved nations) are influenced by Islamic tones embroiled with Turkey's historical, cultural, and geographical ties with multiple local and global regions. Within this trajectory, the conservative political elite in Turkey perceives humanitarian aid as Turkey's manifest destiny (Kardaş 2013, p. 3). The reflection of manifest destiny is seen most prominently in the Balkans and Africa where Turkey's development partnerships have extensive networks through state and non-state institutions. President Erdoğan's UN address is reflective of Turkey's narration as one that stands by aggrieved nations (United Nations 2016).

Similarly, selective historical consciousness—regarding the Ottoman historical presence and power—plays a key role in the deployment of the idea of Turkish manifest destiny and Ottoman benevolence.

---

[5] Ahmet Davutoğlu, a former academic, was chief advisor to Prime Minister Erdoğan from 2003 to 2009, Foreign Minister from 2009 to 2014 and Prime Minister from 2014 to 2016. With the reshuffling of the AKP government in 2016 Davutoğlu's foreign policy formulation and Davutoğlu doctrine has lost its once popular presence in the political narrative.

Hence, the politics and rhetoric of humanitarian aid highlights Turkey's historical connections with the generous Ottoman image in congruence with contemporary aid initiatives. The overarching narrative is that of Turkey being a safe haven for immigrants takes credence from Ottoman benevolence towards Sephardic Jews during the Inquisition, European Jews during World War II (Güleryüz 2009), Balkan migrations during the early twentieth century and in the 1980s, as well as the Kurdish refugee influx from Iraq between 1988 and 1991. Ottoman benevolence can currently be traced to the plight of Syrian refugees (Ihlamur-Öner 2013). From this perspective, Turkey is characterized as a country with the potential to shape the course of regional development by contributing to the resolution of regional conflicts (Davutoğlu 2013b). This characterization is in line with Turkey's contemporary nation branding, which showcases itself as a "generous country"/"donor state." To illustrate, Turkish foreign policy rhetoric draws upon foreign aid and connects it to Ottoman history. Former Foreign Minister Ahmet Davutoğlu—in relation to aid to Somalia—stated that "this is our historical duty, besides this is our humanitarian duty and this is an integral part of our active diplomacy in Africa" (MFA 2015b). At the same time, historically infused rhetoric about foreign aid mobilizes and consolidates the electorate, while facilitating the exertion of power in these regions. Simultaneously, the historical narratives give rise to an ecological structure, a functional foreign aid system consisting of a humanitarian and development network that mobilizes Turkey's Islamic social capital.

PUBLIC DIPLOMACY POLICY AND IMPLEMENTATIONS: INSTITUTIONAL LANDSCAPE

A thorough description of Turkey's public diplomacy landscape is crucial in understanding the network overview and structure. The KDK is the main institution in Turkish foreign policy as it has the mandate to coordinate all existing public diplomacy initiatives. The KDK monitors and publicizes Turkey's ODA. The official circular announcing the establishment of the KDK explicitly acknowledges the existence of "various public foundations and institutions" that are already given the task of "formulating strategies and promoting the country abroad to increase the country's reputation in the eyes of international public opinion" (Başbakanlık 2010). The KDK's official *raison d'être* is to

ensure coordination and cooperation not only between these public establishments but also the civil society organizations (Başbakanlık
2010). Despite this *raison d'être*, the KDK has been mobilizing most of
its efforts on domestic public affairs, such as promoting Turkey's foreign policy objectives and positions to the domestic audience. This contradiction stems from Turkey's interpretation of public diplomacy, the
interconnectedness of its foreign and domestic policies, and the highly
partisan structure of the KDK. The institution, which was established
under the AKP government, has lacked the non-partisan structure that
some institutions such as the Ministry of Foreign Affairs possess. As a
result, the KDK has overwhelmingly served as a tool to increase the
popularity of the AKP and the personality cult of President Erdoğan
amongst domestic constituencies. In short, the KDK rather became an
apparatus of populist politics in Turkey emphasizing "Turkey as a central country" and the slogan "The world is bigger than 5" suggesting
the United Nations Security Counsel needs a sixth member which in this
case it is implied should be Turkey. To further illustrate, catchphrases like
"Erdoğan as a world leader," "Erdoğan as the man of the people," "The
conqueror of Davos," and "Chief" all feed into the "New Turkey" discourse (Selçuk 2016) and in turn into the foreign aid and public diplomacy narrative.

Turkey's foreign aid efforts are grounded in its foreign policy formulation and have been an indispensable part of its public diplomacy framework. As such, Turkey's foreign aid demonstrates a functional ecosystem
of multiple actors, stakeholders, and benefactors that display Turkey as
a benevolent/donor state. This complex aid ecosystem represents the
elements of the network presented in the previous section. In terms of
development-related public diplomacy activities, the Prime Minister's
Office has three additional practitioner institutions that partake in public diplomacy initiatives: the Turkish Cooperation and Coordination
Agency (TIKA) was established in 1992 with the objective of helping
develop the Turkic republics that gained their independence following
the collapse of the Soviet Union. TIKA in the 1990s was a technical
aid organization that was connected to the Ministry of Foreign Affairs
with departments based on functions such as the Economic, Trade,
and Technical Cooperation Office and the Educational, Cultural, and
Social Cooperation Office. In 1999, TIKA was transferred to the Prime
Minister's Office. Yet, especially with the current government's new foreign policy initiatives that have increased international outreach, TIKA

has transformed into a global aid agency. The organizational schema that gives a certain degree of autonomy to its global offices reflects this change. In 2011, TIKA was reorganized with departments based primarily in regions, such as the Central Asia and Caucuses Office, the Balkans and Eastern Europe Office, the Middle East and Africa Office, and the East and South Asia, Pacific, and Latin America Office.

The Housing Development Administration of Turkey (TOKI) was established in 1984, predominantly to build infrastructure (low-cost housing, urban reconstruction, schools, arenas, stadiums, etc.) within the country. The 1984 establishing decree includes two references to projects abroad, one authorizing the agency to work in construction projects beyond the country's borders and another one authorizing the agency to take foreign loans. It should be noted that TOKI did not have much presence in either of its two international activities until 2005 when it initially funded construction in Pakistan following the earthquake (TOKI 2016). In 2004, the administration was transferred to the Prime Minister's Office and still functions as one of its parts. Since then, TOKI became more active in the international arena, working closely with TIKA and the KDK in its construction projects ranging from mosques in Somalia and Sudan to housing in Indonesia and Sri Lanka (TOKI 2015).

Alongside organizations such as TIKA that focus on infrastructure, the Disaster and Emergency Management Presidency (AFAD) focuses on efforts towards rebuilding and rehabilitating the effects of natural disasters. AFAD is the institution managing post-disaster emergencies, and works as an umbrella organization overseeing emergency humanitarian relief. AFAD has responded to disasters and emergencies taking place across the globe and has also carried out evacuation and humanitarian aid operations during the social upheavals that took place in Libya, Tunisia, Egypt, and Syria (Sancar 2015). In addition to these institutions the Turkish Red Crescent and the Directorate of Religious Affairs are also key actors in the foreign aid apparatus with the latter gaining more traction since 2013.

Turkey's development assistance builds its internal and external connections through a number of non-governmental actors. Since the rise of the AKP to power, faith-based business and relief NGOs have become convenient tools of policy-making, strengthening the ties between multidimensional active foreign policy and its numerous stakeholders. Turkish civil society groups have been actively involved in international development projects for a longer time than the Turkish state. Turkey's key public diplomacy actors with international recognition have risen from these political conditions, while Islamist grassroots act as catalysts for the new conservative bourgeoisie. Faith-based aid NGOs such as IHH, Cansuyu, Yeryüzü Doktorları (Doctors Worldwide), Deniz Feneri (Lighthouse Association), Kimse Yok Mu, Beşir Derneği (Basher Association), and Hüdayi Vakfi/Aziz Mahmud Hüdayi Vakfi (Hüdayi Foundation) are manifestations of conservative politics (Çevik 2015). The faith-based charity structure is widespread across civil society development groups in Turkey. The International Blue Crescent Relief and Development Foundation (IBC), Deniz Feneri, and Kimse Yok Mu[6]—three of the largest charitable organizations in the country—all have religious tendencies and operate predominantly within the Muslim geography. Despite these groups' involvement in international development projects, Gaza Freedom Flotilla was the first time they received widespread national and international press coverage based on their relief activities. The flotilla was not necessarily impressive in terms of aid size or contents. But the clash with Israeli Defense Forces and the subsequent tensions between Israel and Turkey brought the Foundation for Human Rights and Freedoms and Humanitarian Relief (IHH)—a Turkish NGO—in the spotlight. An organization known as an Islamic charity (nearly) all IHH campaigns have had the objective of helping Muslims living outside Turkey and have received criticism for being supportive of illegal organizations.

The state–civil society partnership works through official and semi-official channels illuminating the network structure. NGO activities admit to a certain degree of connection with the government, though frequently they do it obscurely. The support base of patrons linked with the Independent Industrialists' and Businessmen's Association (MÜSİAD)[7] and the Turkish Confederation of Businessmen and Industrialists

---

[6]The Kimse Yok Mu Association has been one of Turkey's strongholds in key regions such as Africa in setting the groundwork for Turkey's state-level engagement. Kimse Yok Mu, an organization affiliated with the Gülenist movement, which in turn designated Turkey as a terrorist organization, was sealed off following the coup attempt in Turkey. The Turkish government accuses the Gülenist network of plotting the coup attempt.

[7]MÜSİAD is believed to have close ties with the AKP government through its membership base.

(TUSKON)[8] as well as other devout Muslims indicates a visible connection between conservative businesses, the pious masses, and humanitarian assistance. The conservative businesses and their social power, gaining traction under the AKP government, are inherently connected to the faith-based NGOs through donations and obscure networks between the private and public sector. In certain instances, as reported by KDK (2015b), these organizations partner with state officials and provide logistical support. In other words, the Turkish state uses the expertise of these organizations in host countries and collaborates with some of these charities. In other instances, the state solely supports rhetorical assistance. The relationship between Turkey and the Gülen movement before 2013 exemplifies such a relationship.[9]

Turkey's development aid ecosystem is an exemplar of clientelism and nepotism where party affiliation provides more political leeway to non-state actors. For instance, the Human Rights Platform, which IHH is a member of, has signed a contract with AFAD, the Turkish Embassy in Chad, and the Chadian Ministry of Health (IHH 2015). Moreover, the IHH Gaza offices welcomed TIKA President Serdar Çam and Turkey's Consul General to Jerusalem (IHH 2014) to discuss aid projects. Hence, efficient and effective delivery of aid is often either overseen by the diplomatic representation or implicitly supported. More importantly, NGOs, which are publicly known to support the government, have more leeway in their overseas operations and donations. For instance, Deniz Feneri Derneği—an NGO known for its obscure ties to the AKP government—was part of a corruption scandal in Europe. Despite the magnitude of the scandal the issue was covered up and Deniz Feneri continued to receive logistical support from the AKP government or party affiliates. To illustrate, AKP officials or card members frequent Deniz Feneri events, or

---

[8]TUSKON is a Gülenist affiliated business organization which was closed in August of 2016 by the government after the July 15 coup attempt.

[9]Gülenist Hizmet movement is a loose international network of organizations and individuals that are influenced by the teachings of Fetullah Gulen, a Turkish preacher. The movement is credit to have operations in over 180 countries, such as in schools and cultural centers. Their work was never directly supported by the Turkish state; however, between 2002 and 2013, there have been numerous public declarations by high-level politicians—including the former Prime Minister and current President Recep Tayyip Erdogan—in support of the Hizmet movement. Following a political dispute in 2013, the government distanced itself from Fetullah Gulen and the movement. Currently in Turkey, the movement is labelled a Fetullah Terrorist Organization.

have visited incarcerated Deniz Feneri members (AK Parti Çorum 2016; Hürriyet 2011). Clientelism also provides economic benefits to non-governmental actors and businesses which exemplifies civil society corruption. For instance, the Port of Mogadishu was constructed by Albayrak İnşaat and the Mogadishu Airport by Cengiz İnşaat. Kolin İnşaat has offices in Uganda overseeing development projects in Rwanda, Ethiopia, and Mozambique. Altınbaş Holding, a corporation that conducts business in areas including gold and that is also a government ally, investigated doing business in Ethiopia (Ethiopia Embassy 2010). Similarly, it can be argued that the Rixos Hotels hospitality group owes its expansion to its affiliation with the AKP political elite. Such conservative businesses also have crucial domestic contracts and some of these corporations also own newspapers in Turkey controlling the flow of information. To illustrate, Kalyon İnşaat, a construction company with close ties to the AKP government, owns two mainstream newspapers (*Sabah, Takvim*), while Albayrak Holding owns one newspaper (*Yeni Şafak*), Sancak Holding owns three mainstream newspapers (*Güneş, Akşam, Star*). As a result, the aid ecosystem not only creates capital for pro-government business but it also sustains Turkey's aid framework through offering perks and domestic and international contracts. On the other hand, the grassroots partake in aid drives by and large through Turkey's foreign policy narrative. In sum, Turkey's aid structure indicates a very close connectedness between Islamic institutions by way of political discourse, which serves the interests of the state, government, NGOs, and other stakeholders.

TURKEY IN SOMALIA

Since the early days of the Republic, Turkish foreign policy has been Western-oriented (Davutoğlu 2013). Relations with European countries and the USA were deemed as the most critical. The first deviation from this norm came with the Turgut Özal administration in the 1980s (Abramowitz 1993). Özal was in power until 1993, first as the Prime Minister and later as president of the country. During his tenure, Turkey reached out to former Soviet states in Central Asia. Following Özal, Turkey refocused on its Western-oriented policy. Turkey embraced a more global foreign policy with the rise of consecutive AKP governments to power since 2002. From 2002 to 2014, Turkey established 65 more embassies/consulates (an increase of 39%), with nearly half of them being in Africa, with 27 new embassies and two consulates (KDK 2015a). The Turkish Embassy in Mogadishu—which ceased operations due to the Somali Civil War of 1991—was one of the new embassies which reopened its doors in 2011 and was officially inaugurated by President Erdoğan in 2016.

The 2011 East Africa Drought was a turning point in Turkey–Somalia relations, which provided opportunities for Turkey's ambitions in the Horn of Africa. Then Prime Minister Erdoğan took almost a personal interest in the issue. Together with an envoy of over 200 people that included politicians, businessmen, celebrities, his wife, and his daughter, he visited Somalia in August 2011 (TRT 2011). Erdoğan became the first Western leader to visit Somalia after the Civil War and Turkish Airlines became the first major airline carrier to fly to Mogadishu (Richman 2012). After his visit, he wrote a piece for *Foreign Policy* entitled "The Tears of Somalia" in which he argued that "nobody with common sense and conscience can remain indifferent to such a drama" (Erdoğan 2011). The domestic publicity around the visit reiterated Turkey's benevolent image amongst domestic audiences. In that regard, the Somalia case exemplifies *communication of development* understanding where Turkey has promoted its "donor state," "benevolent country" status to domestic audiences. Somalia is also an exemplar of network structure and strategy. The *Sabah* newspaper—a Çalık Holding company—started a donation drive for Somalia in August of 2011 as Prime Minister Erdoğan was visiting there. Çalık Holding CEO Mr. Çalık donated TRY 500,000 to the campaign (Sabah 2011). In addition, Albayrak Group, another AKP affiliate, not only constructed Somalia Airport but also has the rights to run the airport for 20 years and has constructed the new Turkish Embassy in Mogadishu (Wasuge 2016).

Turkey still provides developmental assistance to Somalia. In 2014, with USD 74.5 million, Somalia was the fourth largest recipient of Turkish aid after Syria, Tunisia, and Kyrgyzstan (KDK 2015b). This amount also puts Somalia at the top of the recipients list among the least developed countries (KDK 2015b). The overall amount of aid is around USD 500 million over a span of five years (Arman 2015). Turkey is the fourth largest donor to Somalia, surpassed by the UK, the USA, and the EU (Saferworld and IPC 2015). Since 2011, TIKA has launched several projects (MFA 2015a). The airport in Mogadishu is being renovated through TIKA funds (Harper 2014). The administration has also implemented education, agriculture, health, and water management projects across the country (Wasuge 2016). TOKI has a couple of projects in the country, including the construction of a hospital, a nurse college, and a mosque (TOKI 2015). The Turkish Red Crescent runs the Mogadishu camp housing 20,000 internally displaced Somalis (MFA 2015a). The reception among Somalis, at least a certain segment of the population, seems to be positive at a personal level as Erdoğan and Istanbul have become popular names for children in the country (Harper 2014).

Relations between the two countries are developing. Erdoğan invited Somalia's President Hassan Sheikh Mohamud to Istanbul in 2013 during the unveiling of a subway line (ensonhaber.com 2013). He visited Somalia again as the president in January 2015 where he demonstrated Turkey's commitment to Somalia's well-being (MFA 2015a). Erdoğan, this time as president, also visited Somalia in 2016, signed new agreements with the Somalia government with the aim to strengthen ties in areas such as the economy, health care, agriculture, education, and security (*Business Insider* 2016). Currently, Turkey is gearing up to establish its first military base in the Horn of Africa in Somalia to train the local army to fight Al-Shabaab terrorists (*Daily Sabah* 2016). Moreover, the private sector keeps investing in the country. The Turkish investment in Somalia is estimated to be around USD 100 million (*Hurriyet Daily News* 2016).

Officially, the Turkish aid framework in Somalia prefers "working with Somalis" over "working on Somalis" (Wasuge 2016, p. 28). In other words, there is a network-based outreach understanding in the field. The link between the civil society network and some of the state network seems to be weak. For instance, the Foreign Ministry and embassies do not enjoy an equal degree of communication amongst one another, which weakens the network. To elaborate, Turkish state agencies (KDK, TIKA, and TOKI) that are made up of political appointees coordinate amongst each other and work with local partners. Similarly, Turkish civil societies partner with local organizations. Yet, the Turkish state or representatives of the state such as the diplomatic offices do not have formal links with Turkish civil society groups. In other words, the Turkish state does not officially sanction or fund any of these groups. However, this does not necessarily mean that there is no communication between these two levels. In the case of Somalia, Turkish officials and civil society representatives make informal ties and communicate about their activities in the field. The informal support and link between the state and civil society groups exists in official declarations and public speeches (Erdoğan 2011; KDK 2015b).

Turkey's aid network in Somalia reflects the ecosystem and state-civil society dynamism. In the Turkish case, business associations and businessmen have taken on the role of citizen diplomats in contributing to the improvement of bilateral economic, commercial and, social ties (Atlı 2011). For instance, when Erdoğan decided to visit Somalia in 2011, his envoy included representatives of business unions. Volunteers involved in foreign aid, as well as businesses operating in the country, have an extensive leverage in listening and communicating with local audiences. They become part of the local community and enmesh with the local values of the recipient society.[10] These representatives are not only acquainted with the culture, language, and traditions of the recipient country, but because of these qualifications they can act as the cultural bridges between two communities, even more so than diplomats. Volunteers and businesses in effect represent Turkey and at the same time maintain the flow of information about the recipient country, as well as interpreting the needs and demands of these communities. Accordingly, volunteers are the eyes and ears of a Turkish state that facilitates the flow of information to and from the community leaders and grassroots. Overall, the role of each actor is important in understanding the domestic appeal of Turkey's foreign aid mechanism.

The key actors in Turkey's foreign aid are empowered by cultural, religious, and economic variables, and at the same time they constitute Turkey's social power. Turkey's foreign aid apparatus showcases the important role of individuals, social capital, and an active public diplomacy audience. The people-to-people interaction between aid workers, ODA offices, and recipients serve as communication pathways to establish genuine relations. The social power of Turkey's NGO field officers and volunteers are the factors that differentiate Turkey's foreign aid framework from those of other new donors.

In terms of network *overview*, the initial step comes from the locals (Wasuge 2016). Turkey does not unilaterally decide on its development objectives, but listens to—or rather monitors—the needs of the countries. Existing projects also increase the country's capacity to engage with audiences and to understand the needs of the people. At the same

[10]Köylü, Mustafa (2013). Personal Interview with one of the authors (Çevik). Cansuyu Derneği President. Ankara. April 2013.

time, existing projects and networks can pose as a limitation in reaching out to diverse recipients. Turkey's investment in Somalia, as well as recent expenditures towards Syria and Tunisia, present further evidence for the existence of a network that is based on the demands of the locals. In both cases, Turkey was keen on providing assistance to the projects that were deemed important by the citizens. This particular policy choice of Turkish civil society and state is supported by a religious and critical communication campaign. The arguments point out that the existing global socio-economic and political systems ignore the needs and demands of the Muslim world. As a result, the networks are overwhelmingly established with communities that are perceived as most vulnerable, in Turkey's case those communities are Muslims.

In terms of network *structure*, the relations are weak, in other words, are predominantly one-time project partnerships that do not go beyond the mandates or time frames of the projects. Turkish understanding of development at both state and civil society levels values capacity building. Even in cases of charitable work undertaken by civil society groups, infrastructural investments are prioritized over short-term aid (with the exception of IBC). Deniz Feneri, for instance, does not deliver fresh water but builds wells. IHH runs an orphanage and a school rather than relocating orphans to Turkey or other countries. Briefly stated, the projects aim to remove the need for further projects on the same topic with the same participants. As the continuing bilateral relations show, locals appreciate this weak structure, thus paving the way for new networks—such as military cooperation.

In terms of network *synergy*, the Turkish–Somali network is closed. Neither the state nor civil society groups seek partnership with "diverse" audiences in terms of religion. The access to these networks is almost exclusive to Muslim groups. No instance of cooperation with non-Muslim partners or developed countries was observed during the study. Given their background, faith-based NGOs have traditionally appealed to the conservative Muslim bases and thus have increased presence during Muslim days of observance such as Ramadan or times of crises that hit co-religionists (e.g. operations against Gaza). These organizations employ religious elements of goodwill and duty and introduce major aid drives during Ramadan and Eid-Al Adha/Eid Al Fitr. Aid drives for co-religionist people in Somalia, Syria, and Myanmar have received significant attention in recent years, together with abundant media coverage. Nevertheless, the public visibility of these NGOs has encouraged new groups, such as secular donors that are traditionally not motivated by religious factors, to begin getting involved in these campaigns. That said, the commitment of the new secular donor group is still very minimal. Yet, this change has the prospect of diversifying the character of faith-based NGOs.[11]

In terms of network *strategy*, both civil society and state networks—regardless of the lack of cooperation between them—claim to perpetuate an almost "post-colonial" understanding of world politics. Within the Turkish model of development aid, according to the dominant narrative, the recipient is not seen as a person in need but rather as "a living individual that witnesses and symbolizes the global injustice and mistaken policies of 'other states' dominating the world-system" (Hasimi 2014, p. 129). In other words, Turkey's humanitarian aid focuses on the countries, in our case on African countries and specifically on Somalia, as the rest of the world ignores the needs of the continent. Thus, the networks aim to position Turkey as a country that is receptive and responsive to the needs of Somalia—a position that is not shared by other countries. In reality, the dominant political narrative that emphasizes Turkey as a change maker in the Somali conflict contradicts the underlying economic and political motivations of Turkey's newly found interest in Africa.

Turkey has proclaimed itself one of the most active development players in Somalia and has also put in large efforts in contributing to Somalia's stability, governance, and security by virtue of its presence in the country. Given Turkey's approach to public diplomacy, which incorporates development aid as a tool of public diplomacy, this presence should be seen as part of Turkey's overall foreign policy goals in Africa. Through two distinct networks—civil society and state institutions—Turkey engages with local civil society groups and individuals and positions itself as a legitimate actor in the continents. Nevertheless, state and civil society lack an official coordination and strategy blueprint in order to expand Turkey's position in Somalia and Africa. The rather unplanned and impulsive ways of communication between state institutions and civil society may undermine Turkey's actual potential in establishing itself as a long-term actor in Somalia and getting more substantial results.

---

[11] Orakçı, Serhat (2014). Personal interview with one of the authors (Çevik). IHH. İstanbul headquarters, Africa Office director. August 2014.

CONCLUSIONS

The main objective of this chapter has been to portray a two-level understanding of public diplomacy and international development, combining the public and NGO sectors. Prior to the research, it was our expectation to observe one single development network that incorporated all the actors. Being aware of the proximity between civil society organizations and the state, we expected the actors to help each other in engaging with local actors and to coordinate their projects. As a result of this cooperation, we expected to build a social network map that included the Turkish state, Turkish civil society organizations, and local actors. However, the case analysis yielded a different reality in which two different networks existed. In terms of working with local actors on development projects, Turkish state and civil society actors did not communicate with each other and established relations with different local groups. However, it should be noted that the Turkish state still sees civil society groups as part of its public diplomacy programs and keeps reporting their successes in the same reports with state-based aid.

A strong and cohesive network can be reached through public diplomacy projects. Technically, such a network requires repetition of links. For instance, an international broadcasting project can partner up with local broadcasters on a variety of projects. A student exchange is implemented on a long-term basis and can be repeated to include more students across the years, establishing stronger links between academic institutions. Yet, the nature of development campaigns should not allow the repetition of these links. These campaigns are expected to help recipient countries develop their own capabilities to cater to the needs of the populations living in their borders. Thus, if a development project is deemed successful, it should have fixed the problem that made the project necessary. Turkish international development projects also embrace this understanding and do not solely rely on sending aid. The Fisheries Training School in Somalia built by TIKA (Ozkan 2014), for instance, is the embodiment of this approach to international development.

Turkey has linked public diplomacy and international development through a brand positioning understanding. As seen in the remarks of Somali President Mohamud (2016), Turkey is known in Somalia as the country that *first* helped Somalia. Erdoğan's symbolic visit in 2011 was seen as a sign of Turkey's fearless commitment to the country. Even after the Turkish embassy in Mogadishu was attacked in July

2013 by Al-Shabaab—killing one Turkish security officer and wounding two—Turkey did not leave the country. Through these symbolic actions and supporting rhetoric, the brand position was established domestically at the state level.

The second level network, in the lack of formal links, provided the opportunity to present further coherent rhetoric. Given the ideological and religious similarities between the Turkish government and the civil society organizations, Turkish religious and post-colonial rhetoric became more persuasive. It was not only the Turkish state that followed a political agenda in addition to helping Somalia develop, but also the Turkish people who were siding with their Somali brethren.

In summary, Turkey embraces the understanding of communication of development to promote its foreign aid in both domestic and international spheres, while it employs communication about development in the field. The country does not see a dilemma in providing development aid and promoting its success. In line with the expansion of Turkish foreign policy, Turkish public diplomacy institutions and civil society groups expanded their outreach. Somalia stands as a crucial case to investigate the two-level public diplomacy network. Even though Turkey does not bureaucratically and logistically coordinate between civil society and state institutions, the rhetorical similarities in between in terms of development understanding, world politics, and religion help Turkey establish a strong and credible position in the eyes of the Somali public. The position has already demonstrated its spillover impact on the economy and trade as well as on the military. Further research, incorporating Turkey's limited yet existent role in non-Muslim regions, will help us better understand the relationship between public diplomacy and international development.

REFERENCES

Abramowitz, M. I. (1993). Dateline Ankara: Turkey After Ozal. *Foreign Policy, 91*, 164–181. https://doi.org/10.2307/1149066.

Achilles, K., Sazak, O., Wheeler, T., & Woods, A. E. (2015). *Turkish Aid Agencies in Somalia.* Istanbul: Saferworld and Istanbul Policy Center.

AK Parti Çorum. (2016). *AK Parti Çorum İl Teşkilatından Deniz Feneri'ne Destek.* Retrieved October 21, 2016, from http://www.akparticorum.org.tr/tr/haber/ak-parti-corum-il-teskilatindan-deniz-fenerine-destek/26666#1.

Arman, A. (2015). *Erdoğan: The Hero of Somalia: Al Jazeera English.* Retrieved March 10, 2016, from http://www.aljazeera.com/indepth/opinion/2015/01/visit-erdogan-somalia-2015121124331818818.html.
Atlı, A. (2011). Businessman and Diplomats. *Insight Turkey, 13*(1), 109–128.
Başbakanlık. (2010). Kamu Diplomasisi Koordinatörlüğü. *Resmi Gazete.* Retrieved from http://kdk.gov.tr/kurumsal/kdk-genelgesi/5.
Business Insider. (2016). *Turkey's President Recep Tayyip Erdoğan in War Torn Somalia.* Retrieved October 21, 2016, from http://www.businessinsider.com/ap-turkey-president-recep-tayyip-erdogan-in-war-torn-somalia-2016-6?IR=T.
Çevik, S. B. (2015). The Benefactor: NGOs and Humanitarian Aid. In S. B. Çevik & P. Seib (Eds.), *Turkey's Public Diplomacy* (pp. 121–152). New York City: Palgrave Macmillan.
Cull, N. J. (2009). Public Diplomacy: Lessons from the Past. *CPD Perspectives on Public Diplomacy.* Retrieved from http://uscpublicdiplomacy.org/publications/perspectives/CPDPerspectivesLessons.pdf.
Daily Sabah. (2016). *First Turkish Military Base in Africa to Open in Somalia.* Retrieved March 10, 2016, from http://www.dailysabah.com/diplomacy/2016/01/19/first-turkish-military-base-in-africa-to-open-in-somalia.
Davutoğlu, A. (2012). *Principles of Turkish Foreign Policy and Regional Political Structuring.* Ankara: TEPAV. Retrieved January 5, 2015, from http://www.tepav.org.tr/upload/files/1336135395-4.Principles_of_Turkish_Foreign_Policy_and_Regional_Political_Structuring_by_Ahmet_Davutoglu.pdf.
Davutoğlu, A. (2013a). *Stratejik derinlik: Türkiye'nin uluslararası konumu.* İstanbul: Küre Yayınları.
Davutoğlu, A. (2013b). Turkey's Humanitarian Diplomacy: Objectives, Challenges and Prospects. *Nationalities Papers: The Journal of Nationalism and Ethnicity, 41*(6), 865–870.
ensonhaber.com. (2013, October 29). *Somali Cumhurbaşkanı Marmaray açılışında.* Retrieved March 10, 2016, from http://www.ensonhaber.com/somali-cumhurbaskani-marmaray-acilisinda-2013-10-29.html.
Erdoğan, R. T. (2011). *The Tears of Somalia.* Retrieved March 10, 2016, from https://foreignpolicy.com/2011/10/10/the-tears-of-somalia/.
Ethiopia Embassy. (2010). *AIGA Forum Horn of Africa.* Retrieved October 21, 2016, from http://www.aigaforum.com/news/A_Week_Horn_Africa_123110.htm.
Fukuda-Parr, S. (2007). *Rethinking the Policy Objectives of Development Aid: From Economic Growth to Conflict Prevention.* Research Paper 2007/032. Helsinki: UNU-WIDER.
Gerring, J. (2009). Case Selection for Case-Study Analysis: Qualitative and Quantitative Techniques. In J. M. Box-Steffensmeier, H. E. Brady, & D. Collier (Eds.), *The Oxford Handbook of Political Methodology* (1st ed.,

Vol. 1, pp. 645–685). Oxford: Oxford University Press. Retrieved from http://www.oxfordhandbooks.com/oso/public/content/oho_politics/9780199286546/oxfordhb-9780199286546-chapter-28.html.

Glassman, J. K. (2008, December). *Public Diplomacy 2.0: A New Approach to Global Engagement.* Speech presented at the New America Foundation, Washington, DC.

Gregory, B. (2008). Public Diplomacy: Sunrise of an Academic Field. *The ANNALS of the American Academy of Political and Social Science, 616*(1), 274–290. https://doi.org/10.1177/0002716207311723.

Güleryüz, N. A. (2009). *The Turkish Jews: 700 Years of Togetherness.* İstanbul: 500. Yıl Vakfı.

Harper, M. (2014). *The Unlikely Love Affair between Two Countries.* Retrieved March 10, 2016, from http://www.bbc.com/news/magazine-30447039.

Hasimi, C. (2014). Turkey's Humanitarian Diplomacy and Development Cooperation. *Insight Turkey, 16*(1), 127–145.

Hürriyet. (2011). *Deniz Feneri Tutuklularını 150 AK Partili Vekil 2 Bakan Ziyaret Etti.* Retrieved October 21, 2016, from http://www.hurriyet.com.tr/deniz-feneri-tutuklularini-150-ak-partili-vekil-2-bakan-ziyaret-etti-18991472.

Hurriyet Daily News. (2016). *Turkey Plans to Enhance Investments in Somalia.* Retrieved March 10, 2016, from http://www.hurriyetdailynews.com/turkey-plans-to-enhance-investments-in-somalia.aspx?pageID=238&nID=95577&NewsCatID=510.

IHH. (2014). *TİKA ve Kudüs Konsolosluğumuzdan İHH'ya Ziyaret.* Retrieved January 5, 2015, from http://www.ihh.org.tr/tr/main/news/0/tika-ve-kudus-konsoloslugumuzdan-ihhya-ziyare/2604.

IHH. (2015). *Türkiye Orta Afrika'ya Umut Taşıdı.* Retrieved January 5, 2015, from http://www.ihh.org.tr/tr/main/region/orta-afrika-cumhuriyeti/146/turkiye-orta-afrikaya-umut-tasidi/2378.

Ihlamur-Öner, S. G. (2013). Turkey's Refugee Regime Stretched to the Limit? The Case of Iraqi and Syrian Refugee Flows. *Perceptions, 18*(3), 191–228.

Kardaş, Ş. (2013). Turkey: A Regional Power Facing a Changing International System. *Turkish Studies, 14*(4), 637–660. http://dx.doi.org/10.1080/1468 3849.2013.861111.

KDK. (2014). *Uluslararası yardımlarda "en cömert ülke" unvanını taşıyan Türkiye'nin yardım seferberliği sürüyor.* Retrieved March 9, 2016, from http://kdk.gov.tr/haber/turkiyenin-dis-yardimlari-2013/494.

KDK. (2015a). *13 yılda 65 yeni temsilcilik: Türkiye'nin yurtdışındaki temsilcilik sayısı 228'e çıktı.* Retrieved March 9, 2016, from http://kdk.gov.tr/sayilarla/13-yilda-65-yeni-temsilcilik-turkiyenin-yurtdisindaki-temsilcilik-sayisi-228e-cikti/41.

KDK. (2015b). *Türkiye'nin 2014 yılı yardımları %47,3'lük artışla 6,4 milyar dolara çıktı.* Retrieved March 9, 2016, from http://kdk.gov.tr/haber/turkiyenin-dis-yardimlari-2014/590.

MFA. (2015a). *Relations Between Turkey and Somalia.* Retrieved March 10, 2016, from http://www.mfa.gov.tr/relations-between-turkey-and-somalia. en.mfa.
MFA. (2015b). Foreign Minister Davutoğlu: We Will Take the Necessary Steps to Strengthen the Brotherhood Between Somalia and Somaliland. *Republic of Turkey Ministry of Foreign Affairs.* Retrieved January 5, 2015, from http://www.mfa.gov.tr/foreign-minister-davutoglu-we-will-take-the-neces-sary-steps-to-strengthen-the-brotherhood-between-somalia-and-somaliland. en.mfa.
MFA. (2016). *Synopsis of the Turkish Foreign Policy.* Retrieved October 21, 2016, from http://www.mfa.gov.tr/synopsis-of-the-turkish-foreign-policy. en.mfa.
Mohamud, H. S. (2016, February). *Speech by Hassan Sheikh Mohamud, President of the Federal Republic of Somalia, at the Opening Session/High Level Partnership Forum Istanbul.* Presented at the High Level Partnership Forum, Istanbul, Turkey. Retrieved from http://hlpfistanbul.mfa.gov.tr/speech-by-assan-sheikh-mohamud-president-of-the-federal-republic-of-somalia-at-the-opening-session.en.mfa.
OECD. (n.d.). *Official Development Assistance—Definition and Coverage—OECD.* Retrieved March 9, 2016, from http://www.oecd.org/dac/stats/officialdevelopmentassistancedefinitionandcoverage.htm.
Ozkan, Mehmet. (2014). *Turkey's Involvement in Somalia: Assessment of State Building in Progress.* Ankara: SETA.
Pamment, J. (2015). Media Influence, Ontological Transformation, and Social Change: Conceptual Overlaps Between *Development Communication* and *Public Diplomacy.* Media Influence, Ontological Transformation, and Social Change. *Communication Theory, 25*(2), 188–207. https://doi. org/10.1111/comt.12064.
Pamment, J. (2016). *Intersections Between Public Diplomacy & International Development: Case Studies in Converging Fields.* Los Angeles, CA: Figueroa Press.
Payne, G. (2009). Trends in Global Public Relations and Grassroots Diplomacy. *American Behavioral Scientist, 53*(4), 487–492. https://doi. org/10.1177/0002764209347635.
Richman, M. (2012). Turkey Takes on Redevelopment Efforts in Somalia. Retrieved March 10, 2016, from http://www.voanews.com/articleprint-view/1204614.html.
Sabah. (2011). *Somali'ye Bağış Yağmuru.* Retrieved October 21, 2016 from http://www.sabah.com.tr/gundem/2011/08/20/somaliye-bagis-yagmuru.
Saferworld and IPC. (2015). *Turkiye ve Somali: Yardimlarin Barisa Hizmet Etmesi* (No. Politika Notu). Istanbul: IPC.

Sancar, G. A. (2015). Turkey's Public Diplomacy: Its Actors, Stakeholders, and Tools. In S. B. Çevik & P. Seib (Eds.), *Turkey's Public Diplomacy* (pp. 13–42). Basingstoke, New York: Palgrave Macmillan.

Seawright, J., & Gerring, J. (2008). Case Selection Techniques in Case Study Research: A Menu of Qualitative and Quantitative Options. *Political Research Quarterly, 61*(2), 294–308. https://doi.org/10.1177/1065912907313077.

Selçuk, O. (2016). Strong Presidents and Weak Institutions: Populism in Turkey, Venezuela and Ecuador. *Southeast European and Black Sea Studies.* http://dx.doi.org/10.1080/14683857.2016.1242893.

Sevin, E. (2014). *Making New Friends: Relational Public Diplomacy as a Foreign Policy Instrument.* Unpublished doctoral dissertation, American University.

Stewart, J. (2012, October 29). *Stop Branding Aid.* Retrieved from http://www.whydev.org/stop-branding-aid/.

Stirk, C. (2014). *Humanitarian Assistance from Non-state Donors: What Is It Worth?* (Briefing Report). Global Humanitarian Assistance. Retrieved from http://www.globalhumanitarianassistance.org/wp-content/uploads/2014/05/Humanitarian-assistance-from-non-state-donors-2014.pdf.

TOKI. (2015). *TOKİ > International Experience.* Retrieved March 10, 2016, from http://www.toki.gov.tr/en/international-experience.html.

TOKI. (2016). *International Experience.* Retrieved October 21, 2016, from http://www.toki.gov.tr/en/international-experience.html.

TRT. (2011). *Erdoğan'dan Somali için Yardım Çağrısı haberi.* Retrieved March 10, 2016, from http://www.trthaber.com/haber_yazdir.php?detayID=6350.

United Nations. (2016). *Turkey's Erdoğan Challenges World Leaders at UN Assembly to End Bloodshed in Syria.* Retrieved October 21, 2016, from http://www.un.org/apps/news/story.asp?NewsID=54972#.WA1xmXhm3ww.

Wasuge, M. (2016). *Turkey's Assistance Model in Somalia: Achieving Much with Little.* Mogadishu: The Heritage Institute for Policy Studies.

Zaharna, R. S. (2007). The Soft Power Differential: Network Communication and Mass Communication in Public Diplomacy. *The Hague Journal of Diplomacy, 2*(3), 213–228. https://doi.org/10.1163/187119007X240505.

Zaharna, R. S. (2014). Network Purpose, Network Design: Dimensions of Network and Collaborative Public Diplomacy. In R. S. Zaharna, A. Arsenault, & A. Fisher (Eds.), *Relational, Networked, and Collaborative Approaches to Public Diplomacy: The Connective Mindshift* (pp. 173–191). New York, NY: Routledge.

CHAPTER 9

Communicating Mexico's International Development Cooperation: An Incipient Public Diplomacy Strategy

Rebecka Villanueva Ulfgard

INTRODUCTION

It should be said from the start that Mexico does not have any proper tradition of public diplomacy. Rather, it has relied on a mosaic of complementary and sometimes competing initiatives for communicating its foreign policy, cultural policy, economic power, and tourist attractions to the outside world, principally through the Secretariat of Foreign Affairs (Secretaría de Relaciones Exteriores), the National Council of Culture and Arts (the defunct CONACULTA), and ProMéxico. Therefore, studying the roles and communication strategies attached to Mexico's IDC (IDC) makes for a particularly interesting case since its institutional structure is still fairly young. Besides, it could be argued that this particular policy area is a new testing ground for the wider ambitions of Mexico's contemporary foreign policy, a point to be discussed in this chapter.

R. Villanueva Ulfgard (✉)
Instituto Mora, Mexico City, Mexico
e-mail: rulfgard@institutomora.edu.mx

© The Author(s) 2018   193
J. Pamment and K. G. Wilkins (eds.), *Communicating National Image through Development and Diplomacy*, Palgrave Studies in Communication for Social Change, https://doi.org/10.1007/978-3-319-76759-8_9

Mexico holds a complex position in the IDC architecture; being a middle income country (MIC) it is both a provider and a recipient of development assistance. This dual role was strengthened by Mexico's entry into the Organisation for Economic Co-operation and Development (OECD) in 1994 and subsequent participation in the OECD-orchestrated Heiligendamm-L'Aquila Process (HAP) from 2007, which included the G8 + G5 as well as seven other countries with a capacity for regional and international influence, which later led to the Group of Twenty (G20). Mexico was the only country participating in HAP that was a member of both the OECD and the G5, a condition which allowed it to consolidate itself as a valid intermediary between DAC donor members and emerging donors (Villanueva Ulfgard and López Chacón 2017).

It should be said that in IDC jargon, there is no universally accepted term or concept used to name these countries. The category used most frequently to describe MICs is as "emerging donors," due to their relatively recent incursion as official development assistance (ODA) donor countries. Along the same lines, they are often referred to as "non-DAC donors" due to having practices and policies similar to the DAC member countries, but without following the same regulations. They are also known as "South–South Cooperation providers" (SSCs), given their involvement in a system established in the 1960s and driven by the Non-Aligned Movement (Zimmermann and Smith 2011). Mexico is, simultaneously, an observer to the DAC and SSC provider, despite its apparent skepticism toward badges of "DAC-ization" or even "DAC-ability" (Lightfoot and Soyeun 2011) while seeking, at least according to official rhetoric, to retain room to maneuver within the IDC architecture (Villanueva Ulfgard and López Chacón 2017). As a "country of multiple belongings," it is aligned with neither the G77 nor with the G8, whereas it is part of the G20, the BRICSAM and the MIKTA (Maihold 2014). Indeed, as an emerging economy and regional "middle power," one that meets its international obligations with firm ties to principles of multilateralism (Cooper 2012; Kirton 2012; Zimmermann and Smith 2011), Mexico has taken on roles of responsibility, which offer opportunities for projecting its IDC in a broader, more effective way (cf. Bracho 2015; Lázaro et al. 2014; Leutner and Müller 2010; Lätt and Öztürk 2008; Piefer 2014). This is reflected in Mexico's National Plan for Development 2013–2018, Chapter V (on being an Actor with Global Responsibility), which refers to consolidating the country as an "emerging power" in world affairs (Presidencia de la República 2013).

Mexico has displayed leadership regarding financing for development ever since it hosted the international conference on this same issue on March 18–22, 2002 ("The Monterrey Consensus"). Many years later, the First High Level Meeting of the Global Partnership for Effective Development Cooperation (GPEDC) was held in Mexico City on April 15–16, 2014. Mexico also served as one of GPEDC's three co-chairs until November 2016 (together with Malawi and the Netherlands). Mexico's Agency for IDC, Agencia Mexicana de Cooperación Internacional para el Desarrollo (AMEXCID) is responsible for coordinating Mexico's participation in the GPEDC and was in charge of drafting the concept note for one of the working groups on the SSC and Triangular Cooperation from the MICs' perspective that formed the basis for discussions at the Second High Level Meeting held in Nairobi, Kenya, from November 28 to December 1, 2016. These are examples of how Mexico is contributing actively to safeguarding a legacy built on the MDG8 ("develop a global partnership for development"), coupled with the present SDG17 ("revitalize the global partnership for sustainable development"), notably through the work by AMEXCID diplomats and officials.

To date, not much has been written for an international audience about Mexico's IDC, and even less from a public diplomacy (PD) perspective. This chapter brings an original analysis of a particular angle of Mexico's IDC, putting focus on AMEXCID, the entity in charge of coordinating and implementing (together with other agencies and secretaries) various programs and activities falling under this policy. Most of the existing literature has been written by Mexicans in Spanish, covering the ex ante AMEXCID period (Ayala and Pérez 2009; Lozoya 2001; Schmukler et al. 2008; Suárez 2006) and the birth and evolution of AMEXCID (Bracho and García 2011; Figueroa 2016; Pérez et al. 2015; Prado 2013, 2015; Vega 2014), many of whom have worked or are still working within AMEXCID or as consultants for the agency, which presents a problem of independent critical analysis. Few attempts have been made at comparing Mexico's IDC with that of other MICs (cf. Sidiropoulos et al. 2015; Soto 2014).

The following sections of this chapter discuss: the institutionalization of Mexico's IDC and structure of AMEXCID; challenges regarding its organization, leadership, and resources; elements of an incipient PD approach for communicating Mexico's IDC; reflections on foundational elements for Mexico's IDC PD; and concluding reflections.

Institutionalization of Mexico's IDC
and Structure of AMEXCID

Mexico's IDC is not a contemporary phenomenon, quite the contrary. The Mexican diplomat, Bruno Figueroa (2016), has traced more than one hundred years of engagement with humanitarian aid and development cooperation. This is a welcome contribution to understand the evolution of Mexico's path to present-day practices of IDC. It is striking how often it seemed to have relied more on individual initiatives than institutional arrangements. Perhaps one could argue that it has not been so much about cooperation as *promotion*, in reality, considering Mexico's national (security) interests with regard to Central America (especially during the 1980s). Figueroa describes how the first forty years were marked by humanitarian aid to natural disasters occurring in Texas, Italy, El Salvador, and Chile. In the 1920s, international cooperation in higher education was launched through the Secretariat of Public Education, focusing on Central American countries. During the 1930s and World War II, Mexico welcomed thousands of refugees, especially from Spain. In the 1970s and 1980s, this happened again with refugees from the political conflicts in Central America. During the Cold War, the famous Estrada Doctrine named after its founder, the Mexican Secretary of Foreign Affairs Genaro Estrada, established that Mexico should not seek to side with either the USA or the Soviet Union "satellites" in Latin America or in any other region in the world. The principles of this doctrine—non-intervention, peaceful resolution of disputes, and self-determination of all nations—came to the fore in Mexico's commitment to bring peace to Central America (through the San José Agreement in 1980 and later the Contadora Group). As pointed out by Figueroa, the Secretariat of Foreign Affairs never had the "monopoly" of exercising Mexico's IDC. In fact, technically driven IDC had very limited resources and impact, whereas other types of initiatives oriented towards developing infrastructure, for example, benefitted from investments under the direct control of the Secretariat of Finance (whose actions are not strictly governed by foreign policy principles).

The institutionalization of Mexico's CID overseen by the Secretariat of Foreign Affairs began in 1971 with the creation of the Directorate General for International Technical Cooperation (Dirección General de Cooperación Técnica Internacional). In 1988, international development cooperation was inserted into the Mexican Constitution (Article 89) as a normative principle of Mexico's foreign policy. In 1998, President Ernesto Zedillo created, by a presidential decree, the first agency within the Secretariat of Foreign Affairs, the Mexican Institute for International Cooperation (Instituto Mexicano para la Cooperación Internacional, IMEXCI). In 2000, the institute was transformed into the General Directorate for Technical and Scientific Cooperation (DGCTC). The idea of creating an agency for IDC was launched by the former Secretary of Foreign Affairs under President Ernesto Zedillo in her capacity as PRI Party (Partido Revolucionario Institucional) Senator, Rosario Green, on March 8, 2007, in a special commission in the Mexican Senate. A series of consultations followed with different stakeholders, with the judicial-political machinery eventually running its course. AMEXCID has its legal foundation in the IDC Act (LCID) made public in April 2011 (Diario Oficial de la Federación 2011), and the agency started operating in September that same year. Embedded in the Secretariat of Foreign Affairs (as *órgano desconcentrado*, which is not the same as a decentralized body but rather an entity with certain self-determination), it is a relatively young cooperation agency still struggling to consolidate its organizational and operational features, but with a clear mandate to project Mexico abroad as "A Mexico of Global Responsibility," as mentioned earlier.

AMEXCID rests on four pillars: Besides the agency, it is sustained by the IDC Program (Programa de Cooperación Internacional para el Desarrollo, PROCID), "the cross-cutting programmatic framework for Mexico's development cooperation [applying] to several Federal public administration entities" (UNDP 2014: p. 22). The trust fund in place since 2015, the National Fund for IDC (Fondo de Cooperación Internacional para el Desarrollo, FONCID), is expected to "enable improvement in the planning of development cooperation projects and increase their impact" (UNDP 2014, p. 23). The National Registry for IDC (Registro Nacional de Cooperación Internacional para el Desarrollo, RENCID) and the Information System for IDC (Sistema de Información de Cooperación Internacional para el Desarrollo, SICID) are two auxiliary mechanisms for "register[ing] projects, agreements, partner institutions, monetary values and other data related to Mexico's development cooperation" (UNDP 2014, p. 23).

AMEXCID's Directorate General oversees five different areas: Directorate General for Educational and Cultural Cooperation (Dirección General de Cooperación Educativa y Cultural, DGCEC); Directorate General for Cooperation and Promotion of International

Economy (Dirección General de Cooperación y Promoción Económica Internacional, DGCPEI); Directorate General for Cooperation and Bilateral Economic Relations (Dirección General de Cooperación y Relaciones Económicas Bilaterales, DGCREB); Directorate General for Technical and Scientific Cooperation (Dirección General de Cooperación Técnica y Científica, DGCTC); and Directorate General for the Mesoamerica Integration and Development Project (Dirección General del Proyecto de Integración y Desarrollo de Mesoamérica). The restructuring of the Secretariat of Foreign Affairs in conjunction with AMEXCID's organizational expansion was not uncontroversial. For example, the area of cultural and educational cooperation that had previously enjoyed a certain degree of autonomy was reluctant to become swamped up by this new "super-structure" (also incorporating tourism with a development focus).

A "flagship" of Mexico's IDC is the Mesoamerica Integration and Development Project (Proyecto Mesoamérica), launched in 2008, formerly known as the Puebla-Panama Plan (institutionalized in 2001–2008), which includes several projects under three major pillars: first, the Central America Integration and Development Project (Proyecto de Integración y Desarrollo de Mesoamérica), which provides mechanisms for high-level political dialogue on technical cooperation, development, and integration for peace and prosperity across this region. Second, the Trust Fund for Infrastructure for Central American and Caribbean Countries (Fideicomiso Fondo de Infraestructura para Países de Mesoamérica y el Caribe), the so-called "Yucatan Fund" (Fondo de Yucatán), which is a financial instrument to support infrastructure projects for connectivity and economic development in the wider region. Third, the Central America Cooperation Program (Programa Mesoamericano de Cooperación) which promotes the exchange of knowledge and experiences within six sectors: education, health, environment, agriculture and fisheries, natural disaster prevention, and tourism.

Challenges for AMEXCID

Reflecting on AMEXCID's key challenges—organization, leadership, and resources—almost since its creation, AMEXCID was criticized for lacking a strong organization. In its early days, the Spanish Agency for IDC (AECID) was a key partner and provider of resources (capital and human). In the aftermath of the economic and financial crisis in 2008,

Spain saw drastic cuts to its IDC, which also led to a significant reduction in projects with Mexico. As the Spanish support diminished, the Germans entered with all their resources and capacities. Accordingly, in 2013, the German Agency for IDC (Deutsche Gesellschaft für Internationale Zusammenarbeit, GIZ) launched the ambitious and comprehensive Institutional Strengthening Project for the Mexican Agency for IDC, which will run until 2019, that is, beyond the 2018 general elections. It could be argued that Germany, in line with what the United Kingdom has sought to attain through bilateral cooperation in higher education and research, is targeting Mexico through this program as a way to strengthen its own nation brand and image. James Pamment (2016) has explored "the role of the nation brands of developed countries in shaping the economic development of developing countries." Obviously, GIZ has far better and more flexible room for negotiation and financial and human resources than AMEXCID, making it a de facto key player of Mexico's IDC. Naturally, this is positive for Germany's foreign policy image; not just as a champion of liberal democracy and respect for human rights but also for efficient development initiatives. As such, one could argue that the GIZ–AMEXCID collaboration forms part of "position[ing] nation brands as a key component of contemporary soft power strategies, which are intended to stimulate growth, instigate infrastructural reform, assert ideational norms, and promote the donor country as a partner of choice" (Pamment 2016). In the light of a growing proportion of IDC funding coming from the private sector or outside actors such as the German GIZ, and the prevalence of executors from other secretariats or government bodies of AMEXCID-sponsored activities, in addition to the fast-growing participation by non-state actors as implementers of Mexico's IDC, AMEXCID's role has become more of a "coordination central" or "facilitator," as AMEXCID officials themselves put it (more about this argument later).

The second challenge concerns the lack of leadership. Since it was created in 2011, AMEXCID has been led by four different executive directors (high-ranked officials and one ambassador), none of them having previous knowledge about IDC issues with the exception of María Eugenia Casar Pérez (who had been working for more than 10 years in high positions in the UN administration), taking over in November 2015. However, during autumn of 2016 she announced that she would be leaving her post, and on April 5, 2017, the President announced that he had designated Ambassador Agustín García-López Loaeza, having served as Mexico's Permanent Representative to the OECD and previously as a key player in setting up the IMEXCI, as successor, from May 8, 2017. In conclusion, frequent changes in leadership have had a negative impact on the prospects for creating an institutional memory; the tradition is that not only the Executive Director leaves the post but also his or her closest collaborators and in some respects this presents a scenario of "back to zero."

AMEXCID's third challenge relates to funding. The Secretariat of the Treasury and Public Credit and the Mexican Congress are the bodies regulating the financial resources for Mexico's IDC. Importantly, the lion's share of Mexico's IDC funding takes the form of "core contributions" to international organizations, meaning that the "same" money might actually return to Mexico through the UNDP, for example. Over the years, AMEXCID has been criticized for lacking sufficient funding to match its political ambitions. The special Mexico–Spain fund, the Mexico–Chile fund, and the Mexico–Uruguay fund operate with limited resources. Concerning wider regional cooperation, such as cultural or health cooperation programs and projects whose allocations are ensured by the implementing agencies, the Secretariat of Health and CONACULTA (the precursor to today's Secretariat of Culture), certain activities have been canceled given the shortage of funding. In addition, the widespread practice within AMEXCID of hiring and firing staff has not helped its image; a workplace associated with uncertainty, excessive working hours for low pay, and a growing young "precariat" frustrated with this situation. It is then relevant to ask: How does AMEXCID seek to convince the financing institutions, or the implementing entities, about the need for solid funding for Mexico's IDC, especially since it is marketed as a way to promote global responsibility?

Finally, there are other challenges with which AMEXCID has to deal, both internally and in collaboration with the Office of the President, other secretariats, and, in particular, organized civil society, for its ambitions of designing a new kind of Mexican soft power to reach a higher level. First, the exclusive recognition of public actors in Mexico's IDC Law; second, the RENCID register is not detailed enough to allow in-depth analysis of AMEXCID's actions, hence there is a lack of transparency about the role of the agency as a donor and recipient of development aid. The direct causes for this are: (a) Mexico's IDC Law is not really inclusive: it rests on a state-centric logic with a limited role for subnational entities, civil society, and the private sector; (b) management and resource problems persist due to technical, financial, and human resource limitations; (c) official reports are insufficient and ill-timed; and (d) the general interest by Mexican society for discussing development issues is scarce, coupled with insufficient knowledge about the potential of Mexico's IDC. As for indirect causes, suffice it to mention clientelism and corruption, lack of credibility and institutional weakness, and negative generalized perception in Mexican society of current IDC practices as based on a Global North–Global South logic (Espinosa 2017).

FEATURES OF THE INCIPIENT PUBLIC DIPLOMACY OF MEXICO'S IDC

According to a joint report by the UNDP Office Mexico and AMEXCID (2014), "the AMEXCID's role is particularly relevant regarding inter-sectorial coordination and the support for institutional and operational capacities of ministries and other Federal entities that as development solutions providers contribute to how Mexico's 'brand' is perceived abroad" (p. 24). But then one may ask: What is the corresponding PD strategy for communicating Mexico's IDC to domestic and foreign audiences? Importantly, Mexico has no tradition of relying on the Anglo-Saxon model of PD (cf. Cull 2009, 2012; Melissen 2005; Pamment 2013; Snow and Taylor 2009) that has been adopted by countries like Australia, Canada, Spain, South Korea, South Africa, and the United Kingdom, to name a few. Now, there is the particular area of cultural diplomacy that complements Mexico's foreign policy (cf. Villanueva 2012, 2015), but curiously, Mexico's IDC is still uncharted terrain for wielding a PD strategy that could possibly inspire other policy areas to develop their own PD strategies according to their needs. This situation arises from the fact that AMEXCID is still a relatively young agency and as it struggles with consolidating its internal organization and leadership, coupled with the lack of resources to carry out fully its mandate, all these factors make prospects for developing a fully fledged agency look quite bleak. In fact, the question is whether the political will exists to allow AMEXCID to grow into a more solid agency in the future.

At the same time, some of the uncertainty regarding what AMEXCID is actually doing has been related to its search for identity. For example, during 2014 some 40 workshops were held with GIZ and other actors aiming to strengthen AMEXCID's identity. One of the challenges concerned how to create a shared statement, a brand for AMEXCID, and

COMPARTIR LO MEJOR DE MÉXICO PARA ENFRENTAR RETOS GLOBALES Y CRECER JUNTOS

COOPERAR ES COMPARTIR

Fig. 9.1 Agencia Mexicana de Cooperación Internacional para el Desarrollo (AMEXCID) logo (Product names, logos, brands, and other trademarks featured or referred to on the cover of or within this book are the property of their respective trademark holders. The trademark holders are not affiliated and in no way imply an association with the publisher or the author. The trademark holders do not sponsor or endorse the publication of this book.) (*Source* www.gob.mx/ amexcid)

to promote ownership and a sense of belonging among the AMEXCID officials. Obviously, all these efforts at securing a better internal communication had another objective to develop a more efficient external communication. The "new" identity of AMEXCID was presented in August 2015, which more or less coincided with the arrival of the new Secretary of Foreign Affairs, Claudia Ruiz Massieu. Needless to say, but as AMEXCID officials have pointed out, the identity construction of the agency is an ongoing process.

The following sections highlight how AMEXCID is communicating Mexico's IDC within the country and the outside world. The special logo (see Fig. 9.1) with the "X" in red and a circle inside this letter was created in 2014, but it was not launched as an official symbol until November 2015. The symbolic meaning of it draws associations with crossroads ("Mexico as a bridging country between the Global North and Global South"), sharing, and openness ("AMEXCID as a facilitating agent for cooperation initiatives").

Another logo reveals a certain national patriotic connotation (cf. chapter by Wilkins in this book); the colors of the Mexican flag are green, white, and red (see Fig. 9.2).

Another rather recent development is a certain streamlining in the presentation of AMEXCID's activities. For many years, Mexico's

AME✕CID
AGENCIA MEXICANA
DE COOPERACIÓN INTERNACIONAL
PARA EL DESARROLLO

Fig. 9.2 Agencia Mexicana de Cooperación Internacional para el Desarrollo (AMEXCID) logo, Mexican flag (Product names, logos, brands, and other trademarks featured or referred to on the cover of or within this book are the property of their respective trademark holders. The trademark holders are not affiliated and in no way imply an association with the publisher or the author. The trademark holders do not sponsor or endorse the publication of this book.) (*Source* www.gob.mx/amexcid)

communication concerning its IDC was ad hoc and improvised. Since January 2015, a special team has been created around the Coordinator of Advisors (Coordinadora de Asesores), currently led by María Esther Pozo who has been working with media and communication strategies for the state and private sector, and her team. AMEXCID also has special coordinators for its outreach and collaboration activities with the private sector, academia, and civil society organizations, among others. Therefore, the task of communicating Mexico's IDC is co-constructed between AMEXCID's Directorate General and the five Directorate Generals responsible for the different thematic areas mentioned in the previous section.

AMEXCID's webpage (www.gob.mx/amexcid) has a streamlined presentation in harmony with the other government secretariats and agencies. This is part of the National Digital Strategy from the Office of the President launched in 2013 to encourage the use of ICTs on a larger scale and bring transparency to activities of government branches through the gradual unification of the platform "gob.mx." In fact, one could argue that AMEXCID's "communicative originality" and more independent forms of socialization with interested parties is based on how the agency makes use of social media, to be discussed below.

In the year 2016, to celebrate its five years of existence, AMEXCID invested resources to strengthen both its internal and external communication (some activities were organized in collaboration with the special program of GIZ). On October 3, the Executive Director published an

204 R. VILLANUEVA ULFGARD

article in a daily newspaper on the achievements and ambitions of the agency in the light of its "5th birthday" (Casar 2016). As for the internal dimension, to strengthen the agency's self-identification and raise staff motivation, various activities took place in order to create a greater "we-feeling," for example a storytelling exercise to develop better understanding of the array of activities performed within the agency's structures, and develop new skills for communicating AMEXCID's activities. The launch of a newsletter to spread information internally about what is going on within the agency also deserves mention. Obviously, all these efforts to strengthening AMEXCID internally are also expected to bring benefits for the external dimension and the perception of AMEXCID's, and by extension Mexico's, image as an emerging economy and ambitious IDC partner, by laying a solid ground for developing a coherent and appealing message to a wider audience.

As for PD, nowadays AMEXCID has catchy slogans like "Sharing the best of Mexico to face global challenges and grow together" (*Compartir lo mejor de México para enfrentar retos globales y crecer juntos*) and "Cooperation is sharing" (*Cooperar es Compartir*), and it is clear that the agency has invested in the link between message and image to present an appealing "total image" of its activities on Facebook and Twitter, the ultimate goal being to reflect Mexico's identity as regards IDC issues. Press releases are another instrument for communicating AMEXCID's activities. There are also fact sheets for public use about AMEXCID and the role of Mexico in the GPEDC. Clearly, there is an incipient PD strategy but the question is whether one day this will be known to the outside world, as in the examples of the Swedish SIDA or the Danish DANIDA.

Concerning *horizontal communication*, since Mexico's IDC does not operate in a vacuum within the Secretariat of Foreign Affairs there is an Advisory Council (Consejo Consultivo), whose mandate is laid down in the statutes for AMEXCID (see Chapter IV of the Law on IDC (Ley de Cooperación Internacional para el Desarrollo, LCID)).[1] It is composed of 17 Secretariats of the State, the National Council for Science and Technology (Consejo Nacional de Ciencia y Tecnología, CONACyT),

---

[1] There is also a technical committee for the Trust Fund on Mexico's international cooperation (Comité Técnico y de Administración del Fideicomiso) with representatives from the Secretary of Foreign Affairs, AMEXCID, and the Secretariat of the Treasury and Public Credit (see Article 38, LCID).

and the National Commission for the Development of Indigenous Peoples (Comisión Nacional para el Desarrollo de los Pueblos Indígenas). Its main task is to contribute to the formulation of the IDC Program and make proposals for its proper implementation. Importantly, although the LCID specifies the functions of the Advisory Council, it is conspicuously silent on the importance of communicating what AMEXCID is actually doing (perhaps one could expect that the role of Mexico's embassies and consulates would be mentioned, for example).

It is fair to say that the uninterrupted PRI governments were not keen on having civil society "meddling in" foreign policy, but since the mid-1990s, which saw Mexican NGOs engaging in transnational NGO platforms around environmental and women's issues in the run up to the North American Free Trade Agreement negotiations (1992), and as a consequence of pressure from various NGOs following conflict with the Zapatista movement (1994), along with the United Nations Economic and Social Council 1996 resolution amending the criteria for NGO accreditation to advisory status, a gradual acceptance of the idea of inviting civil society to participate in deliberations on Mexico's foreign policy has taken place (Villanueva Ulfgard 2017). Today, virtually all public policy areas have an international dimension to them that requires international cooperation and an effective form of *multi-stakeholder communication*. Hence, the field of IDC is not exempted from this trend. But, as mentioned elsewhere, Mexico has been slow to adopt a constructive and viable PD paradigm for its strategies about how to communicate its IDC activities. Now, AMEXCID has a specific ad hoc mechanism called Technical Councils (Consejos Técnicos) for the involvement of academics and scientists, the private sector, local governments, civil society, and a high-level advisors' council. The major civil society organizations (CSOs) in Mexico such as Oxfam Mexico, Save the Children Mexico, Transparency International, ALOP (Asociación Latinoamericana de Organizaciones de Promoción al Desarrollo), and others like Equipo Pueblo, CEMEFI (Centro Mexicano para la Filantropía), and Sustenta Ciudadanía, to name a few, participate in AMEXCID orchestrated actions and events, for example around Mexico's implementation of the 2030 Agenda for Sustainable Development, participation in the G20, the COPs, and other international conferences on biodiversity, climate change, and environmental policy, and the GPEDC. These organizations are led by professional advocacy members, tweeting and retweeting during events (sometimes in self-congratulatory mode), commenting on blogs, television, radio, and newspapers about Mexico's foreign policy and the role of civil society. Hence, they also give a certain spin to official messages before passing them on to new audiences.

However, some CSOs have expressed cautious sentiments about the advisory role and how meaningful it really is to partake in this mechanism. A phrase commonly heard is that of: "We sometimes feel that we are little more than nice scenery." Criticism that I have witnessed over the years relates precisely to this rather "protocol-driven" approach to civil society participation in the foreign policy domain. The cherished multi-stakeholder approach is sometimes said to be little more than a smart buzzword for preaching inclusiveness in the 2030 Agenda or the GPEDC contexts, while actually preserving unequal power relationships when such different kinds of actors are lumped together and said to be on an equal standing when it comes to advocacy and participation (Alejo 2016). In conclusion, some voices argue that it has been difficult for CSOs to be reckoned as a valid interlocutor to AMEXCID.

Regarding *communication through social media*, it is important to clarify that during the first years of its existence, as an entity embedded within the Secretariat of Foreign Affairs, AMEXCID's press releases had to pass through the central office of social communication. With the migration of AMEXCID's webpage to the gob.mx platform in 2015, the window of opportunity for using social media was left open and in fact AMEXCID made clever use of it. At another level, this illustrates how different kinds of diplomacies coexist and that traditional diplomacy with fixed channels and practices for communication are now complemented with more swift, social media based communication tailor made for specific situations engaging a variety of actors implementing Mexico's foreign policy (cf. Terrés 2011).

In order to communicate its activities and hence influence knowledge creation or simply to raise interest within the Mexican population and beyond, both AMEXCID's Facebook page (www.facebook.com/AMEXCID/?fref=ts) and its Twitter account (https://twitter.com/amexcid?lang=es) exhibit a constant flow of new tweets and retweets about Mexico's IDC related activities within the country and in the international arena. AMEXCID has a YouTube channel (www.youtube.com/user/amexcid), which is an excellent source for communicating the agency's activities. There is a concise presentation of AMEXCID's activities in Spanish with English subtitles (www.youtube.com/watch?v=7-2LF9UMiZk). However, presentations on Mexico's IDC in English are scarce. For example, there is a presentation of some of AMEXCID's officials (the Executive Director, diplomats, high-level officials, and technical staff) but without English subtitles (www.youtube.com/watch?v=vSnF-NXtjTpw). Indeed, YouTube could be used more efficiently for promoting AMEXCID, for example by live streaming more of its public events. In conclusion, it seems that the preferred channels are Facebook and Twitter, while more outreach could be desired for a non-Spanish speaking audience.

REFLECTIONS ON THE INCIPIENT PD STRATEGY FOR MEXICO'S IDC

It could be argued that Mexico's strategies for making progress with a "digital government" and greater transparency in public administration fits in with its foreign policy commitments, notably Millennium Development Goal number 8, target "F" about access to landline telephones, cellular subscribers, personal computers, and internet connectivity. According to data presented in the Mexican government's 2015 report on the accomplishment of the MDGs, in the year 2000, only 5% of the population had access to the internet, while by 2014, this benefit reached 44% (Villanueva 2017, p. 123). Moreover, Mexico (together with 75 participating countries) forms part of the Open Government Partnership, which is a "multilateral initiative that aims to secure concrete commitments from governments to promote transparency, empower citizens, fight corruption, and harness new technologies to strengthen governance" (Open Government Partnership 2015).

James Pamment reasons that the confluence of "PD, soft power and Devcom ... represent the harnessing of the participatory nature of a networked society, and the shaping of consensus through dialogue, inclusion, shared values and social practices. They support a form of persuasion based around strategic influence over knowledge, actors, technologies, norms and rules" (see Chapter 2, p. 36). According to Pamment, the objective is to seek "long-term structures of influence." Now, it is fair to say that AMEXCID has quite some road to travel in this regard, also given the fact that it has not yet evolved into a proper brand for Mexico (cf. Anholt 2003, 2012); it is still quite unknown among Mexicans and not seen as a major player among those middle income countries boasting an IDC agency such as Brazil, Chile, South Africa, and Turkey. AMEXCID's PD on SSC at best resembles a "good neighbor policy" aimed mainly at Latin American audiences. Hence it is not surprising that AMEXCID's publicity spots are mostly in Spanish since this is the language of its collaboration partners (according to AMEXCID's own tracking, roughly 85% of followers on social media are Spanish-speaking), whereas the English material is rather for a specialized wider audience involved in IDC activities. That said, reasoning with Karin Wilkins in this volume, "development branding needs to be situated within a public diplomacy framework, in which strategic communication is used to convey positive sentiments toward aid programs" (see Chapter 3, p. 51). Now, if AMEXCID does not promote itself sufficiently or sufficiently well in the current context, the question is how to communicate better Mexico's IDC to domestic and foreign audiences (cf. Del Río 2012; Inagaki 2007; Mefalopulos 2008; Storm 2012; SIDA 2006; Wilkins et al. 2014). To begin with, not all communication regarding Mexico's IDC passes through AMEXCID's official channels but is also undertaken *directly* by different collaboration partners in AMEXCID projects. This is a feature in public–private partnerships, for example, where the private stakeholders are "free to" communicate how they see their participation in specific IDC projects. It could also be interpreted as an indirect channel for AMEXCID to socialize with collaborators and recipients. As pointed out by AMEXCID officials, there is an increasing interest from Mexico's embassies and consulates, especially in Latin America, to acquire new knowledge and spread information about Mexico's IDC through AMEXCID. Therefore, AMEXCID has engaged in special information campaigns and provided tool kits (infographics), and there is a strategy for follow up (through small surveys, for example) and close dialogue with these entities.

Clearly, there is a need to communicate better the fact that Mexico's IDC forms an integral part of its foreign policy (as part of Chapter V in the National Plan for Development (2013–2018), "A Mexico of Global Responsibility") and the benefits of this relatively new policy area for Mexico in terms of the image it projects to other countries as a modern, emerging economy. AMEXCID is also helping to construct communication between different international cooperation initiatives of which it forms a part, such as the Mesoamerica Project, the "Friends of Monterrey," and the Social Cohesion Laboratory together with the European Union. While these are rather examples of internal communication between cooperation partners, nonetheless they demonstrate that communication is much more than a "nice accessory."

AMEXCID could also focus on more efficiently communicating the results of Mexico's IDC, especially in the area of SSC, by carefully identifying, selecting, and then showcasing instances that transmit "good practices" and inclusion of societal actors, like the one of "Mesoamerica Sin Hambre." This information exercise is best undertaken in a constructive dialogue between AMEXCID's "communication office," on the one hand, and secretariats, agencies, embassies, and CSOs working closer with entities in charge of implementing Mexico's IDC activities, on the other (employing more of a network approach, as can be perceived in the case of Turkey; cf. Chapter 8).

Communication with traditional media (TV, radio, and daily newspapers) about AMEXCID's achievements also needs to improve, especially considering criticism along the following lines: "Why should we Mexicans give money to poor people in Honduras when in the states of Chiapas or Guerrero people are living under conditions of extreme poverty?" Not many people in the streets know what AMEXCID is doing, and even less about its targeted programs to alleviate extreme poverty in Central American countries, for example. Therefore, to promote greater transparency and debate about development cooperation is essential, centering on, for example, Mexico's international commitments (this dimension is essential since the lion's share of Mexico's funding for IDC activities takes the form of "core contributions" to international organizations), its priorities, programs and projects, methodologies for implementation and evaluation, and challenges confronted at the implementation stage. In conclusion, continued mapping of target groups through ICT tools and engaging in broad and well-planned communications activities through both traditional and new types of media, all under the premises of participation and inclusion by a broad range of stakeholders, is key for AMEXCID's future PD strategy.

It is interesting to observe that AMEXCID officials nowadays talk about the agency in terms of a "translator" between different regions in the world; for example, AMEXCID and Mexico's National Council for the Evaluation of Social Development Policy (CONEVAL) sharing with authorities in Algeria, Morocco, Mauritania, Tunisia, and South Africa methodologies for measuring multidimensional poverty (CONEVAL 2015), and as a "facilitator" between different parties, for example, between Mexico's Secretariat of Health and corresponding counterpart in another country. Accordingly, there is an opportunity, a space, for AMEXCID to articulate this role and thereby create a narrative around a certain cooperation initiative and convey the special meanings around it. This could take the form of a storytelling exercise emphasizing the value added of this specific collaboration initiative, which also generates a positive spill over for the image identity of AMEXCID itself. In brief, AMEXCID has set out to identify good stories that are loaded with positive meaning and value added for the ongoing construction of its identity, or its brand.

To quote an AMEXCID official:

> It happens in many institutions that the areas of Monitoring and Evaluation amass information [evidence of the value added of a particular policy, in this case the IDC] that never has exited neither from the institutional area of communication, nor is it used to feed into political decision making, which ultimately impacts on the efficacy and direction of that soft power. … There we also have a function, to materialize these narratives in a responsible way with focus on quality, not only on quantity.

It should be pointed out that AMEXCID has recently engaged in a process of institutionalizing an Evaluation Policy for itself. According to the same AMEXCID official, "the vision that we had in launching this evaluation policy had different components: of course, one of them was to seek evidence to gradually improve the way in which we do cooperation, but in a complementary way, we also had the objective that evidence would constitute the substance allowing us to tell more solid stories about the changes and results of our cooperation, that is, to have evidence of soft power." With regard to challenges: "What Mexico has to do is capitalize better on the results of its IDC [available in the RENCID register], that is, find evidence of the degree of success of this policy. Until the impact of Mexico's IDC actions can be fully accounted for, it is only then possible to say more precisely where to invest specific resources to communicate (better) these actions." In other words, the "match" between PD strategy and outcome (a better image for Mexico's CID) awaits this first step. How, then, does AMEXCID seek to identify these changes on the ground? One strategy is to collect testimony from recipients and get people to change their perceptions of Mexico, according to the AMEXCID official.

Conclusion

In this chapter I have discussed the central features of Mexico's IDC and the role of AMEXCID as the coordinator, "nodal point," and implementer of this particular policy. I have also outlined elements of its incipient PD strategy to help position or "brand" Mexico as an emerging economy with the capacity for undertaking global responsibility through its IDC programs and actions. Hopefully, a more integrated and vigorous PD strategy for communicating Mexico's IDC could help position the country even better in the ongoing dialogue with other IDC agencies in Latin America and elsewhere on issues of implementing and monitoring SDGs, for example in the G20. For this to happen two factors are essential: political will and leadership; but both have been in short supply and it remains to be seen what new course of action or strategy the current Executive Director of AMEXCID will adopt.

Another challenge for developing an original PD strategy is that Mexico today is firmly locked into structures that form part of a global consensus on the desired directionality of IDC in the future aligned with neoliberal principles, in which civil society is little more than a decoration in the overall scenography. On balance then, one could ask with Gray and Gills (2016) whether Mexico over the years has contributed to "(cosmetically?) reformed institutions of global governance," thus taking part in "the consolidation of a global elite consensus on development" (p. 560), which has little concern for the criticism that the predominant development paradigm exacerbates inequalities between, and within, the Global North–Global South. Perhaps, at the end of the day, Mexico's commitment to communicating *with* and *for* other MICs on IDC is rather of a "symbolic solidarity" with the Global South, actually bringing it closer to the discourses and practices of the Global North.

One thing is certain: the increased engagement of MICs in the IDC architecture has helped tackle problems such as poverty, migration, climate change, and the effects of economic crises, which forces a rethinking of the workings of IDC architecture to adjust it to a new reality and, by extension, to lead it toward meeting the Sustainable Development Goals by 2030. Mexico in its role as "bridge" between the Global North and Global South is currently undergoing a process of consolidating its own IDC policy, while at the same time AMEXCID is championing Mexico's SSC across the region. However, two caveats should be made. First, the influence of Germany's GIZ is noticeable, effective, and, last but not least, has been made permanent (and it extends into other public policies as well: energy, agriculture, social issues). It is justified to raise concern with this exercise of German soft power as regards both the premises and scope of AMEXCID's institutionalization and activities. Second, there is a need for debate on the growing presence of public–private partnerships in SSC and what some of the risks are with this practice in MICs like Mexico, a country plagued by corruption, lack of transparency, and without functioning accountability mechanisms. This is why it is urgent to discuss the PD strategy for Mexico's IDC under a genuinely open approach and not in isolation (conducted within the Secretariat of Foreign Affairs, with or without German influence) but *together* with major stakeholders such as the private sector, international/ regional organizations, civil society organizations, and academia—and beyond the mere rhetoric of a multi-stakeholder approach.

Acknowledgements The author wishes to thank Juan Carlos Chimal, Samantha Reyes, and Juan Carlos Varillas for their help with background research, and Edgar Domínguez, Iván Espinosa, and Lorena López for their comments. Important insights into AMEXCID's organization and communication strategies were provided through interviews with AMEXCID diplomats and officials, and representatives from civil society organizations. A special thanks to James Pamment for valuable input at the draft stage of this chapter.

REFERENCES

Alejo Jaime, A. (2016, October 28). *Diplomacia de las Organizaciones de Sociedad Civil en un mundo global.* Lecture Delivered at the Master's Program in International Cooperation for Development, Instituto Mora, Mexico City.

AMEXCID (Agencia Mexicana de Cooperación Internacional para el Desarrollo). (n.d.). Cooperación Internacional Para el Desarrollo Otorgada Por México en 2014. Retrieved from https://infoamexcid.sre.gob.mx/amexcid/ccid2014/index.html.

Anholt, S. (2003). *Brand New Justice: How Branding Places and Products Can Help the Developing World.* Oxford, UK: Elsevier Butterworth-Heinemann.

———. (2012). Mito y realidad. La imagen internacional de México. *Revista Mexicana de Política Exterior* 96 (pp. 109–129). Mexico: Instituto Matías Romero.

Ayala Martínez, C., & Pérez Pineda, J. A. (Eds.). (2009). *México y los países de renta media en la cooperación internacional para el desarrollo: ¿hacia a dónde vamos?* Mexico: Instituto Mora, Cideal: FLACSO México.

Bracho, G. (2015). *In Search of a Narrative for Southern Providers. The Challenge of the Emerging Economies to the Development Cooperation Agenda* (Discussion Paper 1). DIE (German Development Institute). Retrieved from https://www.die-gdi.de/uploads/media/DP_1.2015.pdf.

Bracho, G., & García, A. (2011). México y el CAD: una relación en construcción, *Revista Española de Desarrollo y Cooperación, La Cooperación Internacional para el Desarrollo de México: Perfiles, retos y perspectivas* (No. 28, pp. 67–79).

Casar Pérez, M. E. (2016, October 3). Cinco años de la Amexcid contribuyendo al desarrollo global. *Excelsior*. Retrieved from http://www.excelsior.com.mx/opinion/mexico-global/2016/10/03/1120262.

Consejo Nacional de Evaluación de la Política de Desarrollo Social (CONEVAL). (2015, February 4). *Firman Coneval y Amexcid convenio de colaboración para impulsar cooperación internacional, comunicado de prensa núm* (No. 1), México D. F. Retrieved from https://www.coneval.org.mx/SalaPrensa/Comunicadosprensa/Documents/Firman-Coneval-y-AMEXCID-convenio.pdf.

Cooper, A. (2012). Las potencias emergentes y el nuevo multilateralismo. *Revista Mexicana de Política Exterior* 94 (pp. 139–162). Mexico: Instituto Matías Romero.

Cull, N. J. (2009). Diplomacia Pública: consideraciones teóricas. *Revista Mexicana de Política Exterior* 85 (pp. 55–92). Mexico: Instituto Matías Romero.

———. (2012). El futuro de la Diplomacia Pública: implicaciones para México. *Revista Mexicana de Política Exterior* 96 (pp. 45–73). Mexico: Instituto Matías Romero.

Del Río, O. (2012). *Comunicación sobre/para resultados de desarrollo de iniciativas de cooperación pública*. Barcelona, España: Programa URB-AL III. Retrieved from https://www1.diba.cat/uliep/pdf/52252.pdf.

Diario Oficial de la Federación. (2011, April 6). LEY DE COOPERACIÓN INTERNACIONAL PARA EL DESARROLLO. Retrieved from http://www.diputados.gob.mx/LeyesBiblio/pdf/LCID_171215.pd.

Espinosa, I. (2017). *Modelling Mexico's Challenges Regarding Its International Development Cooperation Policy*. Executive Director, Observatory for International Cooperation (Observatorio Cooperación Internacional), Instituto Mora, Mexico City. Unpublished material.

Figueroa Fischer, B. (2016). *Cien años de cooperación internacional de México, 1900–2000: Solidaridad, intereses y geopolítica*. Ciudad de México: Secretaría de Relaciones Exteriores/Acervo Histórico Diplomático.

Gray, K., & Gills, B. K. (2016). South–South Cooperation and the Rise of the Global South. *Third World Quarterly, 37*(4), 557–574.

Inagaki, N. (Ed.). (2007). *Communicating the Impact of Communication for Development: Recent Trends in Empirical Research* (World Bank Working Paper No. 120). Washington, DC: The World Bank.

Kirton, J. J. (2012). El G20, el G8, el G5 y el papel de las potencias en ascenso. *Revista Mexicana de Política Exterior* 94 (pp. 163–200). Mexico: Instituto Matías Romero.

Lätt, J., & Öztürk, A. (2008). *Change, Power, and Responsibility: Emerging Powers as New Partners for Global Structural Policy*. DIE, Productor. Retrieved from https://www.die-gdi.de/uploads/media/Column_Laett.OEztuerk_09.02.2009.pdf.

Lázaro Rüther, L., Ayala Martínez, C., & Müller, U. (Eds.). (2014). *Fondos y redes globales: reduciendo la brecha entre políticas globales y la implementación nacional*. Mexico: Instituto Mora.

Leutner, J., & Müller, U. (2010). Ownership in Practice. In S. Frenken & U. Müller (Eds.), *Ownership and Political Steering in Developing Countries* (pp. 47–59). Baden-Baden: Nomos.

Lightfoot, S., & Soyeun, K. (2011). Does 'DAC-ability' Really Matter? The Emergence of Non-DAC Donors: Introduction to Policy Arena. *Journal of International Development, 23*(5), 711–721.

Lozoya, J. A. (2001). La nueva política de cooperación internacional de México. *Foro Internacional, XLI*(4), 931–938.

Maihold, G. (2014). BRICS, MIST, MIKTA: México entre poderes emergentes, potencias medias y responsabilidad global. *Revista Mexicana de Política Exterior* 100 (pp. 63–79). Mexico: Instituto Matías Romero.

Mefalopulos, P. (2008). *Development Communication Sourcebook. Broadening the Boundaries of Communication*. Washington, DC: The World Bank.

Melissen, J. (Ed.). (2005). *The New Public Diplomacy. Soft Power in International Relations*. London and New York: Palgrave Macmillan.

Open Government Partnership. (2015). ACERCA DE LA ALIANZA PARA EL GOBIERNO ABIERTO. Retrieved from http://www.opengovpartnership.org/about.

Pamment, J. (2013). *New Public Diplomacy in the 21st Century. A Comparative Study of Policy and Practice*. London and New York: Routledge.

———. (2016). Towards a New Conditionality? The Convergence of International Development, Nation Brands and Soft Power in the British National Security Strategy. *Journal of International Relations & Development*, 1–19. https://doi.org/10.1057/s41268-016-0074-9.

Pérez Pineda, J., Ayala Martínez, C., & De la O López, F. (2015). *Diagnóstico sobre la cooperación internacional para el desarrollo*. México: Instituto Mora.

Piefer, N. (2014). *Experiences of Middle-Income Countries in Development Cooperation*. Study prepared for Agencia Mexicana de Cooperación Internacional para el Desarrollo (AMEXCID) and Deutsche Gesellschaft für Internationale Zusammenarbeit (GIZ). México, DF. Retrieved from https://www.researchgate.net/publication/277877710.

Prado Lallande, J. P. (2013). La cooperación internacional para el desarrollo de la política exterior del presidente Calderón. *Foro Internacional, LIII*(3–4), 816–844.

———. (2015). *Mexico's Role in Development Cooperation: Bridging North and South*. United Nations University Centre for Policy Research. Retrieved from http://ssc.undp.org/content/dam/ssc/documents/news/2015/UNUCPR_MexicosRoleinDevelopmentCooperation_Lallande_.pdf.

Presidencia de la República. (2013). *Plan Nacional de Desarrollo 2013–2018*. Mexico City: Presidencia de la República. Retrieved from http://pnd.gob. mx/wp-content/uploads/2013/05/PND.pdf.

Schmukler, B., Ayala Martínez, C., & Sánchez Gutiérrez, G. (Eds.). (2008). *Construyendo los temas clave de la cooperación internacional para el desarrollo en México*. México, DF: Instituto Mora, Porrúa.

Sidiropoulos, E., Pérez Pineda, J. A., Chaturvedi, S., & Fues, T. (Eds.). (2015). *Institutional Architecture & Development: Responses from Emerging Powers*. Midrand, ZA: South African Institute of International Affairs.

Snow, N., & Taylor, P. M. (Eds.). (2009). *Routledge Handbook of Public Diplomacy*. London and New York: Routledge.

Soto Narváez, F. (2014). New Schemes of Horizontal Cooperation Among Emerging Countries: The Mexico-Chile Fund. In L. Lázaro Rüther, C. Ayala Martínez, & U. Müller (Eds.), *Fondos y redes globales: reduciendo la brecha entre políticas globales y la implementación nacional* (pp. 273–280). Mexico: Instituto Mora.

Storm Braskov, R. (2012). *Social Media in Development Cooperation*. Malmö, Sweden: Ørecomm Centre for Communication and Glocal Change. Retrieved from https://orecomm.net/wp-content/uploads/2012/04/SocialMediaOrecomm2011.pdf.

Suárez Dávila, F. (2006). México en la transformación de la OCDE: 1997–2000. *Políticas públicas para un mejor Desempeño Económico. Experiencias del Mundo para el Desarrollo, México 10 años en la OCDE*. Paris: Organisation for Economic Co-operation and Development.

SIDA (Swedish International Development Cooperation Agency). (2006). *Dialogue and Strategic Communication in Development Cooperation*. Stockholm, Sweden: SIDA. Retrieved from http://www.sida.se/contentas-sets/b4b1a8018a804e02848e716ca71cacb7/dialogue-and-strategic-commu-nication-in-development-cooperation_1399.pdf.

Terrés, C. G. (2011). Diplomacia pública 2.0: una propuesta virtual para un mundo real. *Revista Mexicana de Política Exterior* 92 (pp. 97–126). Mexico: Instituto Matías Romero.

United Nations Development Programme (UNDP). (2014). *Towards a Global Partnership for Development. The UN and Mexico's South–South Cooperation*. Mexico City. Retrieved from http://www.mx.undp.org/content/dam/mex-ico/docs/Publicaciones/PublicacionesGobernabilidadDemocratica/css/UNDP-MX-CSS-English.pdf.

Vega, B. (2014). Country Study Mexico. In N. Piefer (Ed.), *Experiences of Middle Income Countries in Development Cooperation. Experiences of Middle-Income Countries in Development Cooperation*. Study prepared for Agencia Mexicana de Cooperación Internacional para el Desarrollo (AMEXCID) and Deutsche Gesellschaft für Internationale Zusammenarbeit (GIZ). México,

DF. Retrieved from https://www.researchgate.net/publication/277877710_
Experiences_Of_Middle_Income_Countries_in_Development_Cooperation.
Villanueva, C. (2012). Imagen país y política exterior de México. *Revista
Mexicana de Política Exterior* 96 (pp. 13–43). Mexico: Instituto Matías
Romero.

———. (2015). The Use of the Spanish Language as a Cultural Diplomacy
Strategy for Extending Mexico's Soft Power in the United States. *Place
Branding and Public Diplomacy, 11*(2), 139–147.

———. (2017). The Image of Mexico Abroad in the Context of the Millennium
Development Goals: Lessons for Public Diplomacy. In R. Villanueva Ulfgard
(Ed.), *Mexico and the Post-2015 Development Agenda: Contributions and
Challenges* (pp. 105–127). New York: Palgrave Macmillan.

Villanueva Ulfgard, R. (2017). Mexico from the Millennium Development
Goals to the Sustainable Development Goals: Congruence and Dissonance in
Development Compromises. In R. Villanueva Ulfgard (Ed.), *Mexico and the
Post-2015 Development Agenda: Contributions and Challenges* (pp. 17–51).
New York: Palgrave Macmillan.

Villanueva Ulfgard, R., & López Chacón, L. (2017). In Search of Making a
Difference: Mexico in the OECD International Development Co-operation
Architecture. *Development Policy Review.* https://doi.org/10.1111/
dpr.12224.

Wilkins, K., Tufte, T., & Obregon, R. (Eds.). (2014). *Handbook of Development
Communication and Social Change* (IAMCR Series). Oxford: Wiley-Blackwell.

Zimmermann, F., & Smith, K. (2011). More Actors, more Money, more Ideas
for International Development Co-operation. *Journal of International
Development, 23,* 722–738.

CHAPTER 10

Power Relations in Development Communication and Public Diplomacy: US and Chinese Practices in Afghanistan

Di Wu

Development assistance and public diplomacy are two intellectual fields emerging from a shared geopolitical and conceptual context (Pamment 2015). Some development assistance programs are seen as a component of public diplomacy or as sharing public diplomacy goals (Kerry 2011). Whereas public diplomacy is defined as managing relationships with foreign publics, development assistance can be regarded as managing social change (Pamment 2016). International development relies much on resource transfer, or simply "foreign assistance." Public diplomacy, as pointed out in Chapter 2, can be defined as attempts to invest resources which produce desired outcomes in foreign societies. In other words, the intersection of public diplomacy and international development lies in the transfer of resources between actors.

D. Wu (✉)
American University, Washington, DC, USA
e-mail: di.wu@american.edu

© The Author(s) 2018
J. Pamment and K. G. Wilkins (eds.), *Communicating National Image through Development and Diplomacy*, Palgrave Studies in Communication for Social Change, https://doi.org/10.1007/978-3-319-76759-8_10

Specifically, resource transaction is mostly manifested in communication *for* development, which is the focus of this chapter. In his recent work, Pamment (2016) proposed three levels of intersection between development and public diplomacy. They are communication *for* development, communication *of* development, and communication *about* development. Communication *for* development refers to actual interactions between development organizations and foreign publics through aid. Communication *of* development involves promoting aid activities, which can, for example, increase the donor county's soft power and improve its national image. Communication *about* development can reach public diplomacy goals through setting agendas and shaping discourses within development communities.

However, even though communication *for* development and public diplomacy share the feature of resource transfer, their distinct objectives suggest the two are walking on different paths. Public diplomacy is the process of exercising soft power for donor countries. It aims to affect the other country to obtain the outcomes it wants through attracting foreign publics rather than through coercion or payment (Nye 2008). The field of development communication is different. It aligns the desired outcomes of both developing and development communities (Pamment 2015). The empowerment framework of development communication even argues that it is preferable for development practices to empower local communities rather than center on the needs of donors (Melkote 2003). Thus, an inconsistency arises between the compatibility of who exercises power and for whose interest.

In order to understand better the intersections and differences of the two fields, in this chapter I try to investigate further the power relations of resource transfer in development communication and public diplomacy. I apply the concept of network theory and rely on a structuralist perspective that uses network centrality measurements to explore the power relations between aid donors and recipients. In this chapter I first introduce the theoretical perspective of power relations in development communication and public diplomacy. I connect the empowerment theory of development with social network theory. Next, I present the two case studies on US and Chinese development assistance to Afghanistan. I then discuss the empirical findings of the case studies and provide implications for practice. I conclude with a summary and limitations.

POWER RELATIONS IN RESOURCE TRANSFER

Traditionally, development communication and public diplomacy have operated in two separate spheres. Over the years, both in scholarship and practice, the two fields show a converging trend. This section untangles the theoretical strands and reveals power relations of resource transfer in the two fields.

INTERNATIONAL COMMUNICATION, DEVELOPMENT, AND PUBLIC DIPLOMACY

Public diplomacy is primarily an instrument used by government institutions to build and manage relationships with foreign publics, influence their perspectives, and mobilize their actions for the purpose of advancing national interests and values (Gregory 2014). As introduced above, three levels of intersection between development and public diplomacy proposed by Pamment (2016) delineate different roles played by communication that connect international development with public diplomacy. Communication *for* development is the process of resource transfer, while communication *of* development is telling this story to the world.

Communicative activities within the framework of development that have public diplomacy implications are considered to be communication *for* development. Within the practice of development and aid, many communication campaigns are utilized to effect development change (Snyder 2003). Different kinds of media have been used by development agencies to spread information rapidly in a local community. The goal is to educate and raise awareness for issues such as health, environment, and family planning (Snyder 2003). In the meantime, disseminating information about specific knowledge can have a spillover effect intentionally or unintentionally, which is the exposure of the donor country. In other words, communication campaigns *for* development can achieve public diplomacy goals. Lee and Smith (2011) as well as Feldbaum and Michaud (2010) have argued that global health has been used by governments to pursue foreign policy goals of increasing the country's soft power. One majority staff report prepared for the use of the U.S. Senate Committee on Foreign Relations stated, "the administration has been using aid to 'win hearts and minds'" (Kerry 2011, p. 4). Another US report from the

Cold War era suggested, "economic development in the South would be good not only for the countries involved, it would, in the view of practitioners, serve the larger purpose of limiting the international spread of communism" (McDowell 2003, p. 8).

Communication *of* development can be seen as a tool to publicize what the donor has done to transfer resource to the recipient country. If public diplomacy is a method to publicize foreign policy, communication *of* development is a process that utilizes communication to promote the action of aid, which in turn reaches public diplomacy objectives such as boosting soft power or changing a foreign policy towards a favorable direction. Therefore, communication *for* development may be composed of indirect impacts; communication *of* development is direct and deliberate. The information aspect of public diplomacy, which consists of publications, speeches, and international broadcasting, is similar to the function of communication *of* development in that they both convey information through various ways to the target population. In the current information era, it also includes communication in cyberspace.

Countries have been utilizing communication *of* development to boost their soft power and national image. For example, Ibahrine (2016) examined the Arab Gulf countries' nation branding that combines national development through sports diplomacy. The message about development was incorporated into nation branding to showcase the country. Another example is Japan's preservation of Angkor, which is part of its public diplomacy that improved its national image and strengthened its regional power (He 2018).

POWER AND EMPOWERMENT IN DEVELOPMENT COMMUNICATION

As suggested above, development communication and public diplomacy have common grounds and sometimes refer to the same diplomatic practices. The two fields represent interests of different actors. According to the definition of public diplomacy, no matter what the means are, public diplomacy always aims to advance national interests and values (Gilboa 2008). These interests and values are achieved by and strengthen the country's increased soft power (Nye 2008). From the perspective of development communication, empowering the recipient country's communication capacity is the core argument of empowerment theory (Melkote 2003). Although a debate exists in development communication between modernization theory and empowerment theory (the former still focuses on the donor), the rising of the empowerment framework in theory and practice calls to shift the paradigm to the aid recipients (Melkote 2003).

Globalization and technological development is driving rapid and dramatic change in communication and, at the core of this changing landscape, is the emergence of network forms of organizations (Monge and Contractor 2003). A network is constituted by a set of actors connected by ties (Borgatti and Foster 2003). For Foucault (1980), power constitutes a network of social relations. Public diplomacy, looking from the perspective of social networks, is a process of a governing actor gaining network power (soft power) through networking with other various actors to manage relationships with foreign publics. In the end, the objective is to obtain or increase the persuasive power to meet the country's national interests.

In contrast to the objective of public diplomacy, development communication is moving towards the empowerment approach. Melkote (2003) suggests two frameworks in theories of communication *for* development: modernization and empowerment. This distinction draws attention to the power relations in development communication. The modernization framework emphasizes the role of mass media on social change and media is an important agent of modernization (Lerner 1958; Schramm 1964). The idea is that by exposure to mass media, people in the Third World can potentially learn modernization with structure of life, values, and behaviors with ones seen in modern Western society (Melkote 2003). Empowerment theory focuses on empowerment of marginalized individuals, groups, and organizations. Empowering theorists believe that power inequality is the major problem to be addressed in development. The problem of the modernization approach is that it ignores the power issue (imbalance between donor and recipient) in development that is seen as critical by empowering theorists (Melkote 2003).

Empowerment is defined as the process in which different social actors gain control over social and economic conditions (Rappaport 1981). As Pamment (2015) pointed out, "the circulation of information is not considered neutral or objective, but rather as a reflection of power relations" (p. 190). The empowering framework in development communication emphasizes the concept of control in the hands of the local community (Melkote 2003). More specifically, empowerment is "an intentional, ongoing process centered in the local community, involving mutual respect, critical reflection, caring and group participation, through which people lacking an equal share of valued resources gain greater access to and control over those resources" (Cornell Empowerment Group 1989, p. 2). An empowerment framework calls for grassroots organizing and communicative social action with those who have been marginalized (Melkote and Steeves 2001). The major objective of empowerment is to "move the locus of control from outsiders and to the individuals and groups directly affected" (Melkote and Steeves 2001, p. 366).

The debate between modernization and empowerment theory points to two distinctive and divergent perspectives of power. The donor and recipient dichotomy in development communication roughly resembles the interactions between two kinds of actors in public diplomacy: government/governing actors versus foreign publics. The debate between modernization theory and empowerment theory portends two divergent discourses of the two fields. First, as pointed out above, power relations exist in both development communication and public diplomacy. Development communication can be a means to achieve donors' political and economic objectives. Similarly, public diplomacy aims to seek power for direct policy change in another country or increased soft power for the governing actor. The second discourse centers around the normative or idealistic notion that development should be empowering local communities and that development communication should be based on participatory communication and dialogical interactions (Dagron 2001). Not surprisingly, some studies in public diplomacy also advocate this view and believe that public diplomacy should be based on two-way communication and pursue mutual benefits (Cowan and Arsenault 2008).

In practice, the two discourses are often intertwined. For the purpose of publicizing foreign aid, communication *of* development usually claims that assistance is for the benefits of local populations. To some extent, this is not just rhetoric. A stabilized country or region can be of a great strategic interest to other countries due to the increasing interdependency brought by globalization. But in fact, communication *of* development represents the interests of the donor country. It publicizes what the donor country has done to help the aid recipients. On the one hand, actions of aid and development assistance should be considering the interests of the recipients. On the other hand, communication *of* development prioritizes the interests of the donor country.

Although the objectives are different, these two interests can peacefully coincide, because the latter does not interfere with the conduct of aid but mainly publicizes the activities.

However, in communication *for* development, there is a tension of power relations. On the one hand, both development communication and public diplomacy are deemed to be serving donor countries' national interests, or are at least based on mutual interests (Fitzpatrick 2007; Hook 1995). As an important actor in development communication, transnational media have been traditionally considered to be tied to national interests (McDowell 2003). In terms of public diplomacy, engaging with foreign publics is considered as the presentation and representation of national interests and often in support of foreign policy goals (Fitzpatrick 2007). This is perhaps the reason why the idea of cultural imperialism was put forward by Schiller (1976). On the other hand, the recent trend of empowering the recipient communities, as argued by the empowerment theorists, benefits the country's development and government (Melkote and Steeves 2001). Similarly, in public diplomacy literature, there is also a paradigm shift to emphasize the relational and collaborative approaches (Fisher 2013; Zaharna et al. 2013). These approaches try to look beyond the traditional communication mode of information dissemination to include relationship-based dialogical interactions that facilitate mutual understanding, cooperation, and co-creation of meanings, which are believed to be effective and influential (Cowan and Arsenault 2008).

So, we not only see the different power relations based on the theories of development communication and public diplomacy, but also witness their intertwined relations in practice. To further understand this empirically, I suggest that social network analysis may be a lens to explore the process.

SOCIAL NETWORK THEORY AND DEVELOPMENT NETWORKS

The two theoretical traditions introduced above indicate a contradiction between a perspective that powers the donor and another that empowers the recipient. To further understand the phenomenon, it is necessary to look at empirical cases. Social network analysis is introduced to this study not only because there is a relational turn in public diplomacy literature (Kent et al. 2016; Zaharna et al. 2013), but also because network theory can help explain how individuals and organizations behave and how relations are linked to patterns in society (Borgatti et al. 2009). Relations do not exist in a vacuum; "individuals are embedded in thick webs of social relations and interactions" (Borgatti et al. 2009, p. 892). Network analysis can help to examine the power relations from the structural perspective.

Multiple measurements of social network analysis can offer explanations for the power relations in the field of development communication. Concerning the overall network structure, there are two perspectives in social network theories: structuralist vs connectionist (Borgatti and Foster 2003). The structuralist perspective (topology) mainly concerns structural capital such as position-based power differentiation. For the structuralist, networks are considered as "the actor's environment or context for action and providing opportunities and constraints on behavior" (Borgatti and Foster 2003, p. 1000). Structuralist approaches tend to neglect the content of the ties and focus on the patterns of interconnection. Conversely, the connectionist perspective focuses on the resources that flow through social ties. A network actor is successful because he or she can access different kinds of resources controlled by his or her connections, including information, money, power, and material aid (Borgatti and Foster 2003). Here the emphasis is on the ties not the network positions (Marsden and Campbell 1984). Tie strength measurements include frequency of contact, mutual acknowledgement of contact, the extent of multiplexity within a tie, the duration of the contact, the provision of emotional support and aid, the social homogeneity of the actors, the overlap of memberships in organizations, and the overlap of social circles (Granovetter 1974; Lin and Dumin 1986; Putnam et al. 1994).

The two network perspectives have a close connection to the concept of social capital. Social capital is defined as "a kind of capital that can create for certain individuals or groups a competitive advantage in pursuing their ends" (Burt 2001, p. 32). Specifically, scholars argue that social capital accessed through interorganizational networks facilitates exchange and provides various kinds of benefits (Inkpen and Tsang 2005; Lin 1999; Nahapiet and Ghoshal 1998; Putnam et al. 1994). Some scholars believe the condition of closure and density in social networks is the premise of social capital (Bourdieu and Johnson 1993; Coleman 1988), while others argue that network structure, especially the structural hole, is "an opportunity to broker the flow of information between people, and control the projects that bring together people from opposite sides of the hole" (Burt 2001, p. 35).

While admitting that both structuralist and connectionist views can offer explanations for the power relations in the field of development communication, in this study I took the structuralist approach and try to illustrate the network structure rather than the nature and strength of ties. In order to do so, I adopted the network measurement of centrality. In social network theory, centrality can measure network power, especially the prominence and importance of a network actor. Freeman (1978) provided three methods for centrality measurement: degree, betweenness, and closeness. Degree measures potential communication activity through the number of ties associated with a network actor (Freeman 1978; Monge and Contractor 2003). Betweenness is an index for control of communication, and it "measures the extent to which a node serves as an intermediary 'between' other nodes in the network" (Monge and Contractor 2003, p. 38). Here node means a network actor. Closeness reflects dependency or efficiency of communication or communication speed (Freeman 1978). It is measured by the extent to which a network actor is directly or indirectly connected to all other actors in the network (Monge and Contractor 2003). In sum, an actor's network power can be measured by its total ties, the probability that it locates between other actors, and direct connections to all other network actors. A network actor needs to connect directly to all other actors in the network in order to obtain network power.

Centrality is a structuralist measurement that focuses on network actors. A traditional view of public diplomacy places governments or governing actors at the center as they quest for soft power. From the perspective of centrality, public diplomacy actors hoping to boost soft power need to access more network power through directly connecting to others in the network, especially the target publics. It should also have more ties and broker more connections. New public diplomacy and relational approaches to public diplomacy slightly moved the power attention beyond solely governmental and governing actors. They at least try to focus on the mutual and collaborative relations. But in the end, public diplomacy is a tool for government or other governing actors to persuade foreign publics (Melissen 2005), thus it places more emphasis on the power of governmental and governing actors.

Communication *for* development or development in general does not necessarily agree with the above power relations that places donors at the core. The goal of empowerment theory is to give power to people, social justice, and build capacity and equity (Melkote 2003). The key is to empower local organizations and communities. Therefore, according to empowerment theory and the network structuralist perspective, local actors or aid recipients need to connect directly to all other network actors and locate more often between other actors. This standpoint that centers around the recipients does not align with the public diplomacy objective that pursues donor country's network power, because public diplomacy first and foremost pursues the country's national interests. The following case study of US and Chinese development assistances to Afghanistan helps concretely to illustrate the difference between the power argument of public diplomacy and the empowerment perspective in development communication.

CASE EXAMPLE: US DEVELOPMENT ASSISTANCE TO AFGHANISTAN

Afghanistan was among the top recipients of US aid worldwide in 2012 (InsideGov). US assistance to Afghanistan covers several areas, the most important two being security support and development assistance. Security support refers to the US "equipment, training, and mentoring to police and army forces" (Tarnoff 2010, p. 10). Development assistance involves economic, social, and political efforts to stabilize and strengthen the Afghan environment (Tarnoff 2010). The US Department of Defense, the US Agency for International Development (USAID), and the Department of State are the key US agencies providing aid to Afghanistan. While development assistance is the focus of this study, it cannot be separated from security support because the latter not only is the largest portion of US assistance but also sets the foundation for other development programs (Tarnoff 2010).

The USA provides aid directly to the Afghanistan government or through contractors. A contractor is an intermediary NGO or for-profit organization hired by the donor to help implement aid projects (Martens et al. 2004). "The U.S. government relies heavily on contractors and sub-contractors in Afghanistan for aid projects. Contractors support direct-hire personnel, implement assistance projects, and address U.S. government workforce shortfalls" (Kerry 2011, p. 18). In fiscal year 2009 and the first half of fiscal year 2010, there were 537,405 contractors in Afghanistan (GAO 2010). During the same period, the Departments of Defense, the Department of State, and the USAID collectively reported obligations of at least $17.2 billion on contracts and various assistance instruments to support US efforts in Afghanistan (GAO 2011).

US outsourcing aid to private parties is thought to provide governments' development assistance agencies with more flexibility, productivity, and cost reductions (Berrios 2000; Huysentruyt 2011; Martens et al. 2004). It started in the 1980s with new directions at USAID (Berrios 2000). The idea was based on the notion that the private sector is the "best engine for promoting development and stimulating growth" (Berrios 2000, p. 12). Adapted from Murrell's (2004) chart, Fig. 10.1 delineates the relationship between donor, recipient, and contractor. The donor government institution (such as USAID) as the donor agent administers the details of the aid program. The recipients are the Afghan government and communities. The contractor is the implementor of the aid project. It has a contractual relationship with the donor and bargaining relationship with the recipient. While using contractors is not without problems (GAO 2011), it still remains one of the major implementors of US foreign assistance.

From the network point of view, contractors locate between US government institutions and local communities (see Fig. 10.1). The contractor is a more powerful actor than both donor agent and recipient principal in this triadic relationship because information or resources has to go through the contractor from the donor to the recipient or vice versa. Therefore, the betweenness score of the contractor is higher than the US government institution. A network actor with high betweenness is critical to the network. Studies of social networks suggest, "when a person is strategically located on the communication paths linking pairs of others, that person is central. A person in such a position can influence the group by withholding or distorting information in transmission" (Freeman 1978, p. 221).[1]

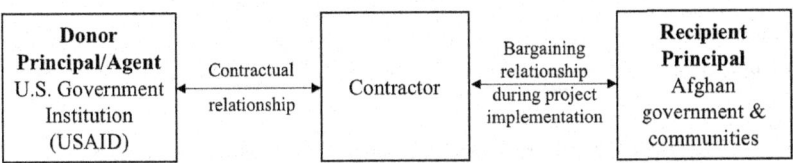

Fig. 10.1 US development aid through contractors (*Source* Adapted from Murrell 2004)

Fig. 10.2   US development aid through local government

Another strategy of US aid to Afghanistan is sending aid directly to the Afghan government (see Fig. 10.2). In order to increase the sustainability of aid programs, the USA has been supporting the Afghan government in providing basic services in security and development (Armitage and Markey 2014). The USA provided training for the Afghan security forces and worked with local officials to reduce corruption of local and national governments (Armitage and Markey 2014). The idea is to allow the Afghan people to develop security forces so that they can defend themselves when the US troops leave; the national and local government continue to provide quality services to the Afghan people; and ultimately the democratic system can be sustained and continue to bring welfare to the Afghan people. The areas of US aid include agriculture, education, economy, and health. Although there are some problems about this approach of aiding the Afghan government (GAO 2014; Olmstead 2014), it is still one major approach of US assistance to Afghanistan.

From the network perspective, the Afghan government locates between the US government institutions and local communities (see Fig. 10.2). In this triadic relationship, the US aid institution has lesser network power than the Afghan government. This can be analyzed not only by betweenness centrality but also closeness centrality. A network actor with high closeness centrality means that it is close to all other actors in the network and can avoid the potential control of others (Freeman 1978).[2] It also measures how quickly the actor can interact with others. The US donor agent does not interact directly with local communities but through the Afghan government. The closeness score of the donor agent is lower than the recipient principal.

CHINA'S DEVELOPMENT ASSISTANT TO AFGHANISTAN

Chinese assistance to Afghanistan focuses on economic rather than military projects because of its strategic considerations (van der Kley 2014). China has avoided becoming entangled in the internal affairs of

Afghanistan (Tiezzi 2014). Chinese official media claimed that Afghan competing forces are represented by foreign interests: Pakistan, India, other countries in central Asia, and Gulf states. Because different countries may have interests that clash with each other, and because they are all China's neighbors and even strategic partners, it is difficult to coordinate China's position on Afghanistan. Once China enters the "battlefield," a loss is probably inevitable (Yuan 2015). Therefore, China's economic aid has been focused on its traditional strength of building basic infrastructure (van der Kley 2014). For example, China has provided diplomatic support, humanitarian aid, and financial assistance to Afghanistan. It has engaged in building hospitals, roads (Karakorum Highway), and water resources (Tiezzi 2014).

Although not comparable to US aid, China's economic aid in Afghanistan has been increasing. Between 2001 and 2013, China provided Afghanistan with a total of RMB 1.5 billion (approximately $240 million) of aid. In 2014 alone, China provided Afghanistan with RMB 500 million ($80 million) of aid and pledged to provide an additional RMB 1.5 billion ($240 million) over the next three years (Zhao 2015). During Afghan President Ghani's visit to China in 2014, he "was rewarded with major new commitments from Beijing—a pledge of 2 billion RMB ($327 million) in aid to Afghanistan through 2017, which will more than double the $250 million China has thus far contributed to Afghanistan since 2001. In addition, China promised to provide personnel training for 3000 Afghanistan professionals as well as helping develop Afghan agriculture, hydroelectricity, and infrastructure" (Tiezzi 2014). China has also invested much in education. It promises to provide 500 scholarships for Afghan students to study in China and offer textbooks and facilities for schools and education institutions (Zhu 2014).

In 2016, as part of its Belt and Road Initiative and the peace mission of the Quadrilateral Cooperation Group, China started to send military aid to the Afghanistan government (Khalil 2016). The aid was to help Afghanistan combat terrorism (Gul 2016). Unlike Western allies of Afghanistan that offered weapons and air fighters, Chinese military aid was mainly limited to training and equipment (Khalil 2016). It was directly sent to the government, especially the Afghan National Defense and Security Forces.

Another important part of Chinese development assistance to Afghanistan is in the form of investment. It is important to note that although foreign investment is different from foreign aid, it can help less developed countries to break the vicious cycle of poverty, bring advanced technologies, managerial, and marketing skills, and easier access to export markets (Soubbotina and Sheram 2000). Therefore, in terms of results, the Chinese state-owned enterprises' investment to Afghanistan is an important part of Chinese development assistance. Two prominent examples are the oil field exploitation and the Mes Aynak copper mine in the Logar province. In December 2011, China and Afghanistan signed a 25-year deal that allowed China's state-owned National Petroleum Corporation to become the first foreign company to develop oil and natural gas reserves (Tiezzi 2014). China has also invested heavily in the Aynak copper mine through state-owned enterprises, China Metallurgical Construction Company and Jiangxi Copper. The Chinese companies also pledged to build more infrastructure, some of which will benefit the broader economy (Downs 2013). For example, a rail line linking the mine to the other parts of the country will be built, thus bringing huge transformations to Afghan society (The Central Government of PRC 2008).

Chinese aid to Afghanistan is sent directly to the Afghan government and through Chinese state-owned enterprises. The Afghan government is the recipient agent while the Chinese government institution and Chinese state-owned enterprises are the donor agents (see Figs. 10.3, 10.4). While some argued that Chinese companies invested in Afghanistan in the pursuit of their own corporate interests, the Chinese government's support to the investments have made a tremendous difference in terms of securing the bids, especially by offering development infrastructure package (Downs 2013). Some even explicitly or implicitly suggest that "Chinese companies in Afghanistan are the brainchild of the Chinese government" (Downs 2013). In some way, different with the situation in the USA, Chinese state-owned enterprises have dual roles: as donor principal and agent. They receive diplomatic and financial support from the Chinese government. At the same time, they also perform

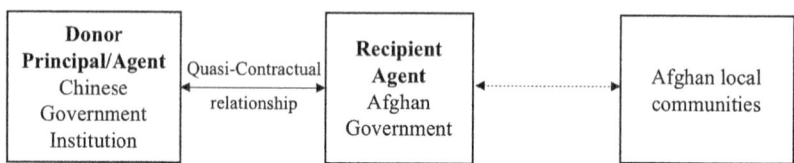

Fig. 10.3   Chinese development aid through local government

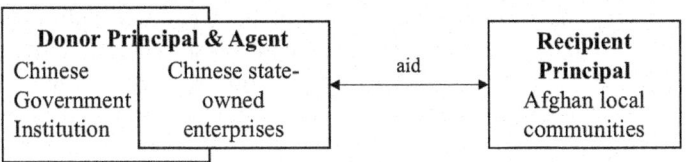

Fig. 10.4 Chinese development aid through state-owned enterprises

under their own interests (Downs 2013). Because of this, the network relations in Chinese aid and investment to Afghanistan is different to the model in the USA.

Again, by analyzing the triadic network, the Afghan government has higher betweenness than the Chinese government. From the perspective of public diplomacy, a lower betweenness score puts the donor agent in a disadvantageous power position. In another scenario where state-owned enterprises are the donor agent, network power resides in the hands of these enterprises. Figure 10.4 is different from Fig. 10.2 in that the Chinese state-owned companies are not contractors as in the US situation; they are both the donor principal and agent that actually do the work. In other words, they represent the country and at the same time interact with local communities. While the Chinese claim that the projects will bring many benefits to the local people, the projects are primarily driven by economic needs. Development assistance is a "side project" after the establishment of the main projects, which means that development sustainability may not be guaranteed. However, because of the possible direct connection with local communities through infrastructure projects, these companies may have high closeness scores in the network. The interaction between the donor agent and recipient principal is easy.

DISCUSSION AND IMPLICATIONS

The above case studies of US and Chinese development assistance to Afghanistan offer some empirical evidence of the power relations in public diplomacy and communication development. Before analyzing the results, it is necessary to clarify that public diplomacy requires governments to obtain network power through direct interaction with Afghan publics. This is because foreign aid as public diplomacy is unique, compared to other types of public diplomacy activities such as cultural and exchange diplomacy. While the content of exchange and cultural activities are explicitly about the country's characteristics, foreign assistance carries limited attributes. For example, without an identification of flag or seal, health equipment or infrastructure may come from any other donor. Visibility is important when we consider foreign assistance as public diplomacy. Therefore, direct exposure to local communities is key in an environment that is not hostile to the donor country (in a hostile environment, using more subtle approaches may be more ideal).

In a network setting, direct connections and interaction is measured by closeness and betweenness centrality. A public diplomacy actor with a high closeness score connects directly to the target audience more often than others, while an actor with a high betweenness score controls more information between a pair of actors between which it is located. Both positions have the by-product of raising the visibility of the donor country in the local community, thus contributing to public diplomacy objectives. On the other hand, empowerment theory of development communication suggests that development assistance should be empowering the local communities including local governments. Thus, network power should reside in the hands of local actors and aid recipients rather than the donors.

From the perspective of communication *for* development as public diplomacy, the strategy of providing aid through agents does not necessarily bring more power, if there is an intermediate agent. Directly contacting local communities as a way to manage relationships with foreign publics can increase power. However, the US private contractor has been the conduit of US aid to Afghanistan, so the opportunity to communicate directly with the local public is limited. From the perspective of development, empowering the local government is beneficial for sustainability. In the context of US aid to Afghanistan, both the Afghan government and local communities are the subject of empowerment. The US approach is a process of empowering the Afghan government which increases its capability to govern, and this is believed to be in the USA's strategic interests.

While the US communication *for* development empowers the contractor and local government to shape empowerment at the tactical level, the Chinese approach empowers state-owned enterprises by giving them the role of both donor principal and agent. Large national state-owned enterprises are seen as the implementor of state aid programs (Gill and Reilly 2007).

As an "extension" of the government, Chinese state-owned enterprises can engage local communities through aid and investment projects, including building infrastructure that is claimed to benefit the Afghan economy. As suggested by a relational approach of public diplomacy, direct two-way interaction between the government and foreign publics helps to sustain long-term relationships which may ultimately fuel the increase of soft power (Zaharna et al. 2013). While it is to be seen whether the infrastructure building will do good to local communities, direct engagement even through special agents such as state-owned enterprises gives an opportunity to build and manage relationships with local communities. The closeness score of the Chinese state-owned companies as the donor agent is high. Here, the Chinese case is special mainly because these large companies carry out some activities including aid that is supposed to be implemented by governments. Therefore, it is highly possible that high network power gained by these enterprises is shared with the Chinese government. Chinese donor agents also provide aid assistance to the Afghan national government. Similar to the situation of US aid, this kind of resource and money flow empowers the Afghanistan government, but it comes with limited contact with local communities. This is a favorable situation based on empowerment theory but not public diplomacy.

The power relations of development aid and public diplomacy has implications for practice. From the perspective of development assistance, taking public diplomacy measurements and objectives into consideration can increase the possibility of a smoother aid implementation. From the perspective of public diplomacy, development assistance is another channel besides traditional education and cultural programs to build and manage relationships with foreign publics. While the network structures of development assistance and public diplomacy emphasize different actors, there are still ways to merge their interests. For example, development assistance can help to increase the visibility of the USA and publicize its activities through the Afghan government. The USA can also redefine the mode of hiring contractors and maybe turn this into public–private partnerships that emphasize the government's presence. The public diplomacy element, on the other hand, can adopt the collaborative and relational approach that addresses the needs and interests of local people. The objective of increasing a country's soft power does not necessarily need to be in conflict with meeting the grassroots needs.

CONCLUSION

This chapter has explored the power relations in the resource transfer of public diplomacy and development communication through network analysis, specifically two network centrality measurements. Empowerment theory focuses on local individuals, organizations, and communities, while the power perspective focuses on state soft power. This study has analyzed US and Chinese foreign assistance to Afghanistan and compared their different network structures. Different actors in development network can obtain structural power by connecting to other actors in the network. From network centrality analysis, we may conclude that US aid to Afghanistan empowers contractors, while Chinese aid gives power to state-owned enterprises.

Although development communication and public diplomacy seem interconnected as development assistance projects can achieve public diplomacy objectives, there is an internal difference between the two fields. As summarized in Chapter 2, development assistance has a more overly ethical and normative purpose, whereas public diplomacy represents the interests of the acting organization and concerns policy outcomes. Different approaches of foreign aid place network power in the hands of different actors. "Public diplomacy almost exclusively retains a governance perspective, placing national or organizational interests and objectives at its core" (Pamment 2015, p. 190), whereas the central issues of power and knowledge of development communication lies in both developing and development communities. The empowerment framework of development communication even places greater emphasis on the development communities. This difference of power relations is supported by the network centrality proposition in this study. On the one hand, development communication intends to provide aid to local communities through granting more power to agents such as contractors and local governments. On the other hand, in order to achieve the donor's interests and unlike other types of public diplomacy, foreign assistance as public diplomacy requires empowering the donor agent.

This study is a first step to investigate the relationship between development communication and public diplomacy from a network perspective. It is important to point out that it only offers an explanation from the structural perspective for the probability and opportunity to obtain and increase network power in development communication. In some circumstances, for the purpose of public diplomacy, unpopular actors may operate through other actors who are less unpopular. Visibility is one thing; pre-existing favorability is another. In other words, centrality measurements only capture a part of the public diplomacy element in development communication. Future study can further explore development networks from the connectionist perspective and examine the content and strength of ties.

NOTES

1. Utilizing Freeman's model, betweenness is calculated by the formula: $C_B(n_i) = \sum_{j<k} g_{jk}(n_i)/g_{jk}$. j and k are two network actors and assuming there is more than one tie between j and k, g_{jk} is the number of ties linking j and k. The probability of using any one of the ties is $1/g_{jk}$. $g_{jk}(n_i)$ is the number of ties linking two actors that contain actor i. Betweenness is the sum of these estimated probabilities that i locates between all pairs of actors not including the ith actor.

2. Utilizing Freeman's model, closeness can be measured by: $C_{c(ni)} = \frac{1}{\left[\sum_{j=1}^{g} d(n_i, n_j)\right]}$. $d(n_i, n_j)$ is the number of ties linking actors i and j. The total distance that i is $\sum_{j=1}^{g} d(n_i, n_j)$ from all other and the index is the inverse of the sum of the distances from actor i to all other network actors.

REFERENCES

Armitage, R. L., & Markey, D. S. (2014). *US Strategy for Pakistan and Afghanistan*. New York: Council on Foreign Relations.

Berrios, R. (2000). *Contracting for Development: The Role of For-Profit Contractors in US Foreign Development Assistance*. Westport, CT: Praeger.

Borgatti, S. P., & Foster, P. C. (2003). The Network Paradigm in Organizational Research: A Review and Typology. *Journal of Management, 29*(6), 991–1013.

Borgatti, S. P., Mehra, A., Brass, D. J., & Labianca, G. (2009). Network Analysis in the Social Sciences. *Science, 323*(5916), 892–895.

Bourdieu, P., & Johnson, R. (1993). *The Field of Cultural Production: Essays on Art and Literature*. New York, NY: Columbia University Press.

Burt, R. S. (2001). Structural Holes Versus Network Closure as Social Capital. In N. Lin, K. S. Cook, & R. S. Burt (Eds.), *Social Capital: Theory and Research*. New Brunswick, NJ: Transaction Publishers.

Coleman, J. S. (1988). Social Capital in the Creation of Human Capital. *American Journal of Sociology, 94*, S95–S120.

Cornell Empowerment Group. (1989). Empowerment and Family Support. *Networking Bulletin, 1*(2), 1–23.

Cowan, G., & Arsenault, A. (2008). Moving from Monologue to Dialogue to Collaboration: The Three Layers of Public Diplomacy. *The Annals of the American Academy of Political and Social Science, 616*(1), 10–30.

Dagron, A. G. (2001). *Making Waves: Stories of Participatory Communication for Social Change.* New York: The Rockefeller Foundation. Retrieved from http://www.communicationforsocialchange.org/pdf/making_waves.pdf.

Downs, E. S. (2013). China Buys into Afghanistan. *SAIS Review, XXXII*(2), 65–84.

Feldbaum, H., & Michaud, J. (2010). Health Diplomacy and the Enduring Relevance of Foreign Policy Interests. *PLoS Med, 7*(4). https://doi.org/10.1371/journal.pmed.1000226.

Fisher, A. (2013). *Collaborative Public Diplomacy: How Transnational Networks Influenced American Studies in Europe.* New York: Palgrave Macmillan.

Fitzpatrick, K. (2007). Advancing the New Public Diplomacy: A Public Relations Perspective. *The Hague Journal of Diplomacy, 2*(3), 187–211.

Foucault, M. (1980). *Power/Knowledge: Selected Interviews and Other Writings, 1972–1977.* New York: Pantheon Books.

Freeman, L. C. (1978). Centrality in Social Networks Conceptual Clarification. *Social Networks, 1*(3), 215–239.

GAO. (2010). *Iraqu and Afghanistan: Dod, State, and USAID Face Continued Challenges in Tracking Contracts, Assistance Instruments, and Associated Personnel.* Washington, DC: United States Government Accountability Office.

GAO. (2011). *Afghanistan: U.S. Efforts to Vet Non-U.S. Vendors Need Improvement.* Washington, DC: United States Government Accountability Office.

GAO. (2014). *Afghanistan: Oversight and Accountability of US Assistance.* Washington, DC: United States Government Accountability Office.

Gilboa, E. (2008). Searching for a Theory of Public Diplomacy. *Annals of the American Academy of Political and Social Science, 616*(1), 55–77.

Gill, B., & Reilly, J. (2007). The Tenuous Hold of China Inc. in Africa. *Washington Quarterly, 30*(3), 37–52.

Granovetter, M. S. (1974). *Getting a Job: A Study of Contacts and Careers.* Cambridge, MA: Harvard University Press.

Gregory, B. (2014). *The Paradox of US Public Diplomacy: Its Rise and "Demise".* Washington, DC: The George Washington University.

Gul, A. (2016). China Delivers First Batch of Military Aid to Afghanistan. *VOA.* http://www.voanews.com/a/china-military-aid-afghanistan/3402178.html.

He, P. (2018). Functional Cooperation and Japan's Cultural Diplomacy: A Case Study of the Preservation of Angkor. In X. Wu (Ed.), *East Asian Studies in the Perspective of Regional Integration.* Shanghai: World Century.

Hook, S. W. (1995). *National Interest and Foreign Aid.* Boulder, CO: L. Rienner.

Huysentruyt, M. (2011). *Development Aid by Contract: Outsourcing and Contractor Identity*. Retrieved from http://personal.lse.ac.uk/huysentr/DevelopmentAidbyContract(Full).pdf.

Ibahrine, M. (2016). Nation Branding in the Gulf Countries. In J. Pamment (Ed.), *Intersections Between Public Diplomacy & International Development: Case Studies in Converging Fields*. Los Angeles: Figueroa Press.

Inkpen, A. C., & Tsang, E. W. (2005). Social Capital, Networks, and Knowledge Transfer. *Academy of Management Review, 30*(1), 146–165.

InsideGov. Compare United States Foreign Aid—Grants and Loans.

Kent, M. L., Sommerfeldt, E. J., & Saffer, A. J. (2016). Social Networks, Power, and Public Relations: Tertius Iungens as a Cocreational Approach to Studying Relationship Networks. *Public Relations Review, 42*(1), 91–100.

Kerry, J. F. (2011). *Evaluating U.S. Foreign Assistance to Afghanistan*. A majority staff report prepared for the use of the committee on foreign relations, US senate (9781437987133). Washington, DC: Committee on Foreign Relations, US Senate.

Khalil, A. B. (2016). The Rise of China-Afghanistan Security Relations. *The Diplomat*. http://thediplomat.com/2016/06/the-rise-of-china-afghanistan-security-relations/.

Lee, K., & Smith, R. (2011). What is 'Global Health Diplomacy'? A Conceptual Review. *Global Health Governance, 5*(1). http://www.ghd-net.org/sites/default/files/Lee-and-Smith_What-is-Global-Health-Diplomacy_Fall-2011_0.pdf.

Lerner, D. (1958). *The Passing of Traditional Society Modernizing the Middle East*. London: Macmillan.

Lin, N. (1999). Building a Network Theory of Social Capital. *Connections, 22*(1), 28–51.

Lin, N., & Dumin, M. (1986). Access to Occupations Through Social Ties. *Social Networks, 8*(4), 365–385.

Marsden, P. V., & Campbell, K. E. (1984). Measuring Tie Strength. *Social Forces, 63*(2), 482–501.

Martens, B., Mummert, U., Murrell, P., & Seabright, P. (2004). *The Institutional Economics of Foreign Aid*. Cambridge: Cambridge University Press.

McDowell, S. D. (2003). Theory and Research in International Communiation: An Historical and Institutional Account. In B. Mody (Ed.), *International and Development Communication* (pp. 5–18). Thousand Oaks, CA: Sage.

Melissen, J. (2005). The New Public Diplomacy: Between Theory and Practice. In J. Melissen (Ed.), *The New Public Diplomacy: Soft Power in International Relations* (pp. 3–27). London, UK: Palgrave Macmillan.

Melkote, S. R. (2003). Theories of Development Communication. In B. Mody (Ed.), *International and Development Communication* (pp. 129–146). Thousand Oaks, CA: Sage.

Melkote, S. R., & Steeves, H. L. (2001). *Communication for Development in the Third World: Theory and Practice for Empowerment*. Thousand Oaks, CA: Sage.

Monge, P. R., & Contractor, N. S. (2003). *Theories of Communication Networks*. Oxford: Oxford University Press.

Murrell, P. (2004). The Interactions of Donors, Contractors, and Recipients in Implementing Aid for Institutional Reform. In B. Martens, U. Mummert, P. Murrell, & P. Seabright (Eds.), *The Institutional Economics of Foreign Aid*. Cambridge: Cambridge University Press.

Nahapiet, J., & Ghoshal, S. (1998). Social Capital, Intellectual Capital, and the Organizational Advantage. *The Academy of Management Review, 23*(2), 242–266.

Nye, J. S. (2008). Public Diplomacy and Soft Power. *The Annals of the American Academy of Political and Social Science, 616*(1), 94–109.

Olmstead, J. (2014, December 23). Fixing America's Aid to Afghanistan and Pakistan. *The Diplomat*. Retrieved from http://thediplomat.com/2014/12/fixing-americas-aid-to-afghanistan-and-pakistan/.

Pamment, J. (2015). Media Influence, Ontological Transformation, and Social Change: Conceptual Overlaps between Development Communication and Public Diplomacy. *Communication Theory, 25*(2), 188–207.

Pamment, J. (Ed.). (2016). *Intersections between Public Diplomacy & International Development: Case Studies in Converging Fields*. Los Angeles: Figueroa Press.

Putnam, R. D., Leonardi, R., & Nanetti, R. Y. (1994). *Making Democracy Work: Civic Traditions in Modern Italy*. Princeton, NJ: Princeton University Press.

Rappaport, J. (1981). In Praise of Paradox: A Social Policy of Empowerment Over Prevention. *American Journal of Community Psychology, 9*(1), 1–25.

Schiller, H. I. (1976). *Communication and Cultural Domination*. Armonk, NY: M.E. Sharpe.

Schramm, W. (1964). *Mass Media and National Development: The Role of Information in the Developing Countries*. Stanford, CA: Stanford University Press.

Snyder, L. B. (2003). Development Communication Campaigns. In B. Mody (Ed.), *International and Development Communication* (pp. 167–188). Thousand Oaks, CA: Sage.

Soubbotina, T. P., & Sheram, K. (2000). *Beyond Economic Growth: Meeting the Challenges of Global Development*. Washington, DC: World Bank.

Tarnoff, C. (2010). *Afghanistan: US Foreign Assistance*. Washington, DC: Congressional Research Service.

The Central Government of PRC. (2008, May 30). *Mcc Signed Afghanistan Aynak Copper Project*. Retrieved from http://www.gov.cn/ztzl/2008-05/30/content_999423.htm.

Tiezzi, S. (2014, October 31). *Can China Save Afghanistan?* Retrieved from http://thediplomat.com/2014/10/can-china-save-afghanistan/.

van der Kley, D. (2014). *China's Foreign Policy in Afghanistan.* Lowy Institute for International Policy.

Yuan, Y. (2015, January 14). China Should Take Over the United States to Send Troops to Afghanistan? *Elite Reference.* Retrieved from http://www.chinanews.com/mil/2015/01-14/6968686.shtml.

Zaharna, R. S., Fisher, A., & Arsenault, A. (2013). *Relational, Networking and Collaborative Approaches to Public Diplomacy: The Connective Mindshift.* New York: Rouledge.

Zhao, H. (2015, February 24). What is Behind China's Growing Attention to Afghanistan? *Carnegie Endowment for International Peace.* Retrieved from http://carnegieendowment.org/2015/03/08/what-is-behind-china-s-growing-attention-to-afghanistan-pub-59286.

Zhu, Y. (2014, May 4). It Is of Strategic Significance for China to Increase Aid to Afghanistan. *Global Times.* Retrieved from http://opinion.huanqiu.com/opinion_world/2014-05/4985761.html.

CHAPTER 11

Ambivalent Perception of China's "One Belt One Road" in Russia: "United Eurasia" Dream or "Metallic Band" of Containment?

Larisa Smirnova

INTRODUCTION

Since President Xi Jinping's accession to power in China and following his unprecedented personal friendship with Vladimir Putin of Russia, it has become rather commonplace in media discourse to associate "Russia and China" and to place this "geopolitical couple" in opposition to the so-called "West" and/or "the United States and their allies" (Chance 2017). As a matter of fact, such association may have greatly contributed to the public communication success that the Chinese project of "One Belt One Road" (OBOR) enjoyed globally in the initial months after its unveiling on March 28, 2015 (Government of China 2015).

An earlier version of this paper was published, for discussion purposes, by "21st Century", a Noravank Foundation journal, No. 1, 2017.

L. Smirnova (✉)
Russian Academy of Sciences, Moscow, Russia

241
J. Pamment and K. G. Wilkins (eds.), *Communicating National Image through Development and Diplomacy*, Palgrave Studies in Communication for Social Change, https://doi.org/10.1007/978-3-319-76759-8_11

The Chinese project, which likely drew inspiration from an earlier American concept of the New Silk Road (McBride, n.d.), was immediately described by epithets such as "ambitious," "grandiose," "far-reaching," and the like. Whereas the Chinese narrative cautiously stressed economic infrastructure as well as "information" (Xu and Mao 2016) aspects, the image of President Xi attending the military parades next to the proven warrior Vladimir Putin added credibility to the Chinese assertiveness. This led the bewildered public to imagine the return of the "Grand Age of Empires" and the possible advent of the finally united Eurasia, a dream that has haunted European history for millennia.

The official part of the Chinese discourse (Xinhua News Agency, n.d.) is structured around the pledge to provide development recipes without challenging the power leverage of local elites in developing countries. The Chinese government is indeed known for opposing violent regime changes, especially the bottom-top "color revolutions" (Jun 2016). At a point when the Western methods of economic and political reforms have come under attack as having led to a recent rise of security-related tensions around the world, it is understandable that the Chinese message, thus presented, has proved appealing (Sputnik News Agency 2016). Itself a non-Western country, China has managed to absorb Western development methods while maintaining its flexibility to select and adapt them to its own cultural taste.

As appears clearer now, however, the international popularity of the OBOR concept has likely surpassed the expectations of the Chinese ideologists of the project. Originally the Chinese policy-makers might have been more preoccupied by domestic policy concerns than by any international ambitions. Among the goals they pursued, there was certainly one of diverting attention from the pressure for political reform by driving their own population's conscience towards exaltation and aspirations for the revival of ancient glory (Smirnova 2014).

This chapter is about the discussion that the OBOR concept provoked in Russian media and expert circles. The sources of data are publications in Russian media and think tanks during the period from March 2015 (the date of the official launch of the OBOR plan) to January 2017 (the time of writing). The research shows that the conceptual launch of the plan was a tremendous success: according to Russia's number one Yandex search engine, the number of publications with key words "One Belt One Road" amounts to 6000; with key words "Silk Road" amounting to 22 million. With these numbers, there is hardly any Russian who would not have heard about the concept. However, and more unexpectedly,

I have found that OBOR has become a subject of domestic speculation in crisis-hit Russia. Specifically, the main line of the Russian debate is in what ways the Chinese plan will challenge the international great power status of Russia and on what terms this will, or will not, be acceptable.

TERMINOLOGY AND METHODOLOGY

Critical Discourse Analysis

The title of this chapter borrows from an article by Sergey Tsypliaev, a Russian statesman working, at the time of writing, for the Russian Presidential Academy of National Economy and Public Administration. In an article published in the daily newspaper *Vedomosti* he points out that if the Russia–China cooperation fails, the "Silk Road risks becoming a 'metallic band' for Russia" (Tsypliaev 2016). The "metallic band" is a metaphorical expression that derives from the Chinese classic novel *The Journey to the West* where a band was placed on the head of the rebellious main character the Monkey King by the Buddhist divinity Guanyin. In the context of Russia–China relations, it sounds like an allusion to the OBOR plan, much like, the Russians believed, its American "New Silk Road" predecessor (Popov 2015) was intended to become a strategy for the "containment of Russia."

In Russian, the term "One Belt One Road" (Russian: "*odin poyas i odin puti*," abbreviated as "OPOP"), which is a literal translation of the Chinese official name for the project "一带一路" (*yi dai yi lu*), sounds rather unnatural. Therefore, it is mostly employed as "professional jargon" by foreign policy specialists. The journalists and experts targeting a wider audience generally refer to the "Silk Road" (Russian: "*sholkovy puti*"), a historic term that, first, carries a Central Asian rather than a Chinese connotation (Frankopan 2016), and therefore, as will be elaborated in more detail below, might or might not include the maritime part of the plan.

The general methodology that is employed here is critical discourse analysis (CDA), which is a methodology closely related to the study of political ideologies. I am fully aware that the Chinese stress that OBOR is not an ideology (Wang 2015). However, since my study is about the impression received in Russia via the Chinese discourse, the recipient's perception matters more than the creator's intention. In the words of Norman Fairclough, the goal of ideologies is "to win acceptance for them as non-ideological common sense," whereas the objective of a discourse analysis that adopts "critical goals" is to "denaturalize" them (Fairclough 2013).

It is often assumed in CDA, based on the democratic theories of government, press, and their mutual relations (Siebert et al. 1981), that those media with most massive public outreach should have most influence on decision-making in a country. However, Joe Straubhaar, in a recent paper, validly challenges the idea that democratization of media systems is a universal trend brought by globalization: "media institutions themselves are becoming more complexly multi-layered as they reach further geographically. Institutional models ... globalize but they are also localized and regionalized as they engage the specific histories and institutions of a variety of cultures, media traditions, and regulatory systems." And further: "when many observers look at cultures these days, they see a top layer of what they might call globalization. Some might suppose that this is perhaps even the dominant aspect of someone's identity or experience. However, ... we realize that these are recent layers, which are important but that they are built over older layers which are still there. While identities change, multiply, and have relative autonomy, they are also tied to *sources of power*" (Straubhaar 2014, my italics).

In Russia nowadays, especially since the unfolding of the Ukrainian and subsequent Syrian crises, the media landscape might fall into the category, according to Teun A. van Dijk's classification, of "various forms of military, policy, judicial or male force" (van Dijk 1993, p. 257). In this context, media indeed become "multi-layered" and some media with marginal circulation, due to their special relationship with power sources, might turn out to become rather influential. Therefore, the works of Yoram Peri on the intersections between the media, politics, and military in Israel might be relevant to the current Russian situation. "Israeli democracy," wrote Peri, "was a formal rather than a liberal democracy" (Peri 2004). He emphasized the impact that national security has on the development of media systems in situations of "intractable conflict" (Peri 2007), explaining how in this situation the mainstream media might lose credibility whereas "sectorial" or marginal media might gain in influence (Tsfati and Peri 2006).

Yet what preoccupies Dr. Peri is Israeli internal politics. The case of Russia and China is different in that we are talking about reciprocal international coverage in two countries with government-controlled mainstream media. It is simply logical that, in the context of "the relations between Russia and China that have never been as good as they are now" (Lavrov 2016), the government-controlled Russian and Chinese media would avoid ostensibly negative coverage of each other. Whether this is truly the case or not (Feng 2014), China has also been presented as Russia's *ally*, even though "tacit" (Romanova 2014), on sensitive matters, such as the "*unification* of Crimea" (the Russian official term) (Zakharova 2017).

Going further, I will attempt to challenge the traditional freedom of speech theory, according to which the information conferred by the Russian media would be deemed all in all unreliable, due to the existing media environment (Freedom House 2016), by arguing that truthful information has not disappeared from the media discourse but has started to be conveyed by other means, at times through an indirect or disguised manner and/or in "sectorial" and "marginal" rather than mainstream media. If the discourse thus became elusive to the general public, it is still understandable to insiders; or rather, the messages conveyed to the general public and those conveyed to insiders now considerably diverge.

Conveying information in an indirect manner is in no case a Russian invention, but rather a feature of repressive, crisis-ridden, or unsafe societies, let alone war-torn societies. Exercising free speech in Russia has been notoriously dangerous: the violent death of journalists who had the courage to take the risks provide convincing evidence in this regard. Before the recent crises, however, it was accepted at the values level, even if not necessarily achieved, that the objective was to make Russia's mass media progress towards more openness (in Stuart Hall's words, "the ideal is a 'perfectly transparent communication'" (Hall 1973, p. 135)) as society evolves towards more safety. However, since society has actually failed to become safer, nowadays the well-foundedness of the freedom of speech principle in itself has become questionable.

Since discourse on war-related events is currently predominant in the Russian media, Russia has developed a sort of "esoteric" journalism. The word "esoteric" is defined by the *Oxford Dictionary* as "intended for or likely to be understood by only a small number of people with a specialized knowledge or interest." Inasmuch as traditional meaningful journalism requires skills, the required set now is different from that required in the free mass media. If the transparent mass media rely on logic, structure, and convincing argumentation, the sectorial media work with metaphors, hints, insinuations, Aesop's language, and may look, to an unprepared reader, extremely strange, unpersuasive, or pseudo-scientific. In his 1973 article "Encoding/Decoding," Stuart Hall described a similar phenomenon with regard to the broadcasting by the media of "problematic or troubling events, which breach our expectancies and run counter to our 'common-sense constructs'" (Hall 1973, p. 134). Likewise, decoding Russian journalism nowadays requires a strong degree of cultural awareness, or in other words, to borrow again from Stuart Hall, a belonging to "a dominant cultural order," "the everyday knowledge of social structures, of 'how things work for all practical purposes in this culture'" (Hall 1973, p. 134). Such cultural familiarity is usually achieved by natives in a country through the education system, especially the system of secondary schooling, but remains difficult to access by foreigners.

Research Approach

In order to sort out the influential articles, I relied, first, on my personal familiarity with the discourses regarding Russia–China relations (since 2014, I have served as an expert on Russia–China relations for the Russian International Affairs Council and, in this capacity, took part in organizing both editions of the highest format conference that exists on these relations) (Lavrov 2016). The full list of quoted articles, in order of citation, is presented in the Appendix.

Second, I added elements of mathematical text analysis to my methodology by submitting a sample of articles (16 articles, a total of 116,026 words) published between March 2015 and January 2017 to computerized text analysis,[1] a process in which the key words are identified by the computer. On a large scale, the methodology of computerized text analysis is being developed by, for example, Kalev Hannes Leetaru.[2] On a smaller and more affordable scale, one of the methods used for this is search engine optimization (SEO) text analysis, which I used. The selected articles come from the following three publications that, to the best of my knowledge, have influence on Russia's decision-making and reflect the two extremes of the Russian political spectrum as well as Vladimir Putin's pledge to "unify" or "balance" the two of them:

---

[1] The function is available at: https://text.ru/.

[2] http://blog.gdeltproject.org/cultural-computing-at-literature-scale-encoding-the-cultural-knowledge-of-tens-of-billions-of-words-of-academic-literature/.

(1) Newspaper *Vedomosti*[3]: Russia's equivalent to the *Financial Times*, printed alike on light salmon pink paper, foreign-launched and focused on quality journalism, circulated in Moscow's busy coffee shops, and popular among the liberal camp. This publication would fall into the category of mass circulation media, and its writing style is rather straightforward and easily understandable.

(2) Newspaper *Argumenty nedeli*[4] (the Russian title of the newspaper literally translates as "*weekly arguments*"): a tabloid written and widely read by the so-called "*siloviki*," a composite term for the employees of various security forces. This publication would fall into the category of "sectorial" media, and its writing style is much more "esoteric," characterized by the abundance of symbolic expressions and metaphors that assume a high degree of cultural awareness from the readers and are only fully comprehensible to insiders.

(3) Analytics pages of the "Valdai Club"[5]: a favorite think tank of Vladimir Putin which he personally launched in 2004. The writing style is policy-suggestions oriented.

Main Findings

1. *The Russians view a China-led "Silk Road" as a challenge to Russia's great power status but have demonstrated openness to cooperation on the basis of equality*

As a context reminder, the Chinese plan, which comprises continental ("One Belt") and maritime ("One Road") parts, was initially intended to concern Russia only to a limited extent. The outline divulged at the Boao Forum on March 28, 2015 described several connection routes between Asia, Europe, and Africa, but only mentioned Russia as part of one of them: "from China through Central Asia and Russia to Europe (the Baltic Sea)." The maritime part of the plan was supposed to focus

[3] http://www.vedomosti.ru/.
[4] http://www.argumenti.ru/.
[5] ru.valdaiclub.com/.

primarily on the Southeast Asian countries with a potential extension deeper into the Pacific Ocean (Government of China 2015).

The Russian foreign policy-makers, however, perceived this as an attempt to downgrade Russia to the position of a "regional" rather than "global" power: a position they firmly regard as premature and unacceptable. The first *Argumenty nedeli* reaction to the Chinese communiqué of March 28, 2015 was a publication of a brief statement by Vice Premier Igor Shuvalov (Source 1). The friendly title of the article "Russia Is Ready to Join Efforts with China" is followed by an extension in the synopsis that Russia "welcomes the Chinese initiative," and that the joint work on it should be carried out "in the format of the Eurasian Economic Union" (EEU), a Russian-dominated project. More straightforwardly, Sergey Ryazanov, a contributor to *Argumenty nedeli*, points out that "many people got nervous about the advancement of the Chinese infrastructural projects .... Some people even called the Great Silk Road a blow to the Eurasian Economic Union and 'an insult to Putin,' as the Chinese had not solicited his opinion in advance" (Source 2).

According to the Russian International Affairs Council, great powers are those countries with "the ability to project the might of the state (*and not always in a destructive way*) anywhere in the world" (Source 3, p. 6, my italics). Parenthetically and taking into account Russia's previous involvement in the controversy over the Treaty between the USSR and the USA on the elimination of their intermediate-range and shorter-range missiles (the INF Treaty) (Arms Control Association 2017), the definition of "anywhere in the world" might be re-opened, for the first time since the end of the Cold War, to hardcore "nuclear military power" interpretations.

In light of the above, the Putin–Xi "Declaration on the coordination between the EEU and the China-initiated Silk Road Economic Belt," signed on May 8, 2015, should be considered as a significant diplomatic breakthrough. The editor-in-chief of *Argumenty nedeli* Andrey Uglanov estimates the value of the Declaration by saying that by its signing "the politics of containment of China was in fact stopped" by the Russian side (Source 4). Achieved in the atmosphere of patriotic fervor on the grounds of World War II memories, it essentially put the Russian and the Chinese projects for post-Soviet countries on the same basis as opposed to the earlier treatment of the Chinese plan as an "initiative" within the Russian framework (Smirnova 2015).

On the same occasion, Alexander Gabuev, the popular observer on Chinese affairs, published an article in the *Vedomosti* with the title that roughly translates as "Dizzy with coordination" (Russian: *Sopriazhenie ot uspekhov*) (Source 5). To a Russian reader, it jolts the memory of an article entitled "Dizzy with Success: Concerning Questions of the Collective-Farm Movement" published by Joseph Stalin on March 2, 1930, which criticized excessive zeal in agricultural collectivization. Pertinently, Gabuev's article is critical of Russia's attitude towards the Central Asian allies "as if they were passive objects whose destinies can be defined in the talks between the two great powers." Indeed, the May 8 Declaration was bilateral and did not solicit the opinion of any other concerned Eurasian countries.

2. *The Russians have strong security concerns but are still interested in Chinese investments*

The Chinese narrative, famous for its materialism officially branded as "pragmatism" (Geng 2017), stresses that the OBOR plan will bring economic prosperity. Whereas it sounds like an irrefutable argument that China was successful in tremendously improving the welfare of its population over the three past decades, the assumption beneath it proposes it as a recipe to be followed by other countries is that other people, too, primarily strive to increase their material comfort. Specifically, the recipe consists in improving accessibility of the geographically remote regions by infrastructure development with the premise that it will boost local economic activities.

The Chinese model works well in regions with high population density and few natural resources. It correctly assumes that the entrepreneurial potential of the people will develop once they have the opportunity, through improved connectivity, to reach out to the outside world. Long before the Chinese economic miracle, this model was sketched by the Hakka merchants of the Southern Chinese provinces. This model, moreover, seems to correlate with increased cultural homogeneity as people need to cooperate to maximize their profits.

However, Russia, and especially Siberia, is a region with geographic conditions exactly opposite to those of China: low population density and abundance of natural resources. As a result, the Chinese arguments do not sound convincing. "Where there are a lot of mosquitos there is also a lot of oil," points out Vyacheslav Shtyrov, a former governor of the Siberian region of Yakutia, in an interview in *Argumenty nedeli* (Source 6). Shtyrov is skeptical about the Chinese investments: "I have had many contacts with the South Koreans, the Japanese, the Chinese ... Negotiations can last for years but the real deals can be counted on the fingers" (Source 6).

Russia's economy largely relies on exports of Siberian resources, and natural resources are a number one item in Russian exports to China (Ministry of Economic Development of Russia, n.d.). Thanks to the exploitation of natural resources, Russia manages to provide to its population material life standards that range from tolerable to comfortable, if not opulent, but that are always above subsistence level. For the Russian businesses, it is far from evident whether improved connectivity would help them to maximize profits or, vice versa, only create more competition for the control over resources.

To verify my findings further, I have submitted 16 articles (six from *Vedomosti*, six from *Weekly arguments*, and four from *Valdai Club*, a total of 116,026 words), all of them dated between the official launch of the OBOR initiative on March 28, 2015 and December 1, 2016, to the computerized SEO keyword search. The full results of the computer analysis are presented in the Appendix.

These are the key ideas identified by the computer:

- A comparatively long peaceful period inside the Central Asian region in the absence of serious conflicts opens opportunities for the development of new technologies;
- The USSR completely exhausted the main resource of industrialization—countryside youth;
- Russia is still not making use of opportunities for economic integration within the Shanghai Cooperation Organization;
- In 2015, the total Chinese foreign direct investment (FDI) in the Commonwealth of Independent States (CIS) countries amounted to USD 27 billion; of this sum USD 23.6 billion went to Kazakhstan;
- The leaders of the Eurasian Economic Union countries started direct dialogue with Beijing, which was evaluated in Moscow almost like a betrayal.

After noting down these and other computer-identified keywords, I have resubmitted the entire keyword list to another round of SEO analysis. Rearranged into a sentence, it reads optimistically: "in the rich in oil and gas region of Central Asia, the coordination between the Eurasian Economic Union and the Silk Road Economic Belt as well as the Shanghai Cooperation Organization should lead to a full economic union."

3. *When reluctant to express their deepest aspirations and concerns openly, the Russians do it through metaphorical language*

The security concerns, openly discussed in the Soviet Union but discarded as a myth in the age of liberal enchantment after its dissolution, are preserved in some of the "esoteric" theories. Often fictional and sometimes sounding like blatantly pseudo-scientific to a Western-educated reader, these theories are no longer viewed as irrelevant nowadays and are in fact powerfully influential on Russian minds. Since, as Hall wrote, a "raw" historical even cannot, in that form, be transmitted by, say, a television newscast, the analysis of such esoteric narrative is rather problematic from a scientific point of view and might be closer to the analysis of fiction literature than information media: "we can never get back to the original meaning that a literary work had for its author" (Labanyi 2010, p. 124).

The narrative of the newspaper *Argumenty nedeli* is particularly abundant in references to these theories. One famous example is the works of Lev Gumilev on the so-called "passion" of nations (Russian: *passionarnosti*). Gumilev's theory (Gumilev 1936) explains the drive for military conquest through the prism of a would-be high psychological energy of nations with abundant young populations living in areas with constrained resources. In an explicitly titled article, "The 'Yellow Dragon' Benefits from the Europe—Russia Dissent, or Geopolitical Risks of the Strategic Alliance between Russia and China," the former mayor of Moscow City Yury Luzhkov calls the "rapprochement" with China "hasty and unnecessarily noisy, as if done only in retaliation to the West," and predicts its failure, as "based on Gumilev's classification, the civilizations of Russia and China are incompatible" (Source 7).

Based on conventional wisdom, the figure of Genghis Khan (Temujin), the notorious Mongolian leader of the Middle Ages, is especially symbolic for anyone who has gone through the Russian or the Chinese system of schooling in history. The connotations however are different. First and foremost, for the collective imagination of the Russians, the Genghis Khan character evokes the fear of a foreign conquest. As a reminder, both Russia and China were conquered by the Mongolians; the difference lies in the fact that the Mongolian conquest is perceived as more humiliating by the Russians, where it was "cross-racial" and became a historical taboo, than by the Chinese, who adopted the historic view of the Mongolian rulers as one of the Chinese dynasties (Yuan dynasty). Meaningfully, Genghis Khan is evoked in discussions of "whether Russia will be able to keep influence in Central Asia" (Source 8). Also, reacting to the September 2015 military parade on Beijing's Tiananmen Square, the Russian newspaper *Pravda*, affiliated with the Communist Party of Russia that has been a part of the ruling alliance since the Crimean events, called the Silk Road a new "Road of Genghis Khan" (Source 9).

The military balance on the Russia–China border has for decades relied on Russia's superior nuclear power. Russian military experts estimate that, taking into account the difference in population sizes is a factor of 10 in favor of China, the Chinese–Russian border is not defendable by conventional weapons (Kashin 2013). The Chinese penetration into Central Asia, especially if coupled with a much feared surge of Chinese nuclear potential, would triple the length of the border and create a direct military threat to Siberia. The Russian concerns, tabooed or metaphorical after the May 8, 2015 Declaration, resurged openly following the incident with the reported placing of the Chinese DF-41 ballistic missiles in the proximity of the Russian border (Source 10).

On the other hand, however, Genghis Khan is associated with the achievability of the "United Eurasia" dream. Much like Napoleon who, besides his image of a conqueror (though, unlike the Mongolians, defeated), is romanticized by the Russians as a symbol of the most acknowledged "European integration" that Russia experienced throughout its whole history, the figure of Genghis Khan has also been associated, for example in the writings of Gumilev's contemporary Sergey Trubetskoy, with the construct of Russia's identity as a "Eurasian" country (Trubetskoy 1925). Looking at things positively from the soft power perspective, although until recently a taboo, it now begins to be acceptable in the media narrative to refer to the Mongolian period as the "beginning of an important stage in the future relations between China and Russia because under the Mongolian yoke (1220–1480), there were as many Chinese in Russia as the Russians in China" (Source 11).

4. *The Russians have presented alternatives to the Chinese projects that take into account Russia's security interests*

Russian thinkers further reacted to the Chinese initiative by proposing their alternative plans for the Silk Road. On the surface, it might even look like the Russians are not at all paying attention to the content of the Chinese suggestions, but only show interest in attracting Chinese funds to support the Russian-designed alternative projects. My argument is that the Russian plans are an attempt to canalize the Chinese investments towards those projects that have been tested by the Russians and are estimated to be safer for them.

For example, between the alternative railway routes that could link China to Europe, the Chinese favor the Central Asian variants and the Russians prefer to stick to the two trans-Siberian ones, especially the Baikal–Amur Mainline (Source 12). Both Siberian railways (Transsib and BAM) were historically built at huge cost and stretch of human and economic resources, and, taking into account the harsh climate and low density of population, their modernization at full length is highly unlikely to pay off economically.

However, the successful Chinese test of the train from China to Georgia that traveled to Tbilisi through Kazakhstan and Azerbaijan bypassing Russia in December 2015 greatly increased the disguised strategic uneasiness in Sino-Russian relations. In the aftermath of the incident, the business newspaper *RBK Daily* ran an article explicitly saying that "despite all the mutual assurances from Beijing and Moscow, the 'Silk Road' and the concept of Eurasian integration promoted by Russia on the basis of the Eurasian Economic Union can hardly be considered complementary" (Source 13).

Infrastructure development being per se a national security-related issue, the Russians view the Shanghai Cooperation Organization (SCO) as the main platform for coordination with China (Luzianin et al. 2015). In the above-mentioned article, the *Argumenty nedeli* editor-in-chief Andrey Uglanov argues that security cooperation is the only realistic roadmap for cooperation with China. "By turning the SCO in the economic direction, we should not forget that it originated as an organization for security and cooperation," he writes. "Logic suggests that it is high time to create a united armed forces of the SCO countries" (Source 4).

Importantly, the Russian experts point out that the security-related incidents in Central Asia are on the rise. Timofei Bordachev, an analyst influential within the Valdai Club circles, in his report "Russia and China in the Central Asia: A Win–Win Game," refers to the July 5, 2016 shootings in Aktobe city, Kazakhstan, and comments that "the incident incited the external observers to suggest that the situation in Kazakhstan, which had been regarded as a good example of stability in the southern part of the post-Soviet space, could tighten significantly" (Source 14).

The Russian proponents of cooperation with China also have their alternative plan for the Maritime Silk Road: the Northern Sea Route that runs through the Russian Arctic. Again, security or "peace-keeping in North East Asia," including around North Korea (Source 2), comes as a · first consideration. Not at all taken into account in the original Chinese plan and recently labeled "Russia's Arctic Obsession" by the *Financial Times* (Hille 2016), the Russian idea actually has strategic implications. If it is true that a great power is a country that is able to project its influence to any part of the globe at any given time, the Arctic is one region where Russia is more powerful than China and likely exercises more control than the USA (Russian International Affairs Council 2016).

POLICY IMPLICATIONS OF MEDIA DISCOURSE

Whereas the relationship between media discourse and its actual policy implications is not always straightforward, the media discourse allows us to predict possible development scenarios.

First of all, the lack of trust between Russia and China, especially around Siberia and in Central Asia, is based on serious grounds. Besides Central Asia being regarded as a military bridge-head to Eastern Russia, it is to be noted that Russia's interests and the interests of the Central Asian countries do not necessarily coincide but often contradict each other. The Central Asian countries are, like Russia, exporters of natural resources, especially gas, to China, and therefore Russia's direct competitors. Second, following the abundance of historic ties, the Russian companies have large stakes in Central Asian natural resources exports (Source 6).

Third, another often disregarded but important factor is competition for human resources. The Central Asian population is the main source of low-skilled labor in Russia. It is true that, as some Russian experts present it (Ryazantsev 2016), remittances from migration are currently a significant revenue income for the Central Asian countries. However, the Central Asian migrants became the most discriminated group in Russia where they are referred to by the German term *"gastarbeiter"* that sounds denigrating in the Russian language. The economic development of Central Asia would put them into a much stronger position vis-à-vis their Russian employers or remove the necessity to work abroad altogether.

Creating a united contingent of SCO members certainly could become a reasonable scale trust-boosting initiative. Since the SCO military drills have already involved China, it is indeed theoretically plausible that a cooperation format could take a more permanent basis. On the other hand, the SCO has already bumped into the lack of trust and common understanding between the participants and therefore expanded to include other, less sensitive aspects, such as research and development (the so-called SCO University), which made the organization more inert.

What can be done in the meantime is that, since both Siberia and Central Asia are too sensitive for Russia from a security viewpoint, infrastructure and other economic cooperation with China might develop in the European part of Russia. This would have the advantage of being located further from the border with China, making an imminent military threat less of an issue, and geographic conditions more suitable for the Chinese model: higher population density and less natural resources.

Appendix: Silk Road-Related Russian Media Articles Cited

1. Shuvalov, I. (2015). Russia Is Ready to Joint Work with China. *Argumenty nedeli*, March 28. Retrieved from http://argumenti. ru/politics/2015/03/393796.
2. Ryazanov, S. (2015). Russia and China: A Planetary Project. *Argumenty nedeli*, February 5. Retrieved from http://argumenti. ru/toptheme/n473/387893.
3. Russian International Affairs Council. (2016). *Asian Players in the Arctic: Interests, Opportunities, Prospects*. Moscow: Spetskniga. Retrieved from http://russiancouncil.ru/common/upload/asia-arctic-report26-en.pdf.
4. Uglanov, A. (2015). A Chinese Elephant in Our Porcelain Shop, July 9. Retrieved from http://argumenti.ru/politics/n495/406728.
5. Gabuev, A. (2016). Peresopriajenie ot uspekhov (Dizzy Over Coordination). *Vedomosti*, June 15. Retrieved from http://www.vedomosti.ru/opinion/articles/2016/06/15/645351-peresopryazhenie-ot-uspehov.
6. Shtyrov, V. (2015). Where There Are a Lot of Mosquitos There Is Also a Lot of Oil, December 24 (A. Uglanov, Interviewer). Retrieved from http://argumenti.ru/toptheme/n519/428362.

7. Luzhkov, Y. M. (2015). "Yellow Dragon" Benefits from the Europe–Russia Dissent, or Geopolitical Risks of the Strategic Alliance Between Russia and China. *Argumenty nedeli*, February 12. Retrieved from http://argumenti.ru/politics/n474/388673.

8. Terentiev, D. (2016). The Party of Genghis Khan: Will Russia Preserve Its Influence Over Central Asia? *Argumenty nedeli*, August 4. Retrieved from http://argumenti.ru/toptheme/n550/461769.

9. Drabkin, A. (2015). Silk Road and the Road of Genghis Khan. *Pravda*, September 14.

10. Khramchikhin, A. (2017). Is China's Nuclear Potential Dangerous for Russia? *Nezavisimaya Gazeta*, January 25. Retrieved from http://www.ng.ru/armies/2017-01-25/2_6911_china.html.

11. Peynichou, C. (2016). Russia and China: The History of Relations During Mongolian Yoke, March 7. Retrieved from http://inosmi.ru/history/20160703/237058674.html.

12. Terentiev, D. (2015). Everything Goes Through Baikal–Amur Mainline (BAM) Railway, November 12. Retrieved from http://argumenti.ru/toptheme/n513/423132.

13. Artermiev, A., and Makarenko, G. (2015). How China Launched the New Silk Road Bypassing Russia, December 15. Retrieved from http://www.rbc.ru/politics/15/12/2015/56703a6d9a7947 f88a89ae7d.

14. Bordachev, T. (2016). *Russia and China in Central Asia: The Win-Win Game*. Valdai Club. Retrieved from http://valdaiclub. com/a/valdai-papers/russia-and-china-in-central-asia-the-great-win-win-game/.

BIBLIOGRAPHY

Arms Control Association. (2017, February). *The Intermediate-Range Nuclear Forces (INF) Treaty at a Glance*. Retrieved from https://www.armscontrol. org/factsheets/INFtreaty.

Artermiev, A., & Makarenko, G. (2015, December 15). *How China Launched the New Silk Road Bypassing Russia*. Retrieved from http://www.rbc.ru/ politics/15/12/2015/56703a6d9a7947f88a89ae7d.

Bordachev, T. (2016). Russia and China in the Central Asia: The Win-Win Game. *Valdai Club*. Retrieved from http://valdaiclub.com/a/valdai-papers/ russia-and-china-in-central-asia-the-great-win-win-game/.

Chance, M. (2017, July 6). *How Russia and China Are Bonding Against the US*. Retrieved from http://www.cnn.com/2017/07/05/asia/russia-china-growing-alliance/index.html.

Drabkin, A. (2015, September 14). Silk Road and the Road of Genghis Khan. *Pravda*.

Fairclough, N. (2013). *Critical Discourse Analysis*. New York: Routledge.

Farzanegan, M., & Schneider, F. (2010). *Factionalized Democracy, Oil and Economic Growth in Iran: Where Is the Curse?* Retrieved from http://www.econ.jku.at/members/Schneider/files/publications/LatestResearch2010/Factionalism_Iran.pdf.

Feng, Y. (2014, March 25). *Chinese Experts Comment on Russia's Policy Towards Ukraine* (L. Smirnova, Interviewer). Retrieved from http://russiancouncil.ru/inner/?id_4=3379#top-content.

Frankopan, P. (2016). *The Silk Roads: A New History of the World*. New York: Alfred A. Knopf.

Freedom House. (2016). Freedom in the World: Russia Country Report. *Freedom House*. Retrieved from https://freedomhouse.org/report/freedom-world/2016/russia.

Geng, S. (2017, March 10). *Foreign Ministry Spokesperson Geng Shuang's Regular Press Conference on March 10, 2017*. Retrieved from MFA China: http://www.fmprc.gov.cn/mfa_eng/xwfw_665399/s2510_665401/2511_665403/t1444983.shtml.

Government of China. (2015, March 28). 经国务院授权 三部委联合发布推动共建"一带一路"的愿景与行动 [Jīng guówùyuàn shòuquán sān bùwěi liánhé fābù tuīdòng gòng jiàn "yīdài yīlù" de yuànjǐng yǔ xíngdòng] "One Belt, One Road" Official Blueprint.

Gumilev, L. (1936). *Ancient Russia and the Great Steppe*. Moscow: Mysl Publishers. Retrieved from http://gumilevica.kulichki.net/ARGS/index.html.

Hall, S. (1973). 'Encoding/Decoding'. In Centre for Contemporary Cultural Studies (Ed.), *Culture, Media, Language: Working Papers in Cultural Studies* (pp. 128–138). London: Hutchinson.

Hille, K. (2016, October 21). *Russia's Arctic Obsession*. Retrieved from https://ig.ft.com/russian-arctic/.

Jun, A. (2016, July 17). Why Hasn't There Been a Color Revolution in China? *Global Times*. Retrieved from http://www.globaltimes.cn/content/994793.shtml.

Kashin, V. (2013). The Sum of All Fears: The Chinese Threat Factor in Russian Politics. *Russia in Global Politics*. Retrieved from http://www.globalaffairs.ru/number/Summa-vsekh-strakhov-15961.

Labanyi, J. (2010). *Spanish Literature: A Very Short Introduction*. Oxford and New York: Oxford University Press.

Lavrov, S. (2016). *Opening Remarks at the Second International Conference "Russia and China: Taking on a New Quality of Bilateral Relations"* (p. 7).

Moscow: Moscow State University. Retrieved from http://russiancouncil.ru/common/upload/Conference-Report-RUCN2016-En.pdf.

Luzhkov, Y. M. (2015, February 12). "Yellow Dragon" Benefits from the Europe—Russia Dissent, or Geopolitical Risks of the Strategic Alliance Between Russia and China. *Argumenty nedeli*. Retrieved from http://argumenti.ru/politics/n474/388673.

Luzianin, S., Matveev, V., & Smirnova, L. (2015). *Shanghai Cooperation Organization: Model 2014–2015*. Moscow: Russian International Affairs Council. Retrieved from http://russiancouncil.ru/common/upload/RIAC-WP-SCO-En.pdf.

Mahdavi, M., & Knight, W. A. (Eds.). (2016). *Towards the Dignity of Difference: Neither "End of History" nor "Clash of Civilizations"*. New York: Routledge.

McBride, J. (n.d.). Building the New Silk Road. *Council on Foreign Relations*. Retrieved from http://www.cfr.org/asia-and-pacific/building-new-silk-road/p36573.

Ministry of Economic Development of Russia. (n.d.). *Analytical Note on the Russia-China Trade Cooperation in 2015*. Retrieved from http://www.ved.gov.ru/exportcountries/cn/cn_ru_relations/cn_ru_trade/.

Peri, Y. (2004). *Telepopulism: Media and Politics in Israel*. Stanford, CA: Stanford University Press.

Peri, Y. (2007). Intractable Conflict and the Media. *Israel Studies, 12*(1), 78–102.

Peynichou, C. (2016, March 7). *Russia and China: The History of Relations During Mongolian Yoke*. Retrieved from http://inosmi.ru/history/20160703/237058674.html.

Popov, D. S. (2015, November 18). *Washington Paves the New Silk Road Bypassing Russia and China*. Moscow: Russian Institute of Strategic Studies. Retrieved from https://riss.ru/analitycs/22989/.

President Rahmon: Extremism and Terrorism Were the Cause of the Civil War in Tajikistan. (2015, June 5). *Ozodagon Information Agency*. Retrieved from http://catoday.org/centrasia/20185-prezident-rahmon-ekstremizm-i-terrorizm-stali-prichinoy-grazhdanskoy-voyny-v-tadzhikistane.html.

Romanova, K. (2014, March 3). China is Russia's Tacit Ally. *Gazeta.ru*. Retrieved from https://www.gazeta.ru/politics/2014/03/03_a_5934609.shtml.

Russian International Affairs Council. (2016). *Asian Players in the Arctic: Interests, Opportunities, Prospects*. Moscow: Spetskniga. Retrieved from http://russiancouncil.ru/common/upload/asia-arctic-report26-en.pdf.

Ryazanov, S. (2015, February 5). Russia and China: A Planetary Project. *Argumenty nedeli*. Retrieved from http://argumenti.ru/toptheme/n473/387893.

Ryazantsev, S. (2016). *Labor Migration from the Central Asia to Russia in the Context of Economic Crisis.* Moscow: Valdai Club. Retrieved from http://valdaiclub.com/a/valdai-papers/valdai-paper-55-labour-migration-from-central-asia/.

Shtyrov, V. (2015, December 24). *Where There Are a Lot of Mosquitos There Is Also a Lot of Oil* (A. Uglanov, Interviewer). Retrieved from http://argumenti.ru/toptheme/n519/428362.

Shuvalov, I. (2015, March 28). Russia Is Ready to Joint Work with China. *Argumenty nedeli.* Retrieved from http://argumenti.ru/politics/2015/03/393796.

Siebert, F. S., Peterson, T., & Schramm, W. (1981). *Four Theories of the Press.* Champaign: Board of Trustees of the University of Illinois.

Smirnova, L. (2014). Fighting Corruption and Political Reform in China: International Experience and Chinese Model. *International Affairs*, 8. Retrieved from https://interaffairs.ru/jauthor/material/1119.

Smirnova, L. (2015). Three Scenarios for Russia-China Relations in 2016. *Russia Direct.* Retrieved from http://www.cemi.rssi.ru/publication/e-publishing/index.php?ELEMENT_ID=9261.

Sputnik News Agency. (2016, September 13). *Russian, Chinese Officials Discuss Color Revolutions.* Retrieved from https://sputniknews.com/world/201609131045247958-russiachina.

Straubhaar, J. (2014). Mapping "Global" in Global Communication and Media Studies. In K. G. Wilkins, J. D. Straubhaar, & S. Kumar (Eds.), *Global Communication: New Agendas in Communication.* London and New York: Routledge.

Terentiev, D. (2015, November 12). *Everything Goes Through Baikal–Amur Mainline (BAM) Railway.* Retrieved from http://argumenti.ru/toptheme/n513/423132.

Terentiev, D. (2016, August 4). The Party of Genghis Khan: Will Russia Preserve Its Influence over the Central Asia? *Argumenty nedeli.* Retrieved from http://argumenti.ru/toptheme/n550/461769.

Trubetskoy, S. N. (1925). *The Legacy of Genghis Khan.* Berlin: Evraziyskoye knigoizdatelstvo.

Tsfati, Y., & Peri, Y. (2006). Mainstream Media Skepticism and Exposure to Sectorial and Extranational News Media: The Case of Israel. *Mass Communication and Society, 9*(2), 165–187.

Tsypliaev, S. (2016, March 21). West or East: Where Should Russia Pivot? *Vedomosti.* Retrieved from https://www.vedomosti.ru/opinion/articles/2016/03/21/634337-zapad-vostok.

Uglanov, A. (2015, July 9). *A Chinese Elephant in Our Porcelain Shop.* Retrieved from http://argumenti.ru/politics/n495/406728.

van Dijk, T. A. (1993). Principles of Critical Discourse Analysis. *Discourse & Society, 4*(2), 249–283.

Wang, Y. (2015, June 16). "一带一路"绝非中国版"马歇尔计划" ["Yīdài yīlù" jué fēi zhōngguó bǎn "mǎxiē'ěr jìhuà] "One Belt One Road" Is Not a Chinese Marshall Plan. *China Daily*. Retrieved from http://world.people. com.cn/n/2015/0616/c1002-27163312.html.

Xinhua News Agency. (n.d.). *Belt and Road Initiative*. Retrieved from http:// www.xinhuanet.com/silkroad/english/index.htm.

Xu, W., & Mao, W. (2016, September 20). Information Silk Road Given Lift. *China Daily*. Retrieved from http://usa.chinadaily.com.cn/china/2016-09/20/content_26836652.htm.

Zakharova, M. (2017, March 16). *Briefing by Foreign Ministry Spokesperson Maria Zakharova*. Retrieved from MFA Russia: http://www.mid.ru/en/web/guest/foreign_policy/news/-/asset_publisher/cKNonkJE02Bw/content/id/2687802.

CHAPTER 12

Conclusion

Karin Gwinn Wilkins and James Pamment

This collection is intended to offer a contribution to our understanding of strategic communication engaged by national governments promoting their image through practices that highlight intersections between public diplomacy and development. We have privileged the role of politics in these communication interventions, considering not only the explicit political agendas articulated in foreign policies, but also the implicit political considerations that guide these communication strategies as particular discourses. National governments engage in soft power as they work to promote their beneficence as development donors and their strength as agencies engaged in international collaboration. We have raised critical questions concerning these efforts to promote appearances that justify projected roles, in bilateral relations, within regions and among global dynamics.

K. G. Wilkins (✉)
University of Texas at Austin, Austin, TX, USA
e-mail: karin.wilkins@austin.utexas.edu

J. Pamment
Lund University, Lund, Sweden
e-mail: james.pamment@isk.lu.se

© The Author(s) 2018   261
J. Pamment and K. G. Wilkins (eds.), *Communicating National Image through Development and Diplomacy*, Palgrave Studies in Communication for Social Change, https://doi.org/10.1007/978-3-319-76759-8_12

As Pamment describes in Chapter 2, we are particularly interested in the intersections across public diplomacy and development communication. We recognize similarities in communication strategies that model processes to achieve particular outcomes, designed to win over public opinion, with a constructed suggestion of public benefit. Although each of these fields remains more diverse than this area of intersection, we believe that the collaborations across national agencies through diplomatic and development programs share similar practices and politics that are worth examining. Our entry here is through a focus on nation branding, but we see more conceptual and methodological approaches worth exploring in future work.

Future research may consider strengthening conceptualizations that connect these political communication strategies to political and sociological theories, economic considerations, and cultural contexts. In this book we have emphasized soft power, given its central importance in diplomatic and development interventions. We have highlighted the implicit politics in discourse and explicit politics in foreign policies when nations create communication strategies meant to promote particular identities in the world. Recognizing that communication interventions are never neutral, but always embody political interests and constraints (despite the idealism of proponents of participatory communication), we encourage scholars to consider the bilateral, regional, and global politics that shape and constrain national interests in their images.

Political contexts also become negotiated given other differences in power, whether in terms of class, race, ethnicity, gender, or other social and cultural identities. In her chapter considering Korean volunteers working in other countries through development programs, Lee highlights the challenges faced by women when serving in host communities, along with other factors that inhibit direct interpersonal contact. These cultural considerations that become manifest through experience are relevant in terms of understanding power dynamics at work. Social and cultural configurations are necessarily relevant to political contexts of development and diplomacy.

We also encourage research that does more to connect these political interests with economic considerations, more often observed as implicitly connected than as directly articulated. Some of the chapters in this volume do reference broader economic concerns. Kaneva references an implied neoliberal agenda in her analysis of nation branding in Kosovo, while Sorzano and Miller attribute Colombia's strategies to promote its national image to an interest in economic gains from foreign tourists; both chapters point to the challenges these economic interests create. Another economic concern to explore will be the strengthening importance of the private sector, complex and varied, particularly in development programs through public–private partnerships. Economic context may be considered in terms of the funding contributed to communication campaigns as well as the assumed expectations manifest through diplomacy and development discourses that are meant to justify projected national images.

In addition to these conceptual directions, we suggest that future projects consider research approaches that engage comparative designs and broader research questions. A strength in this collection is the varied nature of the cases examined. By including a wide variety of national strategies across regions, we are expanding our scope from Northern and Western donors to include emerging development agencies in Korea, China, Russia, Mexico, Turkey, and others. The cases presented, such as Åkerlund's consideration of Sweden's education exchange programs, Lee's analysis of Korea's volunteer program, and Kaneva's discussion of Kosovo's "Young Europeans" campaign, offer compelling research in case study form. Di Wu's comparison of US and Chinese aid to Afghanistan, along with Wilkins's consideration of bilateral branding among OECD-DAC donors, offer initial steps toward comparative analyses. Future research could strengthen this through comparative designs that consider donor strategies in similar areas or countries, within regions, and in relation to global politics. Moreover, future research may consider contrasts over time, given the importance of political leadership to bilateral and global dynamics, as relevant in the case of Turkey.

Overall it is the research question that matters the most in guiding methodological decisions as well as conceptual frameworks. We encourage scholars to consider critical analysis that leaves room for unintended consequences as well as intended outcomes, in order to recognize the implicit politics that become manifest through communication practice. If our scholarship is to contribute to these contemporary concerns, we must engage critical research with relevance and clarity.

INDEX

© The Editor(s) (if applicable) and The Author(s) 2018
J. Pamment and K. G. Wilkins (eds.), *Communicating National Image through Development and Diplomacy*, Palgrave Studies in Communication for Social Change, https://doi.org/10.1007/978-3-319-76759-8

CPSIA information can be obtained
at www.ICGtesting.com
Printed in the USA
LVOW13*0859110518

576724LV00013B/268/P

9 783319 767581